BACKROADS & BYWAYS OF NEW MEXICO

BACKROADS & BYWAYS OF

NEW MEXICO

Drives, Day Trips & Weekend Excursions

Sally Moore

The Countryman Press
Woodstock, Vermont

We welcome your comments and suggestions.
Please contact Editor
The Countryman Press
P.O. Box 748, Woodstock
VT 05091, or e-mail
countrymanpress@wwnorton.com.

First Edition

ISBN 978-0-88150-757-7

Book design, composition, and map by Hespenheide Design
Cover and interior photographs by the author

Published by The Countryman Press, P.O. Box 748, Woodstock, VT 05091

Distributed by W. W. Norton & Company, Inc., 500 Fifth Avenue, New York, NY 10110

Printed in the United States of America

10 9 8 7 6 5 4 3 2 1

To my husband
1 Corinthians 13

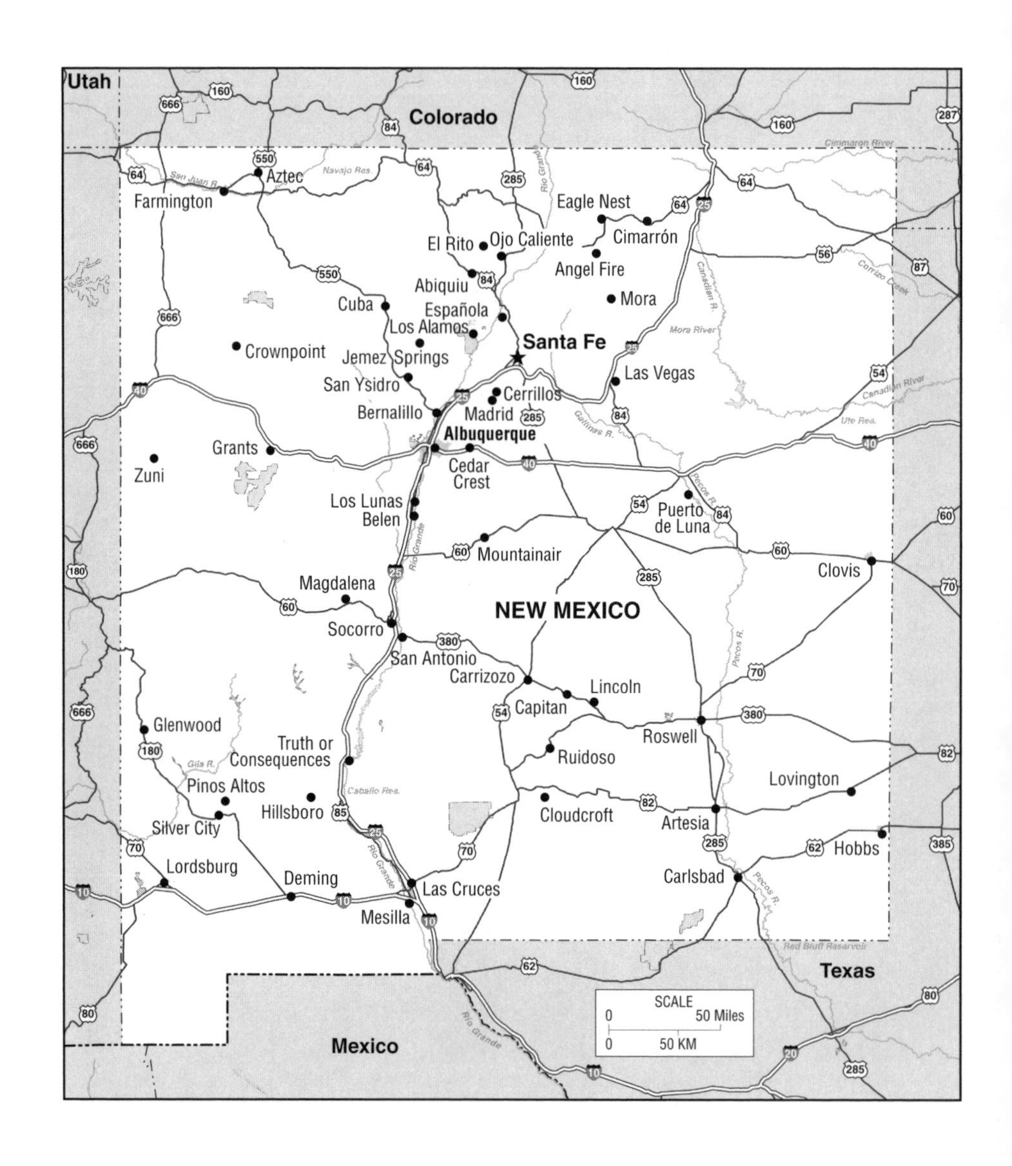
Utah
Colorado
Farmington
Aztec
Eagle Nest
Cimarrón
El Rito
Ojo Caliente
Angel Fire
Abiquiu
Cuba
Española
Mora
Los Alamos
Santa Fe
Crownpoint
Jemez Springs
Las Vegas
San Ysidro
Cerrillos
Bernalillo
Madrid
Albuquerque
Grants
Zuni
Cedar Crest
Los Lunas
Belen
Puerto de Luna
Mountainair
Clovis
Magdalena
NEW MEXICO
Socorro
San Antonio
Carrizozo
Lincoln
Capitan
Glenwood
Roswell
Truth or Consequences
Ruidoso
Lovington
Pinos Altos
Hillsboro
Cloudcroft
Artesia
Silver City
Hobbs
Lordsburg
Deming
Carlsbad
Las Cruces
Mesilla
Texas
Mexico
SCALE
0
50 Miles
0
50 KM

Contents

Introduction

The minute I saw the brilliant, proud morning shine high up over the deserts of Santa Fe, something stood still in my soul, and I started to attend. There was a certain magnificence in the high-up day, a certain eagle-like royalty. . . . Ah, yes, in New Mexico the heart is sacrificed to the sun and the human being is left stark, heartless, but undauntedly religious.

—D. H. Lawrence

New Mexico is a seducer of the most potent sort, a wily beguiler whose siren lure would captivate a born-and-bred easterner whose roots go back to 17th-century Massachusetts. Many years ago, when I first came to New Mexico, I knew at once that it was home. Time passed, as it will, taken up with the necessity of managing a family and job. Eventually the circumstances were right, and with hardly a glance back, I returned to the land which had beckoned me for so long and in which I had traveled extensively.

This guide is the result of a love affair with New Mexico. Not every place is represented, and you may wonder at the exclusion of Santa Fe, Taos, and Albuquerque. So much has been written about these cities that another guide centered on their considerable attractions seems redundant.

The choices are selective. Routes frequently cover many miles and require more than a single day's journey. Basically, I've aimed at giving you, the reader, a sample of the many elements of geography, history, and wide cultural diversity that make up "The Land of Enchantment."

A word about the land itself. It is not all desert, or mountains, or forests. It is all of the above. With 122,666 square miles, New Mexico is the fifth-largest state. It has a diverse landscape that includes sections of the Rocky Mountains, the Great Plains, the Colorado Plateau, and six of the seven climatic life zones, from the Lower Sonoran (2,876 to 5,000 feet) to the Arctic/Alpine (higher than 12,000 feet). Each zone has its own cast of plants and animals, and often it is possible to detect your elevation by checking the landscape from your car window.

The Rio Grande, which runs from its headwaters in southern Colorado to Brownsville on the Gulf of Mexico, cleaves the state in two from east to west. In its more northern reaches, or Rio Arriba, it can be a raging torrent, but once it reaches the plains, or Rio Abajo, it slows to a broad, silty stream. The lifeblood of many civilizations from Archaic to modern times, the river has been indispensable to the state's development.

The history of man in New Mexico begins around 12,000 B.C., perhaps even earlier. Crude tools and animal bones of prehistoric big game hunters were found at Sandia Cave near Albuquerque, and finely chipped projectile points were discovered at the Folsom Site in the northeast and the Clovis Site near Anderson Basin.

Toward the latter part of the Archaic period, the concept of agriculture filtered up from Mexico, and dependence on game lessened. Groups became more sedentary and built semipermanent dwellings such as pit houses. Over time these evolved into the cliff dwellings and freestanding apartment complexes of the Mogollon and Ancestral Puebloan people.

By the 1500s, rumors of great Indian civilizations and gold brought the Spanish to New Mexico. The first encounter with Native Americans occurred in 1539, when a Franciscan friar, Marcos de Niza, led a party from northern Mexico into today's Arizona and New Mexico. At Háwikuh, near today's Zuni, his advance party was repulsed and the good friar fled back to Mexico.

In response to the priest's exaggerated tales of riches, in 1540 Francisco Vásques de Coronado, governor of Nueva Galicia, Mexico, led 300 soldiers

Quarai is one of three pueblos/missions that make up Salinas Pueblo Missions National Monument.

and 800 Indians from Compostela to Háwikuh. He found no cities of gold, only the pueblos whose straw-enriched adobe glistened in the sun.

Following the Entrada (Spanish entry), Don Juan de Oñate marched north accompanied by troops, priests, colonists, and cattle to secure New Mexico by the cross and the sword, and in 1609 Don Pedro de Peralta established Santa Fe, the capital of the region.

The Spanish maintained dominance until 1680, when under the leadership of Popé, a San Juan Indian living at Taos, the pueblos revolted, expelled their oppressors, and killed many of the priests. The Spanish reestablished control in 1692, when Captain General Diego de Vargas Zapata Lujan Ponce de León y Contreras led a small army from El Paso, subdued the pueblos along the way, and easily wrested control of Santa Fe from the Indians.

With the signing of the Treaty of Córdova on August 23, 1821, Mexico received its independence from Spain, and New Mexico became a part of the new nation. The Mexican regime lasted until 1846, when U.S. Army Brigadier General Stephen Watts Kearny led the Army of the West down the Santa Fe Trail and declared New Mexico an American territory. This was ratified at the end of the Mexican War by the Treaty of Guadalupe Hidalgo.

During the long territorial period, the people of New Mexico tried many times to gain admittance into the Union, but it wasn't until January 6, 1912, that President William Howard Taft signed the bill admitting New Mexico as the 47th state.

With its history, it is easy to see why New Mexico is so culturally diverse, its Hispanic, Anglo, and Indian population supplemented by a 20th-century infusion of African Americans, Middle Easterners, and Asians. This rich cultural tapestry makes for an intricate and complex society.

The state's American Indian population can be divided into three major groups: Pueblos, Navajos, and Apaches. Of the three, the Puebloan people have been here the longest, tracing their ancestry, as they do, to the Ancestral Puebloans who built the old cities of Chaco, Aztec, and Bandelier. The Navajos and Apaches came much later, probably not a great deal before the Spanish Entrada.

The Pueblo Indians live in 19 villages, most located in the northern part of the state bordering the Rio Grande. They speak five distinct languages: Zuni (Zuni), Towa (Jemez), Tewa (Nambe, Pojoaque, San Ildefonso, O'ke Owingeh, Santa Clara, and Tesuque), Tiwa (Isleta, Picuris, Sandia, and Taos), and Keresan (Acoma, Cochiti, Laguna, San Felipe, Santa Ana, Santo Domingo, and Zia).

They are a deeply religious and private people, always gracious, but preferring to keep their beliefs secret. Many practice the arts, whether the medium is clay, silver, or stone, and their contributions to Southwestern creative vision is legend.

If you wish to visit a pueblo and be a welcome guest, keep the following cautions in mind:

- Native American territory is part of a sovereign nation. Observe all posted requests or regulations, especially speed limits and prohibitions against photography, sketching, or recording. Photography is an especially sensitive issue. If permitted, images are only for private use, not to be reproduced or sold without written permission from the tribe, a difficult and time-consuming process.
- Many pueblos charge an admission fee. Some charge a photo fee, while others allow no photography, sketching, or recording at all.
- Try to check in at the tribal office or call the pueblo governor's office or the tourist center prior to visiting. Some pueblos welcome visitors, others do not except on feast days.
- Certain areas of the pueblo may be off-limits, and they may or may not be posted. These most generally include cemeteries, kivas (ceremonial chambers), and private homes.
- Tribes hold traditions, customs, and religion in high regard. Some actions and/or questions may be offensive. Dances are religious ceremonies, not performances. When attending, remain silent and do not applaud. And do not walk across the dance area, look into kivas, or talk to the dancers or onlookers during the ceremonies.
- The best times to visit a pueblo are on feast days, which are held annually, regardless of the day of the week. Photography of dances is generally not allowed due to their religious nature.
- Do not bring alcohol or drugs onto the pueblo.
- Finally, remember these communities are not theme parks. They are people's homes and should be treated with respect.

Unlike the Pueblo people, most Navajos do not live in towns but prefer to space their hogans over the 25,000-square-mile reservation in the Four Corners area. They are consummate metalworkers, crafting ornate bracelets, necklaces, rings, concha (shell) belts, and other jewelry in silver and turquoise. Navajo women are world-famous for their beautiful rugs, which they painstakingly weave on traditional upright looms.

New Mexico's diverse landscape ranges from desert to mountains, and includes six of the seven climatic life zones

The Apaches are from the same linguistic stock as the Navajos. Fiercely protective of their people, land, and customs, they suffered intense persecution during the settlement of the West. Today fewer than 4,000 live on two reservations in New Mexico: the Jicarillas, with 800,000 acres between Chama and Farmington, and the Mescaleros, with 450,000 acres in the White Mountains south of Ruidoso.

No guide to New Mexico would be complete without a discussion of the cuisine. Do not confuse New Mexican food with Tex-Mex or Mexican. It has a flavor all its own, which owes its distinctive nature to Hispanic–Native American blend. From the Indians we have the trinity: corn, beans, and squash. This translates into tortillas, refried beans, and calabacitas. No meal is complete without chile, and New Mexicans are most serious about their capsicums, both red and green. Utilized in many strengths from the mild, meaty poblanos to the mouth-blistering habaneros, they are found in salsa, gracing a plate of enchiladas, or in the marinade for carne adovada. Many consider green chile stew the signature New Mexican dish, and when natives return from far away, that's likely to be the first meal they crave.

Before setting out on your New Mexico adventure, you should be aware of several idiosyncrasies endemic to Southwestern travel. Life proceeds at a slower pace, attuned to its own internal rhythms. In small towns, business hours frequently are flexible, and change with the seasons or sometimes with the whim of the owners. If something is a "must see," a call ahead forestalls disappointment.

Every part of the state receives abundant sunshine, but the climate varies from place to place, often depending on the elevation. Snowfall ranges from less than 2 inches in the Rio Grande Valley to almost 300 inches in the north-central mountains. During the monsoon season in July and August, thunderstorms are common.

During any day the temperatures may vary by 30 degrees, so it is always wise to be prepared and dress in easily adjusted layers.

In an arid climate, dehydration is a concern, and the wise traveler always carries a supply of water. If you're going to be driving long stretches on little-traveled roads, an emergency stash is good insurance, and if you plan moderate day hikes, a quart per person is recommended. In addition, it's a good idea to tote a reserve of nonperishable food in the very real eventuality that you are miles from the nearest café when hunger strikes.

Despite every effort to make the routing clear, there's always the possibility of a wrong turn. Wise road warriors use a GPS or at least have a simple compass mounted on the dashboard, and avail themselves of detailed maps, especially if they plan to try any of the state's many backcountry byways. The *New Mexico Road & Recreation Atlas* published by Benchmark Maps of Berkeley, California, is the best of the bunch and may be purchased in almost any New Mexico bookstore.

Finally, dust off your curiosity, put aside preconceived notions, and open your heart. You are about to have an adventure in an extraordinary and mysterious land, "a land of vast spaces and long silences . . . a land of enchantment, where Gods walked in the cool of the evening." (Source: *Land of Enchantment: Memoirs of Marian Russell along the Santa Fe Trail,* Marian Sloan Russell, University of New Mexico Press, ISBN 0-8263-0571-7.)

CHAPTER

1

A Jemez Journey

Getting there: From Albuquerque's Big I (the intersection of I-25 and I-40), take I-25 north 20 miles to Exit 240, Bernalillo. From I-25, Exit 240, take NM 313, East Avenue, 0.6 mile to NM 473, and turn right onto Camino del Pueblo, which then intersects with US 550 north of town. Follow US 550 northwest 24 miles to San Ysidro. Bear north on NM 4 through Jemez Springs to the edge of the caldera, where the road completes a horseshoe turn southeast to Bandelier National Monument. Leaving Bandelier, follow NM 4, then turn west onto East Jemez Road to Los Alamos. From the city, NM 502 skirts San Ildefonso Pueblo and ends at US 285, Pojoaque, 24 miles north of Santa Fe.

Highlights: A journey of a day or longer takes you off the interstates into some of New Mexico's most spectacular mountain country—from canyons once sheltering ancient cliff dwellers to the city the atom built, **Los Alamos.** Along the way you'll visit historic **Bernalillo** and **Valles Caldera,** the 15-mile-wide basin formed by surface collapse in an area of once-primal volcanic activity. Native American pueblos, hot springs, two wineries, and the tiny All-American city of **Jemez Springs** round out your Jemez Mountain encounter.

The road between Albuquerque and Santa Fe is familiar to many visitors, who vary their route occasionally by heading north on NM 14 or the Turquoise Trail. A longer but largely undiscovered route heads northwest through the Jemez Mountains with their spectacular panoramas of red rock cliffs, deep, pine-filled canyons, and serene pueblo villages.

Valle Grande

Let's Go: Heading out of the hustle and bustle of Albuquerque, the state's largest city, you find the pace slackens and time moves more slowly in the old Hispanic town of **Bernalillo.** The site of the annual **Labor Day New Mexico Wine Festival,** the village has a historic main street, once part of the celebrated El Camino Real. Like so many small, quiet villages, Bernalillo's assets are not obvious to the casual passerby. Look closer. In the 900 block of Camino del Pueblo, an old building with a deceptively modern front houses **Rose's Pottery House and Art Gallery; The Range Café;** and **Home on the Range** gift shop. Rose's Pottery House is a treasure trove of Native American art, both classic and current. In this unimposing storefront, Rose Silva, a trader's daughter and granddaughter of a Lebanese immigrant, maintains her father's 90-year collection of Native American art, which rivals anything seen in the West's more sacred repositories.

Aficionados of pueblo pottery will be captivated with rare pieces by Maria Martinez, legendary San Ildefonso potter, or prehistoric gems like a snowflake olla from Chaco Canyon or a jug from Mesa Verde. Complementing the museum collection, Rose stocks and sells a variety of Southwestern art, from the storytellers of Cochití's Helen Cordero to the impressive silver concha belts of Navajo silversmiths.

Next to the pottery, Matt DiGregory and Tom Fenton run **The Range Café,** a popular local eatery specializing in the kind of home cooking Mom would have produced had she been a talented and innovative chef. Daily specials include pasta dishes like scallop pasta with red chile linguine, cilantro cream, and pine nuts, or Tom's meatloaf with roasted garlic mashed potatoes and gravy. Breads and confections are available on-site for consumption or takeout.

Sandwiching the restaurant to the north and south with twin shops, Lynne Bladergroen stocks her **Home on the Range** with "lots of cool stuff you don't really need." There are all sorts of paraphernalia related to the restaurant: T-shirts, caps, aprons, and Range salsa and dressings. Local artists contribute paintings, santos and retablos, and decorated gourds. A large selection of Navajo folk art sits cheek by jowl with Ben Forgey's furniture and Windmill Works frames and mirrors.

Off NM 313 just a short distance north of its intersection with US 550, **La Hacienda Grande** is tucked away down Barros Road. Melody and Scott Troy purchased the old adobe bed and breakfast from Shoshanna Zimmerman in 2003. Prior to Zimmerman's renovation, it had remained in the Gallegos and Montoya families, who had settled the area in 1695 after the Pueblo Revolt. The gracious bed and breakfast has six spacious suites, cozy sitting and reading areas, an intimate dining room, and a large, secluded, open-air courtyard with a covered portico. A near-mystic ambiance pervades, and there are tales of treasure. It is rumored that as the Confederates retreated south after the Civil War battle of Glorietta Pass, they buried their valuables under the hacienda floor. Many have searched for the gold, but none have been successful. Perhaps it is still there, or perhaps this is just a tale.

Leaving Bernalillo, you turn onto US 550 and cross the Rio Grande. On the river's west bank in the shadow of the bosque, **Coronado State Monument** commemorates the ancient Tiwa pueblo Kuaua and the place Francisco Coronado and his men spent the winter of 1540–1541. Today a visitor's center traces the history of the site and displays original kiva murals, which deal with the Native American population's complex relationship with the earth and heavens. There are trails through reconstructed ruins, which include a kiva, or ceremonial chamber, similar to the one which originally housed the images.

As you head north, you pass Santa Ana Pueblo's commercial complex and **Jackalope,** a multiacre compound that advertises "folk art by the truckload." A Mexican-style market with a plethora of pottery, blankets, baskets, rugs, tinware, etc., from all points south, Jackalope is a diverting place to shop for a piece of cedar and pigskin equipale furniture from Guadalajara, a painted terra cotta figure by Irene Aguilar of Oaxaca, or merely an inexpensive souvenir of your visit.

US 550 follows the Jemez River valley past **Zia Pueblo,** whose rayed sun sign is the symbol of New Mexico and appears on the state flag. The peaks of the Jemez Mountains rise in shades of red, ochre, and umber to the west, and during the spring, summer and fall, the sage- and juniper-dotted roadsides are carpeted in wildflowers—blue flax, Indian tea, and yellow clover. At the small farming community of **San Ysidro,** the route veers onto NM 4. Named for the patron saint of farmers, the somnolent village is the site of a famous dinosaur dig that took place from 1978 to 1980. The large Camarasaurus skeleton on display at the New Mexico Museum of Natural History in Albuquerque was discovered there, and another dinosaur, Seismosaurus, was uncovered at a nearby site. Your route through town passes a picturesque church and Shirley Powell's **Columbine Pottery.** A working studio and gallery, the shop carries Marion Ball's sculptured bears and cats, mezuzahs and menorahs by Pat Callahan, hamsa hands (Hebrew house blessings) by Hava Tiger, Pat's wife, and pottery by Shirley in emerald green, Jemez blue, and a purple blend called amethyst.

Following the river into a verdant valley rimmed by red cliffs, you arrive at **Jemez Pueblo.** Among the Jemez (pronounced HEM-mus), the village traditionally is called Walatowa, a Towa word meaning "this is the place." It is among the most traditional pueblos. The Jemez people believe their ancestors originated from an underworld place, Hua-vu-na-tota, and migrated from the Four Corners area to the "Cañon de San Diego" region. When Europeans reached the region in 1541, the Jemez had an estimated population of 30,000 and numerous pueblos scattered around Walatowa. Now a tribe with more than 4,000 members, the Jemez people are consummate artisans, best known for their work in clay—bowls, seed pots, sgraffito vessels, wedding vases, and their famous storytellers.

The pueblo requests that visitors go directly to the visitor's center. Wandering around the village is not permitted, but if you wish to visit a particular artist and make arrangements in advance, allowances generally can be made. In particular, the Fragua family, whose storytellers are world-famous, welcomes buyers, and Sal and Flo Yepa encourage shoppers to visit their **Sun and Fire Gallery Pottery House** on the main road. Sal, from Jemez, and Flo, part Laguna and part Jemez, specialize in two distinct types of pottery: earthenware, which combines red clay and fine white sand temper, and stoneware, which is temper-free. Their home-studio is a warm, friendly place, and they are always willing to spend a few minutes with gringos, educating them on the fine points of the potter's art.

The **Walatowa Visitor Center** is located across from Red Rocks natural amphitheater. It houses a gift shop, a reconstructed traditional field house, and a free museum that traces the history of the Jemez people through photographs and pottery displays. On special days they schedule interpretive programs, bread-baking demonstrations, and traditional dances. Spring and fall bring arts and crafts shows at Red Rocks, where on off-weekends you may find women selling fresh bread from beehive-shaped ovens called hornos.

Leaving pueblo land, you'll find many shady picnic spots along the Jemez River. If you'd like a cold bottle of wine to accompany your alfresco lunch, be sure to take the turn down NM 290 to the **Ponderosa Valley Vineyards & Winery.** The vineyards planted by Henry and Mary Street in 1976 have consistently produced award-winning Rieslings as well as exotic local specialties like Cactus Apple New Mexico Prickly Pear. Mary is usually found pouring for oenophiles at the tasting counter, while Henry is busy in the fields or among the vats. If he's not terribly preoccupied, you might convince him to give you a tour of the winery.

Beyond Ponderosa, the road makes multiple forks and becomes dirt or gravel as it reaches into San Juan and Paliza canyons. Backtrack to the main road, NM 4, and continue through Cañones toward Jemez Springs. As you enter deeper and deeper into the canyon of the Jemez River, the precipitous walls of Bandelier volcanic tuff rise to the east and west. The tawny pink rock with its eroded "Swiss cheese" cavities is the product of the two great eruptions that shaped the Jemez Mountains. The "tent rocks" that line the cliffs are thought to represent cones of hardened ash that once surrounded volcanic vents. The green of the river valley, the fleetness of the clear, boulder-filled stream, and the glow of the ruddy rock make an unforgettable drive.

Several miles south of Jemez Springs at Mile Marker 11, **Shangri La West Gallery and Trading Post** is housed in a lovely adobe compound freshened by a fountain and bursting with flowers, birds, and dragonflies. Owners Rodney and Andrée Moen stock Native American arts and crafts, including a prime selection of the famous storytellers of the region. Through their years as traders, they have developed a rapport with many artists with whom they deal directly. They showcase the work of many different tribes: Zuni fetish carvings, Hopi silver overlay jewelry, Jemez pots, Oaxaca wood carvings, Casa Grande pottery, Tarahumara drums, Zia pottery—the list is endless. Both Rod and Andrée are jewelers, and in addition to the Native American ware, you'll find their unusual handcrafted pieces, which include Rod's Egyptian primitive earring designs.

First-time visitors to **Jemez Springs** always get a chuckle when they discover this small resort town was named an "All-America City" in 1995. The award was presented in response to the cleanup and beautification of the grassy park at the town center. Although the corporate limits encompass a couple of Catholic retreats, a Zen center, a general store, restaurants, and various accommodations, Jemez Springs' primary draw is its therapeutic hot springs. The **bathhouse,** which sits on the edge of the park, was built in the 1870s and added to in the 1940s. Flower beds surround the cottage-like structure, and the main room's gift shop is filled with a selection of natural health and beauty supplies. Mineral bathtubs are to the rear, with private sections for men and women. Herbal or sweat wraps and massage are nice additions to the experience, and for those seeking a group

The Jemez Springs bathhouse, built in the 1870s, offers mineral bathtubs with private sections for men and women.

encounter, an outdoor cedar tub with a capacity of six is available by reservation.

After a relaxing soak, you'll be ready for some sustenance, and at **Deb's Deli Restaurant & Mercantile** you can order up the best lunch in town, a hot espresso, or an ice-cream parlor delight. Steve and Helen Nichols serve up particularly toothsome burgers, and all their breads, rolls, and pastries are baked on premises. The side porch, with its view of the town's comings and goings, is the most popular spot in Jemez Springs on a warm spring or summer afternoon.

Jemez State Monument, a couple of miles north of town, embraces the prehistoric ruins of the 13th-century Towa pueblo of Guisewa and the 17th-century Spanish mission of San José de los Jémez, founded in 1622 by Franciscan Fray Alonso de Luga, who came to the New World with Oñate in 1598. Guisewa, meaning "place of boiling waters," was an ancestral home of present-day Jemez Pueblo people. Stop at the monument visitor's center to learn more about Jemez history and mythology, and take a few minutes to examine the artifacts recovered from the rubble. A path from the center takes you to the partially excavated pueblo and the impressive church ruins.

As the road climbs beyond the monument, you'll notice cars stopped by the right side of the road. **Soda Dam,** a calcium carbonate–travertine dike over the river, was formed over the centuries by deposits from a spring surfacing nearby. The colorful formation is 300 feet long, 50 feet high, and 50 feet wide at the base. Kids play in the shallow caves at the base, and photographers burn frame after frame of film on the massive, rust-streaked protuberance.

If you'd like the experience of no-frills natural hot springs where bathing suits are optional, continue up the hill to Battleship Rock picnic area near Mile Marker 23. In the shadow of the prowlike formation, a rather steep trail leads to **Battleship Rock hot spring,** a 30-by-40-foot pool surrounded by pines.

The trail to perennially popular **Spense hot springs** is just 2 miles north of Battleship Rock picnic area, between Indian Head and Dark Canyon campgrounds. Two rock pools with a series of mini waterfalls are about 100 yards above the river. The water at the top is warmest, cooling as it descends to the lower pool and waterfall.

If your energy starts to sag and you're searching for a place to stay, you could do no better than the **Cañon del Rio Bed and Breakfast** a couple of miles south of town near Mile Marker 16. Owner Pam Grider's quiet oasis on the Jemez River felicitously combines the qualities of a healthful and spiritual retreat with graceful accommodations in the Southwestern style. While adults are welcome at the main inn, an adjoining, refurbished, century-old casita serves the needs of traveling families. Special yoga retreats are scheduled during the year.

When you leave Jemez Springs, the road climbs consistently upward, past the turnoff to Fenton Lake State Park, Seven Springs Fish Hatchery, and Jemez Falls. Rounding the southern flank of Redondo Peak, you are greeted by an extraordinary sight: a huge, grass-covered bowl with dimensions so staggering that buildings, cattle, and ranch vehicles are reduced to microscopic proportions. Once thought to be the site of the world's largest volcano, some 15,000 to 25,000 feet in height, Valle Grande and its sister valleys, Valle San Antonio, Valle Toledo, Valle Jaramillo, and Valle de los Posos, are believed to be a caldera, a basin formed by the collapse of the surface as a result of volcanic activity. Eruptions from this caldera during the Pleistocene period sent a blanket of volcanic ash 1,000 feet thick over a 400-square-mile area, which erosion carved into the mesas and canyons of the Pajarito Plateau. For many decades Valle Grande was private grazing land with restricted access. Made a national preserve under the Valles Caldera Preservation Act of 2000, the **Valles Caldera National Preserve** attracts a wide range of admirers. Now that the property is public land, the opportunities to study and learn on the preserve are growing. Managed by a nine-member board of trustees, seven of which are appointed by the president of the United States, the caldera is a new model of public land management. There are hikes, winter skiing and snowshoeing, trail rides, fishing, sleigh and wagon rides, van and group tours, and elk hunting. Limited enrollment in these activities ensures the pristine nature of the caldera is maintained.

The seismic forces that shaped Valle Grande are also responsible for creating Frijoles Canyon, home of **Bandelier National Monument.** As you drive the winding road from the mesa top, you can understand why the Ancestral Puebloan people made the canyon home. El Rito de los Frijoles (Little River of Beans) bubbles its way down the canyon floor, bestowing a permanent source of water for man and beast. Along the stream's edge, fertile volcanic soil provides a growing medium, and the canyon's north wall of friable volcanic ash, called tuff, contains natural apertures that were enlarged into cavelike shelters. Unlike Chaco Canyon, which today is a barren, inhospitable place, Bandelier is a haven in the desert.

When you visit, stop at the visitor's center, where you will get an orientation to the 50-square-mile park. A 10-minute slide show, "The Bandelier Story," introduces you to what has been called "one of the largest concentrations of archeological sites in the Southwest." You'll learn park history and be introduced to Adolph Francis Bandelier, the Colorado rancher and self-trained scholar who was the first to study and report on the ruins. Static exhibits interpret the occupation of the area from about 1200 to the present, and during the summer, regularly scheduled ranger-led walks originate here.

Stroll the canyon floor along the pretty loop trail bordered in wildflowers. In a quarter mile you'll come to the Tyuonyi Pueblo ruins. Almost immediately to your right, cliff dwellings pock the face of the escarpment. Climb in and around them. These one- to three-story talus villages that extend along the base of the northern wall for approximately 2 miles. Many have cave rooms gouged out of the tuff, while others show holes where vigas (wooden support beams) extended the natural shelter. If you have time, say two hours or more, continue to the ceremonial cave. The cave is reached by a 140-foot climb up four steep wooden ladders; the ascent is not for the fainthearted or those suffering from vertigo. However, the view from the top is spectacular.

Cottonwood Picnic Area provides shaded bowers for lunch-munchers, and those seeking more extensive hiking trails will discover nearby trail heads to Upper and Lower Falls, the Rio Grande, Frijolito ruins, and the backcountry.

Wooden support beams called vigas provide access to the multistory cliff dwellings at Bandelier National Monument.

Leaving Bandelier, you climb Frijoles Mesa and head out NM 4 toward **White Rock,** where you'll find a winery with a most impressive view. Former Los Alamos nuclear chemist John Balagna's **Balagna Winery** possesses a splendid overlook of the White Rock Canyon of the Rio Grande River and the Sangre de Cristo Mountains. Here you can promenade the porch of the tasting room, sipping vintages and gazing down and out at a panorama nonpareil. John's wines are a reflection of his Italian heritage, and he unashamedly displays his Dago Red along with other gentler vintages like zinfandel and chardonnay. La Bomba Grande, a blend of zinfandel, pinot noir, and merlot grapes, is one of John's most popular items. Part vin ordinare and part souvenir of the Atomic City, it is bottled with a label depicting a gigantic mushroom cloud.

For directions to the winery, copies of a self-guided walking tour of **Los Alamos,** a diagram of the buildings of the National Laboratory, and other helpful information, stop at the **Visitor's Center** on Rover Boulevard or at the chamber of commerce office downtown.

Los Alamos is unlike any other town in New Mexico. One of your first observations might be that the cultural mix, so obvious in the rest of the state, is missing. Instead of Native Americans, Anglos, and Hispanics, you find an international amalgam of highly educated nuclear physicists, chemists, and representatives of other branches of science. At your quarters, you breakfast with a Ph.D. from Helsinki instead of a traveling couple from St. Louis. You also become aware of the absence of typical New Mexico adobe architecture.

If you think back, you'll begin to understand why this place is so different from its sister New Mexico cities. In 1917, in what is now the heart of Los Alamos, a wealthy Detroit businessman with the unlikely name of Ashley Pond purchased the Harold H. Brook homestead. His dream was to create a school dedicated to transforming sheltered boys from wealthy families into robust, learned men through participation in the active, outdoor life. By 1918, Pond's vision was a reality, and for almost 25 years the Los Alamos Ranch School prospered.

During the dark days of World War II, the U.S. government embarked upon a highly secret project headed by General Leslie Groves. His task was to assemble the top minds in physics to tame the power of the atom. In searching for a spot for a clandestine laboratory, he considered five crucial factors: available housing for 30 scientists, land owned by the government or easily acquired in secrecy, an area large and uninhabited enough to permit safe separation of experimental sites, easy control of access for security, and sufficient cleared land so new building could be started immediately.

Los Alamos Ranch School was selected because J. Robert Oppenheimer, the director of scientific research, was intimately familiar with the school and knew it fit all the criteria. His family's summer home was in the mountains at the headwaters of the Pecos River, and as a boy he'd ridden over the mesas of the Pajarito Plateau on pack trips.

On December 7, 1942, the government gave notice that it was taking over the school, and shortly thereafter work on the secret laboratories began. By January 1, 1943, the University of California was appointed to operate the facility, and a formal nonprofit contract was drawn with the Manhattan Engineer District of the Army. The Manhattan Project, as it became known, was a reality.

Over the next two years, some of the greatest minds in science toiled frantically in the ramshackle town of temporary structures. The old school buildings were pressed into service: Fuller Lodge became a restaurant, the classrooms were the Post Exchange and other shops, and the masters' houses were residences for top project administrators. As these homes were the only houses to offer tubs instead of showers, they were collectively dubbed "Bathtub Row."

On July 16, 1945, the scientists' efforts reached fruition when the first atomic bomb was successfully tested at the Trinity site, a remote spot on White Sands Missile Range. Three weeks after the Trinity test, "Fat Man" was dropped on Hiroshima, and on August 9 a third explosion leveled the city of Nagasaki. Japan gave up five days later, and formal surrender ceremonies were held on September 2, 1945.

Although its prime purpose had been accomplished, the city did not die but gradually evolved. Research goes on at the Los Alamos National Laboratory, but now half its effort is devoted to the peaceful uses of atomic energy. The government has turned back commercial and residential properties on the hill to private ownership or to the county of Los Alamos, which was created in 1967. It is almost, but not quite, like any other town.

The best place to begin your visit would be the **Los Alamos Historical Museum,** housed in what was the Ranch School's infirmary and later guest quarters during the Manhattan Project. Here, more than anywhere else in the city, you get an idea of the flow of time and events. Exhibits deal with area geology and prehistory, homesteading, the Ranch School, and the

Fuller Lodge originally served as the dining and recreation hall for Los Alamos Ranch School. Today it provides space for community meetings and events.

Manhattan Project. A well-stocked bookstore sells a selection of books dealing with area history.

Some of the museum's most interesting displays depict the Ranch School years with pictures of the boys and masters partaking in vigorous outdoor activities. Since toughening spoiled easterners was the aim, both teachers and pupils wore shorts and knee socks, even during the cold, snowy winters. Two better-known graduates are author Gore Vidal and Antonio J. Taylor, brother to Lady Bird Johnson.

Fuller Lodge, perhaps the most imposing structure left from Ranch School days, is next to the museum. Listed on the National Historical Register, the jackal log structure with massive front columns originally served as the school's dining and recreation hall. The logs were said to have been hand-selected by noted architect John Gaw Meem and Ranch School Director A. J. Connell.

Today Fuller Lodge is a county-run, multiuse building providing meeting space for laboratory conferences and community events. In addition, the south wing houses the **Art Center at Fuller Lodge,** which sponsors arts and craft fairs in August and October and mounts juried shows throughout the year. Docent tours of the building are available by reservation through the Los Alamos Historical Society headquarters at the museum.

If you've been sightseeing all morning at Los Alamos's 7,400-foot altitude and have developed a ravenous appetite, head for the **Hill Diner** on Trinity. Originally the Good Eats Café, the Hill, with its knotty pine paneling and camp lodge atmosphere, dishes up a mean platter of chicken-fried steak, bowls of homemade soup, and tasty burgers. Leave room for dessert, however, because their banana cream pie is out of this world. Meltingly ripe chunks of banana rest on a flaky crust, topped with rich cream filling and a halo of whipped cream. The portions are monstrous, so you might want to share with a friend.

Save time in the afternoon for the **Bradbury Science Museum,** named not for Ray Bradbury of science-fiction fame, but for Norris Bradbury, director of research at what is now Los Alamos National Laboratory after Oppenheimer's departure. With more than 130,000 visitors per year, it is easily the most popular attraction in town. The modern structure at Central Avenue and 15th Street in the heart of downtown has 8,500 feet of exhibit space dedicated to interpreting the role of the laboratory to the lay public.

In all, there are 40 high-tech exhibits on Manhattan Project history and current and historical research projects. Technocrats, students of all ages, and even those who think they're scientifically challenged will enjoy the interactive computer programs, which allow visitors to learn about lasers and light, computer research, and weapon design. The displays of the Fat Man bomb case, a cruise missile, and models of satellites are impressive.

Local, national, and international visitors find the 18-minute film, *The Town That Never Was,* a satisfying and comprehensible explanation of the Manhattan Project and life in Los Alamos during the last days of World War II. Historic black-and-white footage graphically portrays world and national events at this critical point in history.

Next to the museum, **Otowi Station Science Museum Shop & Bookstore** is one of those wonderful stores where you can browse for hours. They stock educational toys, hiking and mountain biking guides, maps, local histories, and books on atomic history, technical sciences, and computers. Tourist information is graciously dispensed, and if you'd like to spend a couple of hours with someone who has the real skinny on Los Alamos, this is where you'll meet **Buffalo Tours** Georgia Strickfaden, a Los Alamos native who knows more about the area than any 10 people combined. Her 90-minute tours feature the historical town site, the laboratory, and the Rio Grande overlook at White Rock. She also tailors special interest tours, including trips to nearby Spanish and Indian villages and excursions to the Jemez Mountains.

Dining in Los Alamos doesn't get any better than the **Blue Window Bistro** on Central. Owner Erik Luedemann presents a varied international cuisine with emphasis on seasonal produce. All pasta, breads, desserts, and ice cream are made on premises, and the Blue Window is one of the few places in the New Mexican outback where you know you'll get immaculately fresh fish, properly prepared. You might want to start with Erik's creamy New England clam chowder, move on to the special chopped salad of field greens, fresh mozzarella, roasted red peppers, candied pecans, and Bermuda onion dressed with white balsamic vinaigrette, then follow that with Prince Edward Island mussels and linguini with tomatoes and green onions in a saffron cream sauce.

Heavenly! Or perhaps you'd prefer the popular Southwest chicken, a tender chicken breast wrapped in phyllo pastry, stuffed with Boursin cheese and chipotle pesto, and served with a basil cream sauce and truffled mashed potatoes.

After such an exhausting and fulfilling day, you'll want a soft pillow and a welcoming room. **Adobe Pines Bed & Breakfast** will fill the bill. Dan and Ann Partin's gracious adobe is on the north side of town, near the 18-hole Los Alamos County Golf Course and Loma Linda Park with its spectacular views and varied hiking trails. Their spacious home, designed by Dallas-born Ann, has five bedrooms, all with king-size beds and private baths. Windows look out onto views of the Jemez Mountains, Pajarito Ski Area, and the city. A plus for traveling businesspeople is a desk and Internet access in every room.

Leaving town, you head out NM 502 and descend a steep hill. If you look sharply, you'll see the remains of the original road to your right and prehistoric ruins to your left at canyon bottom. After the intersection of NM 502 and NM 30, you pass the entrance to **San Ildefonso Pueblo.** If you take the first marked road, you encounter **Babbitt's Cottonwood Trading Post,** what has to be the most visually pleasing example of its kind in the West. With adobe construction, sky blue wood trim, pots of colorful flowers, and a plethora of hummingbird feeders with their greedy guests, Cottonwood has a small and select stock. Trader Judith Babbitt blends the needs of local Indians with the interests of San Ildefonso Pueblo visitors. There are old and new Navajo rugs, Zuni fetishes, Navajo, Zuni and Hopi jewelry, pottery from San Ildefonso, Acoma, and Santa Clara, and examples of Maria Martinez's famous work.

Continuing beyond the tree-shaded trading post, you enter the pueblo proper, home of potters Maria and Julian Martinez, who revolutionized design with their black-on-black ware. It is still a village of potters and one of the prettier pueblos. Stop at the visitor's center to register, pay a fee, and get a map, which will delineate those areas open to guests. It is pleasant to walk the dusty streets, visit with the potters in their home studios, and examine the duel plazas divided by the giant grandfather cottonwood. Perhaps at journey's end you'll carry home a piece of world-renowned San Ildefonso pottery, a remembrance of hours of enjoyment exploring the Jemez Trail.

Contacts:

Art Center at Fuller Lodge, 2132 Central Avenue, Los Alamos, 87544. Call 505-662-9331. Mon. through Sat. 10–4. Web site: www.artfulnm.org.

Babbitt's Cottonwood Trading Post, R.R. 5, Box 320, Santa Fe, 87501. Call 505-455-2954. Located 9 miles west of junction US 285/NM 502, San Ildefonso Pueblo. Tues. through Sat. 9:30–4:30.

Balagna Winery, 223 Rio Bravo Drive, Los Alamos (White Rock), 87544. Call 505-672-3678. Tues. through Sun. noon–5. Web site: www.nmwine.com/wineries/balagna.

Bandelier National Monument, 15 Entrance Road, Los Alamos, 87544. Call 505-672-3861, Ext. 517. Visitor's center, summer, daily 8–6; spring and fall, daily 9–5:30; winter, daily 8–4:30. Frijoles Canyon and Tsankawi, daily dawn to dusk. Fee. Web site: www.nps.gov/band.

Blue Window Bistro, 813 Central Avenue, Los Alamos, 87544. Call 505-662-6305. Brunch, Sat. 8:30–2:30; lunch, Mon. through Sat. 11–2:30; dinner, Mon. through Sat. 5–9. Web site: www.bluewindowbistro.com.

Bradbury Science Museum, Central Avenue and 15th Street, Los Alamos, 87544. Call 505-667-4444. Tues. through Sat. 10–5, Sun. and Mon. 1–5. Web site: www.lanl.gov/museum.

Buffalo Tours, P.O. Box 726, Los Alamos, 87544. Call 505-662-5711. Fee. Web site: buffalotours.home.att.net.

Cañon del Rio Bed & Breakfast, 164455 NM 4, Jemez Springs, 87025. Call 1-800-809-3262 or 505-829-3262. Web site: www.canondelrio.com.

Columbine Pottery, 311 NM 4, San Ysidro, 87053. Call 505-834-7687. Tues. through Sat. 9–5, Sun. 12:30–5. Web site: www.columbine pottery.com.

Coronado State Monument, 485 Kuaua Road, P.O. Box 95, Bernalillo, 87004. Call 505-867-5351. Located 1 mile west of Bernalillo on US 550. Wed. through Mon. 8:30–5. Fee. Web site: www.nmstatemonuments.org.

Deb's Deli, 17607 NM 4, Jemez Springs, 87025. Call 505-829-3829. Summer, Mon. through Fri. 8–3:30, Sat. and Sun. 8–4; winter, daily 8:30–3.

The Hill Diner, 1315 Trinity, Los Alamos, 87544. Call 505-662-9745. Summer, daily 11–9; winter, daily 11–8. Web site: www.hilldiner.com.

Home on the Range, 925 Camino del Pueblo, Bernalillo, 87004. Call 505-867-4755. Daily 9–9. Web site: www.rangecafe.com.

Jackalope, 834 US 550, Bernalillo, 87004. Call 505-867-9813. Mon. through Thurs. and Sun. 9–6, Fri. and Sat. 9–7. Web site: www.jackalope.com.

Jemez Springs Bath House, 062 Jemez Springs Plaza, NM 4, Jemez Springs, 87025. Call 1-866-204-8303 or 505-829-3303. Summer, daily 10–8; winter, Mon. through Thurs. 10–6, Fri. through Sun. 10–8. Web site: www.jemezspringsbathhouse.com.

Jemez State Monument, 18160 NM 4, P.O. Box 143, Jemez Springs, 87025. Call 505-829-3530. Wed. through Mon. 8:30–5. Fee. Web site: www.nmstatemonuments.org.

La Hacienda Grande, 21 Barros Road, Bernalillo, 87004. Call 505-867-1887. Web site: lahaciendagrande.com.

Los Alamos Historical Museum, 1921 Juniper Street, Los Alamos, 87544. Call 505-662-4493 or 505-662-6272. Summer, Mon. through Fri. 9:30–4:30, Sat. and Sun. 11–5; winter, Mon. through Sat. 10–4, Sun. 1–4. Web site: www.losalamoshistory.org.

Los Alamos Visitors Centers, 85 Rover Boulevard, White Rock, 87544. Call 505-662-8105. Downtown at chamber of commerce, 109 Central Park Square, Los Alamos, 87544. Call 1-800-444-0707. Mon. through Sat. 9–4. Web site: www.visit.losalamos.com.

Otowi Station Science Museum Shop and Bookstore, 1350 Central Avenue, Los Alamos, 87544. Call 505-662-9589. Mon. through Fri. 8–8, Sat. 9–6, Sun. 11–6. Web site: www.otowistation.com.

Ponderosa Valley Vineyards and Winery, 3171 NM 290, Ponderosa, 87044. Call 1-800-WINEMKR or 505-834-7487. Tues. through Sat. 10–5, Sun. noon–5. Web site: www.ponderosawinery.com.

The Range Café, 925 Camino del Pueblo, Bernalillo, 87004. Call 505-867-1700. Breakfast, daily 7:30–3; lunch, daily 11–3; dinner, daily 5–close; brunch, Sat. and Sun. 8–3. Web site: www.rangecafe.com.

Rose's Pottery House and Art Gallery, 2000 Camino del Pueblo, Bernalillo, 87004. Call 505-867-5911. Tues. through Sat. 8–6, Sun. 10–5.

San Ildefonso Pueblo. For pueblo office, call 505-455-2273. Visitor's center open Mon. through Fri. 8–5. **Maria Poveka Martinez Museum** open Mon. through Fri. 8–noon and 1–4. Call 505-455-3549. Pottery shops open Mon. through Fri. 10:30–5.

Shangri La West Gallery & Trading Post, Mile Marker 11, NM 4, Jemez Pueblo, 87024. Call 505-829-3864. Weekends 10–5 or by appointment. Web site: www.shangrilawest.com.

Sun & Fire Gallery Pottery House, 4514 NM 4, Jemez Pueblo, 87024. Call 505-834-7717. Daily 8–6.

Walatowa Visitor Center, 7413 NM 4, P.O. Box 100, Jemez Pueblo, 87024. Call 1-877-733-5687 or 505-834-7235. Daily 8–5. Web site: www.jemezpueblo.org.

CHAPTER

2

Georgia O'Keeffe Country

Getting there: From Albuquerque, take I-25 north 35 miles to St. Francis Drive, Exit 282, Santa Fe. North of Santa Fe connect with US 84/285. Follow St. Francis Drive out of Santa Fe, past the National Cemetery and the turnoff to the Santa Fe Opera. Head north on US 84/285, 24 miles to Española, where US 84 divides from 285 and heads northwest 22 miles to Abiquiu, through the small towns of San Pedro, Hernandez, and Chili. Ghost Ranch and the Living Museum are off US 84 north of town.

Leaving Abiquiu, take NM 554 northeast 16 miles to El Rito. Outside the village, NM 554 meets NM 111, which continues east and south for 9 miles. Turn south onto US 285 and drive 2 miles to Ojo Caliente. Leaving the hot springs, continue on 285 south to Española, 25 miles.

Highlights: For a three- or four-day excursion into this region of mystery and color, follow the path of artists and aesthetes to Abiquiu. Visit the **Georgia O'Keeffe Home** and **Ghost Ranch,** refresh your spirit with the Benedictine monks at the **Monastery of Christ in the Desert,** discover **El Rito,** an old community where new and old arts flourish side by side, and bathe in the healing waters of **Ojo Caliente** hot springs.

Let's Go: When Nature created northern New Mexico, she gathered her forces to shape the spectacular and expanded her color palette to include shades seldom seen in terrestrial forms. Of all the sites in a state known for its colorful scenery, the region around Abiquiu is perhaps the most wondrous and exotic.

The 20th-century American painter Georgia O'Keeffe made the mesas, cliffs, and buttes of Abiquiu famous in her intensely colored paintings, but even for O'Keeffe devotees, a trip to this small Hispanic town on the banks of the Chama River is a revelation. The mystery of "the white place," the vibrancy of the red and yellow cliffs at Ghost Ranch, the imposing form of the flat-topped Pedernal Mountain, all are there in shape and shade but not greatly changed from the artist's representation.

It is only a short journey from Santa Fe to Abiquiu. Leaving "the city different," you climb the hill past the National Cemetery and begin a long descent toward Española. The four-lane divided highway hums along past the entrance to the Santa Fe Opera and Tesuque Pueblo.

At Pojoaque Pueblo's stunning adobe complex, the **Poeh Center,** you can trace the efforts of the northern Rio Grande Valley pueblo communities to preserve and revitalize their cultures through their arts and crafts. **The Poeh Museum's** permanent exhibit, "Nah Poeh Meng," or "Our Continuous Path," traces the revitalization of Tewa art and cultural traditions from their earliest days to the present. An 11,000-square-foot Indian Arts and Crafts Gallery and tourist information center feature a huge selection of northern New Mexican Indian pottery as well as jewelry, sculptures, kachinas, and sandpaintings. Seasonal activities at the complex include dances and bread baking in the traditional beehive-shaped adobe hornos (ovens). Even if you arrive in midwinter, the soft-crumbed pueblo bread is usually available both in the gallery and at Ó, a restaurant specializing in pueblo and regional foods.

A short distance down the pike on Española's outskirts, **David Dear's** small showroom is the place to shop for elegant silver and gold jewelry. David is a self-taught jeweler who works in noble metals and draws inspiration from traditional Southwestern designs. Part of the Museum of New Mexico and the Santa Fe Wheelwright Museum's permanent collections, David's jewelry is designed, cast, and hand-finished locally in Arroyo Seco. His concha belts, bolo ties, tip sets, belt buckles, pins, earrings, cuff links, and studs are meticulously cast and exquisitely finished.

Entering Española, you cross the Santa Cruz River. A farming and ranching community founded in the middle of the 19th century, the area served for many years as the shipping point for produce grown in the Española Valley. Today the city's main product appears to be low riders, automobiles that have been specially modified. The basic low rider has had its chassis adapted to accommodate a smaller set of wheels set on a wider axle. The steering wheel is often replaced with welded chain link, and the paint job can be customized to reflect the owner's artistic taste, whether it's a vision of Our Lady of Guadalupe or a space-age scene. Some low riders are equipped with a special hydraulic system, which enables the car to hop, rise up and down, and perform various maneuvers. The pride and joy of Hispanic males of all ages, the low rider is mucho macho.

If you have developed an appetite, it's time to divert from the road to Abiquiu and head into town on Riverside Drive. Española has several restaurants dealing in northern New Mexican food. The first place you encounter will be **Jo Ann's Ranch O Casados.** The Casados family grows its own red and green chiles and corn products in their nearby valley farm. They serve breakfast all day, and their blue corn tortillas make a wonderful base for enchiladas.

Another modest but genuine purveyor of New Mexican cooking is **Matilda's Restaurant,** located a block off Riverside on Corlett. Matilda and Phillip Guillen have been serving their food to Española's citizens for 50 years. It's a place favored by locals, and you're more likely to encounter families out for dinner than transplants from Santa Fe.

El Paragua, a block off Riverside on Santa Cruz Road (the Taos High Road), is perhaps the most famous of Española restaurants. Larry and Pete Atencio started the business as a taco, tamale, and lemonade stand in 1958. Their dad, Luis, provided them with a beach umbrella to shade them from the hot sun, and it became the stand's namesake, El Paragua, or "the umbrella." As good things will, their taco stand flourished, expanded, and matured into a restaurant, enveloping the former tack rooms of the family home and the plumbing shop next door. Additions continued through the years, creating the El Paragua sprawling complex that exists today.

Oddly enough, although the menu runs the gamut from a rib-eye steak topped with whole green chiles to lightly breaded, pan-fried trout, the house specialty is still the Tacos Estilo El Paragua, which marries deep-fried tortillas with succulent beef shreds moistened with a reduction of tomato and a hint of cumin.

If you don't want the full restaurant treatment, the Atencios have an adjoining taco stand named **El Parasol.** You can drive up, place your order, and enjoy your lunch in the shade of the ancient cottonwood trees.

In your meandering around Española, you might encounter individuals in white robes, their hair confined by snowy white turbans. They are members of the Sikh Dharma community, an East Indian religious sect with many non-Indian followers. They have an ashram nearby, which draws followers from all parts of the globe, especially during the summer solstice in June.

Before leaving Española, you should spend an hour with Leo Polo-Trujillo and his partner, Beryl D. Steuart, at the **Chimayo Trading Post/Marco Polo Shop.** This New Mexico landmark is the quintessential trading post, with its solid adobe walls and cavernous, wood-beamed interior. Located where Sandia intersects Riverside Drive, the post was founded in the nearby village of Chimayo by Leo's dad, the late Esquipula de Aguero "E. D." Trujillo, a prominent figure in Rio Arriba. Following an unneighborly dispute in 1926, E. D. moved both family and trading post to Española, where he constructed a new compound consisting of the post, the family home, and the Ramona Hotel, named for his wife. In June 1939 fire destroyed the post and residence. Undeterred, E. D. rebuilt around the baked adobe walls.

The post prospered through the '30s and '40s as a regular stop on Fred Harvey Tours, but the building fell into disrepair after E. D.'s death. Leo returned to his childhood home in the 1980s after a 30-year career as a bursar with Pan American Airlines. The place was a wreck, suffering damage from years of neglect and having lost many of its unique architectural elements to vandals. Not content to see his heritage destroyed, Leo and his partner Beryl, who had retired from Air France, dug in and restored the buildings.

Opened in 1983 as the Marco Polo Shop at the Trading Post and named to the state list of cultural properties, the mercantile sells much the same merchandise as the original. There are objects for all pocketbooks. Silver jewelry, old pawn, pueblo pottery, and beautifully carved santos fill the antique glass cases. Leo and Beryl's personal collection with NFS (not-for-sale) tags rests among the New Mexican crafts, baskets from Pakistan, and Zapotec weaving. The partners sit at the entrance, available to anyone interested in a specific item or just wishing to talk about the history of the post and the area. A symbol of their hospitality to travelers is the perennial coffeepot sitting on the burner, free java to anyone in need of a fix.

Leaving the city, you head northwest on the Chama Highway. Passing the small village of Hernandez, you might recall one of photographer Ansel Adam's best-loved and most widely recognized prints, "Moonrise Hernandez," which shows a full moon rising over snowcapped mountains. If you give in to the temptation to search for the scene, chances are you will be disappointed. Modern development has all but obliterated the

With its adobe walls and wood-beamed interior, the Chimayo Trading Post/Marco Polo Shop is the quintessential New Mexico trading post.

simple arrangement of church, village, and cemetery. However, if you stop at **Romero's Fruit Stand** on the west side of the road, Jake or Clarabelle will be happy to point you in the right direction. In addition to information, they stock an incredible supply of New Mexican products: long and short ristras (ropes of chiles), ristras in the shape of hearts or wreaths, 14 varieties of beans and bean soup mixes, 10 varieties of red and 6 varieties of green chiles, and corn products like panocha, chaqueque, atole, and harina.

Heading north and west, you pass the junction of the Rio del Oso, the Rio Ojo Caliente, and the Rio Chama near Chili. Keeping the Rio Chama's waters to the east, you enter the outskirts of Abiquiu. Several commercial services line the highway, but like some medieval fortress, the village itself sits atop a hill.

Abiquiu was first settled around 1744 by a handful of Spaniards and genizaros, Christianized Indians freed from slavery. The village, built on top of an old Tewa pueblo on the banks of the Chama River, was a center of trade and the starting point of Fathers Dominguez and Escalante's 2,000-mile trek to California.

For years the village slumbered in relative anonymity. As in many northern New Mexican towns, life centered around home and church. Traditionally, the men supported Los Hermanos de Nuestro Padre Jesus Nazareno, or Los Penitentes, a clandestine Christian flagellant group whose members, in addition to practicing penance during Lent, also contribute to the welfare of their communities through acts of charity. Their gathering place, or morada, occupies a prominent place on Abiquiu's hill.

Before Georgia O'Keeffe bought the ruin overlooking the river and the road to Santa Fe, there was little reason for outsiders to visit the village. O'Keeffe had been living at her home on Ghost Ranch, but the soil was poor and would not support a garden. She wearied of depending on the stores in Española or Santa Fe for fresh produce, and the Abiquiu property had both garden space and water.

In the 1970s strangers appeared in the village, seeking the famous artist, and both she and the townsfolk grew tired of constant intrusions on their cherished privacy. She is said to have greeted one overardent visitor who wanted to "see" her with four words: "front side," a turn to the rear and "backside," and a slamming door accompanied by "good-bye."

With this history, it is not surprising that the town maintains an uneasy truce with guests. No photos are permitted in the village, and should you wander up the hill to the community out of curiosity, you will be treated courteously but with a distinct touch of reserve.

The artist's home, administered by the Georgia O'Keeffe Museum, is open for tours, and guests will find the museum is a faithful guardian. Regulations limit the number of visitors, and there is a prohibition on photography, note-taking, and recording. Many rooms may be viewed only at a distance. This creates a fine line between making the home accessible to O'Keeffe's legion of admirers and maintaining an old adobe property that was never intended to host legions.

Tours are small (a maximum of 12), last approximately an hour, and must be booked in advance through the tour office. Demand is great, especially during the warm months, and it behooves you to phone ahead as early as possible.

It's all worth it. The gardens are lovingly maintained, even though they are not as extensive as when the artist was in residence. The home, which is kept as it was 1984, is larger than expected, about 5,000 square feet. The main house is divided into quadrants: storage, living areas, service, and guest quarters.

The house was built around an interior court in the plazuela style, and most rooms open onto it, including the sitting room with its ceiling vigas and cedar rajas. A wall of windows, a familiar O'Keeffe signature, overlooks ancient tamarisk trees, and an aged jade plant fills a corner of the living room. Furniture is minimal. Adobe bancos (benches) line the kiva fireplace wall, and a rattlesnake skeleton is seductively displayed under glass at one end. Chairs are by classic designers Charles Eames and Eero Saarinen.

The view from the dining room is extended through "the roofless room," an adjoining outdoor atrium shaded by a screened roof. The table is a model O'Keeffe had made from a design by Rudolf Schindler, a designer for several Frank Lloyd Wright homes. Utilizing hinges, the plywood table opens to accommodate guests or folds for more intimate dining.

The bright kitchen houses another plywood table, this time supported by sawhorses, and the cabinets are recessed deep into the thick adobe walls on one side of the kitchen. There is a Chambers gas range and an old KitchenAid dishwasher.

The "Indian Room" is a small rectangle off the kitchen. The chamber features a shepherd's bed elevated above the fireplace so the warmth of the adobe could toast a traveler's bones on cold nights. O'Keeffe used the space mainly to dry herbs and store fruits and vegetables.

The pantry and laundry also adjoin the kitchen. It is interesting to discover how involved O'Keeffe was with the running of her household. Some of the pantry's jars are labeled in her handwriting, grown somewhat spidery in her old age. To those who consider the artist's retreat to New Mexico a withdrawal from the conveniences of the modern world, it may come as a surprise to discover she had not only a dishwasher but two freezers and a mangle.

The artist's studio and living area were created where the original barn had stood on the property. The studio is breathtaking, particularly with brilliant sunlight entering through the windowed wall. Looking out the window, O'Keeffe could view the Sierra Negre Mountains; the "white place," which she often painted; and the yellow domes of the Dar al Islam mosque. O'Keeffe's collection of stones lines the windowsills.

The bedroom off the studio is quite small and spare, with two windows at right angles and a small kiva fireplace. The hand of Buddha in the "fear not," or mudra position, and more simple rocks are the spare decorations.

After your midday tour, your immediate need will be for bodily fortification. Your best bet both for meals and lodging is the **Abiquiu Inn.** The dining room has a traditional menu with specialties in Middle Eastern fare, lamb, and northern New Mexico cuisine. A gift shop adjoining the lobby carries selections from around the world as well as work by native and local artisans.

Accommodations vary from plain motel rooms to lovely casitas overlooking the river. With woodstoves, eat-in kitchens, talavera-tiled baths, and separate bedrooms, the casitas are the best choice, especially in the off-season, when you will have to rustle some of your meals.

Abiquiu's vibes continue to inspire painters, weavers, potters, photographers, and the like. With more than 60 artists and craftspeople working in the area, the visitor has a wonderful opportunity to take home original work. Every Columbus Day weekend the artists and townspeople get together to put on their annual studio tour, augmented by a bake and book sale and special northern New Mexico foods.

The El Farolito Restaurant in El Rito is known for its green chile dishes.

Bode's General Merchandise is on the main highway at the base of the hill. Founded in 1919, the store was once located in the heart of the village. It carries everything from rabbit feed and fishing lures to a complete line of groceries, including some herbal remedies and natural food items. Prepared food is limited to deli soups, salads, and sandwiches, fresh pastries, rotisserie chickens, or the hot pot full of fresh tamales by the counter.

Most locals and visitors in the know make the 16-mile drive to El Rito and **El Farolito Restaurant.** For 15 years Dennis and Carmen Trujillo have been serving up some of the best green chile in New Mexico from their modest café. Dennis goes through more than 100 sacks of chile a year, making up his "secret recipe" from three varieties that he selects from crops in Los Cruces and Romero's in Hernandez. All their entrées are excellent, but ah, those green chile burritos! There's just enough heat to leave that little tingle around the lips that chile-heads savor.

A visit to Abiquiu should last more than a single day. Take an afternoon to visit **Ghost Ranch,** 13 miles northwest of the village. Part of the 1766 21,000-acre Piedra Lumbre Land Grant, the property and some adjacent parcels were purchased in the 1930s by Mr. and Mrs. Arthur Pack for a guest ranch.

In 1929 Georgia O'Keeffe first visited Taos at the urging of Dorothy Brett and the indomitable patron of the arts, Mabel Dodge Luhan. But Taos and its arts scene were too public for O'Keeffe, and in 1934 she found the spectacular valley of remote Ghost Ranch more to her liking. Renting from the Packs for several summers and returning every winter to New York and her husband, noted photographer Alfred Stieglitz, O'Keeffe finally convinced Arthur Pack to sell her his own residence, Rancho de los Burros, and 7 acres of land. She owned this property concurrently with the Abiquiu house, and Ghost Ranch environs are the subjects of much of her best-loved work: the red and gray hills across from the roadside park south of the ranch, Kitchen Mesa's red and yellow cliffs, and flat-topped Pedernal Mountain.

In 1955 the Packs donated Ghost Ranch to the Presbyterian Church. Now an adult study center with a variety of programs focusing on the northern New Mexico environment, Ghost Ranch's ties to the O'Keeffe story are largely in the past. The artist's former home is on private land with no public access. There are no Georgia O'Keeffe originals at the ranch, no O'Keeffe museum. For some basic information, stop at the Ghost Ranch Piedra Lumbre Education and Visitor Center on US 84, where you'll find two museums, one dedicated to the cultures of northern New Mexico and the other to natural history.

If you venture into the complex, you'll find guests are welcomed, and with sufficient notice you can join students of all ages for cafeteria-style meals or in the simple ranch-style accommodations. There's even an RV area set aside for campers. The center's hiking trails, including the trail to the top of Kitchen Mesa, are open to everyone. A map and sign-in sheet are available at the office reception desk.

In addition, the **Florence Hawley Ellis Museum of Anthropology** and the **Ruth Hall Museum of Paleontology** are open to the public. The anthropology museum, constructed on the design of a great kiva, illustrates

12,000 years of life in the Rio Grande–Chama–Gallina Valleys. Examples of Indian crafts, both historic and prehistoric, line the displays. The re-created workshop of Max Roybal, santero and longtime teacher of wood carving at the ranch, is riveting for lovers of Hispanic arts. Many of his solemn wooden saints keep watch on the foibles of mortals from their nichos (niches) by his workbench.

The Museum of Paleontology focuses on the Triassic period, a time when most nearby fossil beds were laid down. Stretching across one wall, Flora and Fauna of the Triassian Twilight features Phytosaur, a giant lizard. A work in progress, the fossilized remains of Coelophysis, earliest known dinosaur, awaits the skilled hands of trained paleontologists commissioned with wresting secrets from its tomb of silt stone.

To visit the **Monastery of Christ in the Desert,** you must turn west on Forest Service Road 151 a couple of miles north of the museum. There is no sign, and the first mile is deceptively paved. You will quickly find yourself on a 13-mile dirt track, which can be impassible in a touring car if there has been any recent rain or snow. Check at Bode's (see page 42) for conditions, and give yourself plenty of time to reach the monastery.

You will be traveling through the Chama River Canyon Wilderness Area, surrounded by its high polychrome bluffs and riverine habitat. The farther you progress from pavement, the more you understand why Father Aelred Wall and his Benedictine monks founded this sanctuary in 1964 to "sing God's praises in the wilderness" and provide a "place apart" for those seeking prayer and meditation. Currently 23 to 25 brothers from places as diverse as Vietnam and Argentina reside at the monastery, practicing Benedict's precepts of common and individual prayer, reading, study, and manual labor.

Upon reaching the monastery, you should park in the designated area and walk to the foot of the chapel, where there is a large bell. Give it a good pull or two, which will summon the guestmaster, your liaison with the monastic community. Whether you arrive on retreat or as a day visitor, you are welcome to attend any of the seven daily services, walk in those places not considered private by the monks, or visit the gift shop to browse its cornucopia of religious books and crafts.

George Nakashima, the famous Japanese American woodworker and architect, designed the chapel. The soaring bell tower backs against red rock cliffs, whose fiery tones reflect through chapel windows in the late afternoon. The altar is a 5-foot block of Colorado granite, and the first monk's choir is graced with a large carving of Our Lady of Guadalupe by Maria Romero Cash.

The second monk's choir contains the tabernacle, also designed by Nakashima. The tabernacle's open doors are painted with representations of a variety of saints, including Gabriel; Benedict; Scholastica, Benedict's twin sister; Francis; and Kateri, the Lily of the Mohawks. A monk from San Juan el Bautista carved the figure of St. John the Baptist, patron of the monastery, and the large figure of the crucified Christ in back of the lectern.

If you come on retreat, you will be housed in the guesthouse, which is spare but comfortable. Woodstoves provide heat in cold weather, and kerosene lamps contribute light. A common bath has hot and cold running water. Meals are taken in silence in the refectory, and according to the Rule of Benedict, the order's founder, no red meat is served.

Before departing Abiquiu, take time to visit **Dar al Islam,** an educational organization dedicated to fostering better understanding between the Muslim and non-Muslim world. It is 2½ miles down CR 155, a well-maintained dirt road. You turn about a quarter mile after crossing the Chama River bridge to the northwest of Abiquiu.

The organization's headquarters were designed by Hassam Fathy, the Egyptian architect, and consist of offices, a mosque, school, summer camp, and teacher training institute. The buildings are beautiful—yellow domes punctuated with carved white stucco screen windows. You are welcome to visit, remembering that Muslim law prescribes modesty—no shorts, halter tops, or the like. A head covering for women is appreciated but not required.

The beautiful buildings of the Dar al Islam headquarters in Abiquiu were designed by Egyptian architect Hassam

Entering the mosque, you'll find benches to remove your shoes and an anteroom to the left containing a tiled tank or fountain for ablutions. A niche, or mihrab, in the wall is oriented to Mecca, and soft rugs carpet the floors. Since religious law prohibits figurative decoration, the mosque's majesty is contained in its series of interlocking arches.

Dar al Islam owns 1,600 acres, including "the white place," one of O'Keeffe's favorite subjects. No special permission is required to hike in the canyon, and you should not miss the opportunity even if you go but a short distance. It is a moving, some might say disturbing, place. Ghostly columns of gray volcanic tuff rise like spirit sentinels, and sections of the canyon wall resemble giant versions of the drip castles you made on childhood beach outings.

Departing Abiquiu, you head for El Rito, and although it may not be obvious upon your first pass through town, it is a community of artists. The second or third weekend in October they hold a studio tour, which includes more than 20 stops. If you visit any other time of year, stop at either Martin's General Store, the big white frame building in the center of town, or at El Farolito across the street. They have lists of studios open to the public.

A sampling might include the atelier of Cindy Talamantes, who weaves exquisite pine needle baskets and crafts cunning Mimbres, animal ornaments of clay disks framed in pine needles and tiny pinecones.

Nick Herrera, a well-known santero, has his studio in his residence 1.4 miles out NM 110. Nick does both modern and traditional versions of the saints. You'll see a Penitente death cart driven by the skeletal Dona Sebastiana as well as his humorous 1990s interpretation, which portrays those dry bones perched on a lowrider motorcycle.

Kathleen Vanderbrook and her husband, Terry, share a studio to the rear of El Llano Mercantile. He is a potter, and she creates handmade paper, prints, and paintings.

After you've visited El Rito's artist community, drive over to **Ojo Caliente** hot springs, which have attracted health seekers since prehistoric times. The ruins of three Tewa pueblos rest on the mesa above the resort. Even Cabeza de Vaca, the 16th-century Spanish explorer, is said to have passed by, and it was he who gave the springs their name.

Perhaps the resort's greatest appeal is the variety of its waters: lithia for "depression, sluggish kidneys and excess stomach gas"; iron to fortify the

"The White Place" was a favorite subject for painter Georgia O'Keeffe.

blood; arsenic for "arthritis, rheumatism, stomach, burn relief, excema [sic], and contusions"; and soda springs for "over acidic stomach problems." Water temperatures range from 80 to 106 degrees, and the springs' output tops 140,000 gallons per day.

The Big Pool is filled with water from the iron and arsenic springs, and the same combination of waters is blended in the upper cliffside pools and three private outdoor mineral pools. Water in the enclosed "steam" pool is piped directly from the Soda Spring, the rock walls creating a soft echo and producing a sense of calm and relaxation. For depression or indigestion, use some muscle and pump and drink from the Lithia Spring, located in what was once the center of the plaza.

Pools are coed and bathing suits are the order of the day except for the private pools available by reservation. If you should visit Ojo during the cool months, be sure to bring a pair of beach shoes and a warm terry robe for dashes from pool to pool.

Part of Ojo's charm is its laid-back, unpretentious, somewhat retro atmosphere, which current owners Sherman and Joyce Scott have tamed by renovating structures and converting all facilities to geothermal heating and cooling. The old mission revival–style adobe hotel, built in 1916, is listed on the National Register of Historic Places. Its simple rooms are clean and somewhat spare, and as was common at spa hotels during the period of construction, there are no showers. Guests were expected to bathe at the springs.

The north and south cottages have been remodeled and now boast television, refrigerators, and DVD/VCR players. Twelve new suites provide upgrades to more funky accommodations. They are in the typical Southwestern style, with 500 square feet of space, kiva fireplaces, viga ceilings, and private patios. Six will have cliffside, private, two-person soaking tubs filled with the mineral waters.

For a group or families, Hill House, Adobe House, and Mauro House are rental homes with full kitchens, baths, and showers. A gift shop, conference center, RV park, and the historic round barn round out the facilities.

Artesian Restaurant at the hotel serves three meals a day and specializes in fresh food prepared to the diner's preference. Vegetarian meals are routine, although the red meat eater won't go hungry. The dinner menu might include a chipotle Caesar salad, cactus dumplings with tahini sauce, piñon trout with wild rice pilaf, or Southwest favorites like enchiladas or fajitas.

The Inn and Mercantile at Ojo is an alternative to the resort lodging. Once a youth hostel and somewhat seedy bed and breakfast, the inn was purchased by the Wimett family and completely redone. The section containing the original B&B rooms was torn down and replaced with an attractive adobe building with all the modern amenities. Zemmie Wimett, a longtime interior decorator and antiques shop proprietor, has furnished the rooms with iron beds and old pine armoires. A full breakfast is served in the cheery common room.

The Shops at the Mercantile are another family venture. Daughter Leza manages the store, which specializes in unusual natural fiber clothing, much of it designed by her sisters, Claudia and Diana Wimett. In addition, an eclectic selection of jewelry—some of her own design and constructed of found objects—is available. There are also pieces by local artists, knitted ware, and assorted bibelots. Zemmie's collection of antiques for sale occupies one wing of the store; she has an especially fine assortment of old quilts.

Charlie Jordan's **Dragon River Herbals** in Ojo is a must-see if you're interested in herbal medicine. He specializes in organic, wild-crafted, or woods-grown herbs, and his selection runs an encyclopedic range from agrimony to yucca. His nostrums are compounded to treat everything from turista to hay fever.

Before completing your loop of O'Keeffe Country, you should make plans to visit the **Rancho de San Juan,** a member of the prestigious Relais & Châteaux group. Created with an eye to

The elegant Rancho de San Juan sits at the base of Black Mesa with sweeping views of the San Juan Mountains and the hills of Ojo Caliente Valley.

elegance and luxury, the inn rests at the base of Black Mesa with vistas of the San Juan Mountains and the hills of Ojo Caliente Valley.

A bonus to guests of the inn and restaurant is a visit to the *Sandstone Shrine, Windows in the Earth.* In the rock formations of the mesa backing the property, owners John H. Johnson III and David Heath provided artist-sculptor Ra Paulette with the medium required to create a grand opus. Burrowing through the pliant rock, the artist created chambers: a space for performance, an egg-shaped meditation room, and a writing room, all lit by arched windows overlooking the Jemez Mountains. The general public is welcome to the unusual construction Saturday through Monday by reservation.

Built in 1993, the inn's hacienda and adjoining casitas are arranged around a center courtyard brimming with flowers and native plants. Each casita has a distinctive decor that blends the elegance of antiques and old world fabrics with the charm of the Southwest. Private Talavera-tiled baths, wood-burning fireplaces, and private porches complete the picture.

The hacienda, which is residence to the owners and Johnson's mother, is also home to David and John's extensive collection of art. The first thing that greets you when you enter the reception area might be a magnificent Tony Abeyta oil of Navajo yei spirits or a weaving by Navajo artist Charlene Laughing. Everywhere you look you discover another treasure—a small pair of furred chaps presented to the elder Johnson when he was 6 by a Sioux lady, the startling mask of the ghost of a drowned whaler carved by a northwestern Maka Indian, or a set of Navajo dance wands.

The main dining room, where breakfast and John's gourmet dinners are served, is a sun-filled expanse opening out onto the patio and garden. A small auxiliary dining room accommodates a carved Balinese mirror against one wall, a breakfront with a collection of carved kachinas and Zuni fetishes, and a high shelf with pueblo pots. A full breakfast is offered to guests (for a fee), and dinner is available by reservation to guests and the public Tuesday through Saturday.

To complete your tour of O'Keeffe Country, be sure to stop at the **Georgia O'Keeffe Museum** in Santa Fe. The first art museum in the United States dedicated to the work of a woman artist of international stature, it is housed in an adobe structure renovated by architect Richard Gluckman. The main building houses the majority of the permanent collection in nine large exhibition galleries that wrap around an outdoor courtyard displaying sculpture by O'Keeffe. With more than 120 paintings, watercolors, drawings, pastels, and sculpture, the holdings represent the largest repository of the artist's work in either public or private hands. Founded in 1995 by philanthropists Anne and John Marion, the museum, though entirely private, has a close association with the Museum of New Mexico and its supporting foundation.

While in the vicinity, don't miss the **O'Keeffe Café** adjoining the museum. The 150-year-old Territorial home, which served as barracks for Union officers during the Civil War, may be old Santa Fe on the outside, but the interior is modern. The stone-tinted walls are hung with large black-and-white photos of O'Keeffe in her kitchen, and the chairs and banquettes are upholstered in vivid hues of lipstick red. Bouquets of long-stemmed red roses grace the tables and reservation desk. Both lunch and dinner are exceptional, with Executive Chef Carmen Rodriguez utilizing classical French technique and culling menu ingredients from the entire culinary universe.

Contacts:

Abiquiu Inn, P.O Box 1010, US 84, Abiquiu, 87510. Call 1-888-2902 or 505-685-4378. Restaurant, summer, daily 7:30–9; winter, call for hours. Web site: www.abiquiu.com.

Abiquiu Studio Tour, P.O. Box 906, Abiquiu, 87510. Call 505-685-4454 or 505-685-4200. Columbus Day weekend. Web site: www.abiquiu studiotour.org.

Bode's General Merchandise, US 84, P.O. Box 100, Abiquiu, 87510. Call 505-685-4422. Summer, Mon. through Thurs. 6:30–7, Fri. 6:30–8, Sat. 7–8, Sun. 7–7; winter, Mon. through Fri. 6:30–7, Sat. 7–7, Sun. 7–7.

Chimayo Trading Post, The Marco Polo Shop, 110 Sandia Drive, Española, 87532. Call 505-753-9414. Summer, daily 9–5; winter, daily 9–4:30. Call to confirm.

Cindy Talamantes, CR 246, #30, P.O. Box 173, El Rito, 87530. For appointment, contact by e-mail, claudius@cybermesa.com.

Dar al Islam Foundation, P.O. Box 180, Abiquiu, 87510. Call 505-6854515, Ext. 22. Web site: www.daralislam.org.

David Dear Inc., P.O. Box 1117, San Juan Pueblo, 87566. Call 1-800-753-8141 or 505-753-8141. Mon. through Sat. 9–5. Web site: www.daviddear.com.

Dragon River Herbals, P.O. Box 74, Ojo Caliente, 87549. Call 1-800-813-2118 or 505-583-2348. Mon. through Fri. 10–4. Web site: www.dragonriverherbals.com.

El Farolito Restaurant, 1212 Main Street, P.O. Box 27, El Rito, 87530. Call 505-581-9509. Summer, Tues. through Fri. 11–2:30 and 4:30–8, Sat. and Sun. 11–8; winter, Tues. through Fri. 11:30–7:30, Sat. and Sun. 11–7:30.

El Paragua Restaurant and El Parasol Drive-in, 603 Santa Cruz Road, Española, 87532. Call 1-800-929-8226 or 505-753-3211. Lunch, daily 11–2; dinner, Mon. through Thurs. 2–9, Fri. and Sat. 2–9:30, Sun. 2–8. Web site: www.elparagua.com.

Española Valley Chamber of Commerce, P.O. Box 190, 710 Paseo de Oñate, Española, 87532. Call 505-753-2831. Mon. through Fri. 9–5. Web site: www.espanolachamber.com.

Florence Hawley Ellis Museum of Anthropology and Ruth Hall Museum of Paleontology, Ghost Ranch Education and Retreat Center, US 84, Abiquiu, 87510. Call 505-685-4333. Summer, Tues. through Sat. 9–5, Sun. and Mon. 1–5; otherwise, Tues. through Sat. 9–5. Web site: www.ghostranch.org.

Georgia O'Keeffe Home and Studio Tour Office, P.O. Box 40, Abiquiu, 87510. Call 505-685-4539. Office, Mon. through Fri. 10–3. One-hour tours are offered April through November, Tues., Thurs., and Fri. at 9:30 and 11 AM, 2 and 3:30 PM. Call for reservations well in advance. Meet at Tour Office off US 84 next to the Abiquiu Inn. Donation due one month prior to tour.

Georgia O'Keeffe Museum, 217 Johnson Street, Santa Fe, 87501. Call 505-995-0785. Tues. through Sun. 10–5, Fri. 10–8. Fee. Web site: www.okeeffemuseum.org.

Ghost Ranch Education and Retreat Center, HC 77, Box 11, Abiquiu, 87510. Call 505-685-4333. Office, daily 8–5. Web site: www.ghostranch.org.

Ghost Ranch Piedra Lumbre Education and Visitor Center, US 84, HCR 77, Box 15, Abiquiu, 87510. Call 505-685-4312. March through October, daily 9–5. Web site: www.ghostranch.org.

The Inn at Ojo, Hot Springs Road, P.O. Box 215, Ojo Caliente, 87549. Call 505-583-9131. Web site: www.ojocaliente.com/pages/inn_and _merc_at_ojo.html.

Jo Ann's Ranch O Casados Restaurant, 938 N. Riverside Drive, Española, 87532. Call 505-753-1334. Mon. through Sat. 7–9, Sun. 7–4. Web site: www.joannsranchocasados.com.

Martin's General Store, NM 554, P.O. Box 9, El Rito, 87530. Call 505-5814567. Mon. through Sat. 8–6.

Matilda's Restaurant, Box 30107, Corlett Road, Española, 87532. Call 505-753-3200. Tues. through Thurs. 10:30–8, Fri. 10:30–9, Sat. and Sun. 9–9.

The Mercantile at Ojo, P.O. Box 215, Ojo Caliente, 87549. Call 505-583-9153. Daily 9–5. Web site: www.ojocaliente.com/pages/inn_and _merc_at_ojo.html.

Monastery of Christ in the Desert, Guestmaster, P.O. Box 270, Abiquiu, 87510. No phone. For retreat accommodations, write well in advance. Do not use Express Mail or Federal Express. Web site: www.christdesert.org.

Nicholas Herrera, Canyon Road, P.O. Box 43, El Rito, 87530. Call 505-581-4733. By appointment only. Web site: www.sanangelfolkart.com/ Herrera.

Ojo Caliente Mineral Springs Resort, P.O. Box 68, 50 Los Banos Drive, Ojo Caliente, 87549. Hotel and spa, 1-800-222-9162 or 505-583-2233. Baths, daily 8–10, Artesian Restaurant, breakfast, daily 7:30–10:30; lunch, daily 11:30–2:30; dinner, Sun. through Thurs. 5–9, Fri. and Sat. 5–9:30. November through March, restaurant closes one hour earlier. Web site: www.ojocalientespa.com.

O'Keeffe Café, 217 Johnson Street, Santa Fe, 87501. Call 505-946-1065. Daily, lunch from 11 AM, wine bar from 3 PM, dinner from 5:30 PM. Web site: www.okeeffecafe.com.

Pojoaque Pueblo: Poeh Museum and Ó Eating House, US 84/285, Santa Fe, 87501. **Museum,** 78 Cities of Gold Road, Santa Fe, 87506. Call 505-455-5041. Mon. through Fri. 9–5, Sat. 9–4. Restaurant, call

505-455-5065. Daily 11–3 and 5–9. Museum Web site: www.poeh museum.com; pueblo Web site: www.citiesofgold.com/PuebloMain.

Pojoaque Pueblo Visitor Center and Gallery, 96 Cities of Gold Road, Santa Fe, 87506. Call 505-455-3460 or 505-455-9023. Mon. through Sat. 9–5, Sun. 10–4.

Rancho De San Juan Country Inn and Restaurant, P.O. Box 4140, Fairview Station, Española, 87533. Call 505-753-6818. Office hours daily 8–6. Dinner Tues. through Sat. by reservation. Web site: www.rancho desanjuan.com.

Romero's Fruit Stand, (US 84/285, 5 miles north of Española in Hernandez), Route 4, Box 179, Española, 87532. Call 505-753-4189. Daily 8–6.

Vanderbrook Studios, No. 2 County Road 246, P.O. Box 254, El Rito, 87530. Call 505-581-4597. By chance or by appointment.

Herb collecting

SECOND PRIZE
THIRD PRIZE
THIRD PRIZE

CHAPTER

3

Trading Posts and Ancient Cities

Getting there: From Albuquerque, take I-25 north 20 miles to Bernalillo, Exit 242. From Bernalillo head northeast on US 550 approximately 112 miles to the entrance to **Chaco Culture National Historical Park.** Take CR 7900 3 miles east of Nageezi (paved the first 5 miles followed by 16 miles of dirt), then turn onto CR 7950. When you arrive in the park, you will encounter blacktop. Leaving Chaco, retrace your route to US 550 and continue 46 miles to Bloomfield, where you turn north onto NM 544 7 miles to Aztec. In Aztec follow the signs to **Aztec National Monument.** Retrace your steps to NM 64 west 3 miles to the Salmon Ruins and from there 10 miles to Farmington. Go south 74 miles on NM 371 to Crownpoint. Outside Crownpoint, head southeast on Navajo 48 10 miles to Borrego Pass. Finish the 19-mile Navajo 48 loop by returning to NM 371. Pass Smith Lake and join I-25 at Exit 53, Thoreau. Stauder's Navajo Lodge is 8 miles west of Thoreau, off the interstate.

Highlights: On this foray into the heart of Indian country, you'll encounter the ruins of the ancient Ancestral Puebloan cities of **Chaco, Salmon,** and **Aztec.** You'll sojourn in the Navajo Nation, where solitary hogans dot the desert and a few trading posts still fulfill their traditional role of supplying the outback. You'll explore **Farmington** and attend a rug auction on the reservation.

Let's Go: This is one of the most challenging and interesting journeys you will make, but before you set out, understand that you will need more preparation than usual if you are to enjoy it to the fullest. Your first consideration should be the extent to which you intend to investigate **Chaco Culture National Historical Park,** a World Heritage Site. As your delight in this expansive ancient city depends on the amount of time you're willing to devote to its exploration, you should be aware that a quick once-over from the seat of your car is going to leave you longing for more. It's a tease, a come-on, and although it's better than not seeing Chaco at all, it is largely unsatisfying. To really understand the wonder and complexity of the site, you need to stay a day or two—generally possible only by camping. Chaco is a remote and primitive park, and visitors should not expect the comfort and conveniences associated with many other sites. There is no food, gas, lodging, or auto repair. Much of the entry road is unpaved, creating access problems after heavy rains. If you have any inkling that the area has received showers, a call to the park is in order before you leave.

Anticipation builds as you set out, bypassing Bernalillo (see chapter 1) and beginning the northwest trek up US 550, the main connector between central and northwestern New Mexico. Not too long ago, this route was a dirt strip, dotted by trading posts at irregular intervals. Now the four-lane highway accommodates heavier traffic between the two points.

Your route takes you through valleys carpeted in wildflowers—Mexican hat, peppergrass, penstemon, and clumps of deep purple asters. Soaring red rock mesas capped with gray thrust into the bluer-than-sapphire sky. You increase in elevation and pass into an area of open plains dotted with piñon and juniper. Pale green lines of cottonwoods thread the ditches, and cattle graze in their shade. To the west Cabezon Peak stands sentinel. The black volcanic plug, visible for miles, is sacred to the Navajos, who believe it is the head of the giant killed by Monster Slayer, one of their twin war gods.

The road takes you in and out of Jemez and Zia Pueblo lands, and eventually leads to Cuba. Travelers passing through town en route to the Four Corners area traditionally have used Cuba as a food and fuel stop. Stop in at Cuba's visitor's center, where you'll find a selection of maps and brochures on the area, friendly service, and advice on the Chaco road conditions. Or drop in on Cleo and Richard Velarde at their store, **Richard's,** where you'll find everything from old pawn to beadwork. The Velardes specialize in Navajo graphic art, and on any day you're likely to find originals by Edie Tsosie and Paul Vigil, or scratch paintings by Sammy Sandoval.

During 2006, Cuba's most beloved restaurant, El Bruno, burned to the ground, leaving a ruin of blackened adobe bricks and disappointed travelers. Take heart. North of town, Pres and Mary Martinez's **Presciliano's** has stepped up to the plate with a varied northern New Mexico menu. You'll find the usual selection of enchiladas, burritos, and tacos as well as "American" specials like chicken-fried steak, roast beef, and pork chops. Lunch service includes burgers, hot dogs, and sandwiches like their turkey and avocado on a fresh wheat roll. It's one of the few places where you can order just a bowl of red or green (chile, that is), with or without beans. And if you're curious about menudo, here's the place to try the famous Hispanic hangover remedy. But be warned: It's not for the fainthearted since it contains large doses of spice and tripe.

After leaving Cuba, you climb again into upland meadows flecked with clumps of large sage and ponderosa pine. Passing into a portion of the Jicarilla Apache Reservation, you drive through rolling, largely barren uplands.

Soon you arrive in Counselor, hardly a blip on the screen of life but home to the **Counselor Trading Post.** If this is your first impression of a post or if you have visited Hubbell's in Ganado, Arizona, a National Park Service and National Historic Site, you may be disappointed. First glance reveals a general store with shelves of Twinkies, Tide, and motor oil. You have to look harder to see the history here. Founded 65 years ago by Ann and Jim Counselor, the store was sold to Leonard Taft, who later took on Harold and Jane "Turk" McDonald as partners in the 1960s. Taft and the McDonalds additionally acquired the Blanco post, and in the 1960s the McDonalds bought out Taft's interest in both enterprises.

Well-known among the Indians of the Checkerboard section of the Navajo reservation, Harold and Turk would put on a huge Christmas party on the Saturday before Christmas each year. Hot dogs, doughnuts, and coffee were liberally dispensed along with sacks of candy for the children. More than 1,200 attended the event some years.

In 1988 a tragedy occurred. As he was closing up shop, Harold was brutally murdered. After his death, Turk sold the Blanco post and concentrated her efforts in Counselor until her death. Pita Lanell now manages the post for Turk's heirs.

Counselor continues to function as a traditional trading post, buying lambs and raw wool, finished rugs, and a small amount of jewelry from the Navajos. If you show an interest, Pita will go to the walk-in safe, which functions as their rug room, and bring out the current selection. They carry about 20 quality rugs from weavers such as Eleanor, Arlene, and Louise Johnson. The selection of patterns is eclectic, ranging from Tree of Life to depictions of Navajo gods, the yeis.

Trucking on, you'll pass natural gas wells scattered among the chamisa and blue flax, and at Lybrook, a gas refinery raises its piped and smoke-plumed head. You forge on past eroded hills, red and gray cliffs, and an outcrop of strange brown boulders resting on black sand hills. A scattering of Navajo homes and hogans breaks up the stark landscape before you arrive at the Chaco turnoff at County Road 7900. The first 5 miles are paved, but soon you hit 16 miles of rough dirt road, County Road 7950.

You may be perturbed to see **Chaco** isn't much of a canyon at all—more of a deep wash. And why, you ask, was this unimposing real estate such a center of Ancestral Puebloan culture? With the area's long winters, short growing seasons, and marginal rainfall, it seems an inhospitable place. Yet a sophisticated culture did flourish here a thousand years ago. People farmed the lowlands and built great masonry towns that connected with other towns over a far-reaching network of roads.

By the year 1000 Chaco was established as a political and socioeconomic center. It is thought that at one time as many as 5,000 people lived in the surrounding settlements, using Chaco as an administrative and ritual hub. What caused them to abandon this well-developed site? Scientists theorize that a prolonged drought in the San Juan Basin between 1130 and 1180 combined with a depleted environment led to food shortages that even the Chacoans' clever irrigation systems couldn't overcome. People moved on to better-watered areas, becoming the ancestors to today's pueblo people.

Your first stop should be the visitor's center, which includes a museum, information desk, theater, bookstore, and gift shop. Picnic tables and shade shelters are located in the parking lot. If your time in Chaco is short, you should check in at the desk to determine if a ranger-led walk is scheduled. This is the best way to learn a lot in a compressed interval.

If you can't connect with a ranger, drive the 9-mile loop, stopping to explore the sites that interest you. When hiking, be sure to wear proper footwear, for segments of the paths are uneven and steep. Don a protective hat and carry water and sunscreen.

There are six major ruins along the loop. Una Vida is close to the visitor's center and can be reached by trail from the parking lot. Only partially excavated, it contains five kivas and about 150 rooms. You'll also encounter

Pueblo Bonito, once four stories high and containing 600 rooms and 40 kivas; Chetro Ketl with 500 rooms and 16 kivas; Pueblo Del Arroyo with 280 rooms and more than 20 kivas; Kin Kletso with 100 rooms and 5 enclosed kivas; and Hungo Pavi.

Casa Rinconada is 6 miles from the visitor's center along the loop. The trail to the ruins and the nearby villages is a half mile long, round-trip. This is the only site that is not part of a community structure, and it encompasses the largest of the park's great kivas, 63½ feet across at floor level. You may view the kiva from the rim, but entrance is now forbidden, as the wear and tear of many feet were damaging the structure.

Casa Rinconada is thought to have astronomical/geometrical orientations. The major and minor axes fall along the lines of the four cardinal directions, and there are six irregularly spaced niches placed around the circumference. On the morning of the summer solstice, light from the sun comes through a small window just east of the kiva's north entrance and shines on the opposite wall directly above one of the six niches. As the sun moves higher, the beam sweeps downward and illuminates the niche.

Hiking trails lead to a number of other sites that require permits available at the visitor's center. Pueblo Alto is on the north rim, and Wijiji is at the canyon's east end. If you tramp the canyon's western end, you will pass Casa Chiquita and come to a large concentration of rock art before reaching the site of Peñasco Blanco. These petroglyphs and pictographs are of great interest to archeo-astronomers because they contain symbols that have led some to believe they represent the Crab Nebula supernova, recorded in Chinese journals of 1054.

This is not the only place that interests the scribes of the sky. On a cliff face near the top of Fajada Butte, three large upright slabs of rock stand in front of two spiral petroglyphs. A dagger of light appears on various points of the spirals during spring and fall equinoxes and winter and summer solstices. You can't climb the butte, but the visitor's center has an excellent film on its exploration and significance.

Chaco does not give up its secrets easily, so do plan to camp and enjoy the full experience. The National Park Service operates Gallo Campground, which has tent and RV sites. It's fairly primitive, with no shade, power, or potable water. You will find tables, fireplaces (bring your own charcoal), and central toilets. Drinking water is available at the visitor's center.

When you finish your inspection of Chaco, retrace your steps to US 550 and head northwest. You'll soon pass **Nageezi Trading Post,** now unfortunately a trash-littered framework. Nageezi is an old post, opened in 1939 by Jim McKuen, and was once the local post office. But there's a new brick post office now, obviating the need to keep the original in working order.

A few miles farther down the pike, **Blanco Trading Post** has undergone a revival thanks to owners Savannah and Justin Higgins, who've been running the place since 2002. They assumed ownership from Justin's family, who purchased it from the McDonalds. In the eye-catching gallery, they stock an impressive array of Navajo craft—mica-flecked, pitch-glazed pottery, jewelry, baskets, and a large selection of rugs. If you're a fan of Navajo folk art, you'll find they have one of the best selections in the Four Corners. The front room of the post stocks a full line of groceries and general merchandise, and at the By The Way Café you can sample traditional Navajo delicacies like mutton stew, chile beans, Navajo tacos, and platter-sized fry bread. Other than the Hubbell Trading Post, you won't find a more vital representative of the old trading post culture.

Just north of Blanco, El Huerfano Mesa rises to the east. A large, isolated, sandstone mesa in the flatlands, El Huerfano, or Dzil Na'oodilii, is one of the Navajos' sacred mountains. Said to be suspended from the sky with sunbeams, it is where Changing Woman gave birth to the Warrior Twins, Monster Slayer and Born for Water. Reputed to be one of the homes of First Man and First Woman of Navajo mythology, the semicircular mesa is off-limits to all but Native Americans. The ruins of two old trading posts are in the badlands just south of the mesa.

Traveling on, you pass through the outskirts of Bloomfield and head north to Aztec. The name of the town was chosen by early settlers to reflect the nearby ruins, which they thought were built by Indians related to the Aztecs of Mexico. Later investigation proved them wrong, as the Ancestral Puebloan builders were influenced first by Chaco and later by Mesa Verde.

Aztec Ruins National Monument celebrates this cultural mix and was named a World Heritage Site in 1987. Considered a Chacoan outlier by scholars, Aztec was first inhabited from 1111 to 1115 by a people who constructed a large, multistory pueblo on rising ground overlooking the Animas River. This huge, D-shaped compound had about 400 rooms on three levels and more than a dozen kivas, including the plaza's Great Kiva. The settlement prospered for several decades as an administrative, trade, and ceremonial center, but it declined along with Chaco and for many of the same reasons. Villagers moved away, and the town was deserted until

A visit to Aztec Ruins National Monument should include a stop at the settlement's Great Kiva.

1225, when a culture similar to that of Mesa Verde arrived, remodeling the pueblo and adding new structures. Like their predecessors, they flourished for a time and eventually departed.

The first Europeans to view the site in 1776 were Spanish padres Dominguez and Escalante; their cartographer, Bernardo Miera y Pacheco, put the location on his map. In a more recent era, the first visitor of record was Dr. John S. Newberry, a geologist. In 1859 he found the pueblo in a fair state of preservation, but in the years following his stay, pot hunters and looters ravaged the ruins. To protect the remnants, they were declared a national monument in 1913. However, it wasn't until 1916, when the American Museum of Natural History began sponsoring excavations, that the site was thoroughly explored. Earl H. Morris headed up the museum's first dig and spent seven years excavating and stabilizing the buildings, and in the 1930s he returned to supervise the reconstruction of the Great Kiva.

Visiting Aztec is a pleasure. The visitor's center is located in back of a grove of trees, which provides shade for a picnic area. The center features exhibits and an excellent 25-minute video, *Hisatsinom,* which introduces guests to the extensive and fascinating pre-Columbian Ancestral Puebloan history of the area. The video is shown on the hour and half hour throughout the day. Books, postcards, slides, posters, and videos are for sale, and you can pick up a trail guide booklet for the quarter-mile self-guided path.

The trail passes through several rooms with intact original roofs as well as the semi-subterranean Great Kiva. Pause a while in the depths of this ceremonial hall and listen while the plaintive notes of a native flute call up the shadows of times past. The dust motes dancing in the rays emanating from the dual entrances call up the whirling ghosts of Ancestral Puebloan shamen, entreating their gods for favor.

Skip ahead several centuries, and venture into the town of Aztec, where you'll find the **Aztec Museum, Pioneer Village,** and **Oil Field Exhibit** on North Main Avenue. Stroll through a doctor's office, sheriff's post complete with a soft-sculpture lawman at his desk, a blacksmith shop and foundry, a pioneer cabin, the general store, the post office, and the Cedar Hill Church, all reconstructed from original buildings in the area.

Don't miss the 1920 Fort Worth Spudder drilling rig with its wooden derrick, and look inside the old "doghouse," a name given to the oilman's office. Traipse through Atwood Annex and peruse its pictorial history of the equipment and personnel of the San Juan County "oil patch."

Visit the main museum, which contains a mineral and fossil display, Southwestern artifacts, farm and ranch tools, and a comprehensive collection of Aztec memorabilia, including a fully equipped barbershop of the era.

At the museum you may check out the gift shop or pick up a copy of "Walking Tour of Historic Aztec," which delineates 24 historic homes, churches, and commercial buildings. Eleven of these are on the National Register of Historic Places and the New Mexico State Register of Cultural Properties.

Take a lunch break at **The Main Street Bistro** on the corner of Main and Blanco. From its origins as a filling station in the 1950s to its time as an oil equipment storehouse in the 1980s, it has morphed into a funky little café open for breakfast and lunch. The interior is bright and colorful, with a sky-blue ceiling dotted with puffy white clouds. An outdoor patio provides alfresco dining in the summer months. Owners Tony and Susan French serve up fresh daily pastries and quiche, homemade soups, and some bodacious sandwiches, including their "Ultimate," a fresh-baked croissant stacked high with sliced breast of turkey, mixed baby greens, alfalfa sprouts, garden tomato, and red onion drizzled with creamy avocado dressing and topped with provolone cheese, fresh sliced avocado, and crispy bacon.

Leaving Aztec, you retrace your route south, turn west onto NM 64 and arrive at the **Salmon Ruins** and the **San Juan County Archaeological Research Center & Library.** A large Chacoan apartment complex constructed during the late 11th century, the excavation is located on an alluvial fan at the base of gravel terraces bordering the San Juan River.

Originally a Chaco outlier constructed between 1088 and 1090 and patterned on the classic C shape, the pueblo contained approximately 217 rooms skirting the Great Kiva. The Chacoans abandoned the site around 1130, and it lay fallow until 1185, when people influenced by the Mesa Verde culture moved in. Their occupation lasted about a century, after which the site was vacant except for a small remnant population.

In the late 1800s, George Salmon homesteaded the area around the ruins and protected it from vandals and treasure hunters for more than

The visitor's center at the Salmon Ruins includes a research center and library, museum, and gift shop.

90 years. His homestead and outbuildings remain nearby. In 1969 San Juan County purchased the 22-acre tract, placed the site on the National Register of Historic Places and the New Mexico State Register, and appointed the County Museum Association to administer the property.

Today, in addition to viewing the ruins, you can visit Heritage Park, a series of exhibits displaying traditional habitations of numerous prehistoric and historic groups of the Four Corners area. There's quite an assortment—an Ancestral Puebloan pit house, Ute and Jicarilla wickiups and tepees, and both a forked stick and a traditional Navajo hogan.

The visitor's center incorporates the research center and library, a museum of artifacts from the site, and a gift shop well stocked with kachinas, rugs, jewelry, and an excellent selection of regional books. The museum's display area contains a reproduction of a room in the ruins as it might have appeared while still in use by the Ancestral Puebloans.

If all this inquiry has you fainting with fatigue and panting with hunger, take heart and head off to Farmington. **Three Rivers Eatery and Brewhouse** is arguably Farmington's most popular restaurant. Located downtown in the Andrews Building, the pub formerly housed the Farmington Drug Store and the *Farmington Times-Hustler* (now the *Daily Times*). With true shabby chic decor, the walls are mostly adorned with items found during the building's multiple renovations. Their menu offers a selection of pub grub, including soups, salads, appetizers, burgers, sandwiches, and entrées, as well as daily specials. Try the Drunken Steak, a rib eye soaked for three days in Chef Jon Weaver's secret marinade, or an 8-ounce biscuit-battered catfish served with fries, coleslaw, and a side of homemade country gravy. Their green chile chicken soup is a favorite, and their take on traditional French onion soup is made with brew house beer and topped with croutons and melted provolone cheese.

Needless to say, there is a huge selection of beer—ales, lagers, ciders, and time-limited specials. Brewers Casey Gwinn and Peter Fieweger brew all 12 beers on tap on-premise. You can buy growlers to go in half- and 5-gallon sizes as well as 15-gallon kegs. For those who don't imbibe, they make their own sodas: root beer, cream soda, and six other seasonals.

If you have a hankering for New Mexican food, trot over to **Los Hermanitos** on East Main or their new location on West Main. Sam and

Chetro Ketl, which has 500 rooms and 16 kivas, is one of six major ruins along a 9-mile loop in Chaco.

Cathy Gonzales have been turning out the posole and tamales since 1992, and their breakfast burritos are billed as "World Famous." Although that might be a bit of a stretch, you have to admit they're mighty fine. Their colorful East Main restaurant boasts a large mural by Leander Begay that depicts Mexican country scenes.

Fed and content, check into **Casa Blanca Bed and Breakfast,** owned and operated by David and Shirley Alford, who have two other delightful properties, the Don Gaspar Inn in Santa Fe and Blue Lake Ranch south of Durango, Colorado.

Casa Blanca is perched on a hill overlooking the town. Its beautifully landscaped grounds, colorful flower beds, and sparkling fountain set the

The living room of Farmington's Casa Blanca Bed and Breakfast is decorated with vibrant textiles, Navajo rugs, and hand-carved furniture.

stage for the elegant interior decor. The mission-style house was designed, built, and decorated in the 1950s by Miriam and Merrill Taylor, owners of the Greasewood Trading Post in Lukachukai, Arizona.

David and Shirley have transformed the property into an elegant and luxurious accommodation in the style of a Spanish hacienda. The gardens are exceptional, and the public rooms are expansive and inviting with richly colored Guatemalan textiles, Navajo rugs, and hand-carved Peruvian furniture. The library is equipped with a wide-screen television and a computer workstation, while the living room supplies a game table and space for relaxing and sharing the day's activities. The elegant dining room is embellished with a house original, a sapphire blue French wall mural depicting exotic birds. A full complimentary hot breakfast is served in the cheery sunroom, and snacks and mementos are available in the small gift shop.

Guest rooms and suites are arranged around individual patios with courtyard or garden views, and there are enough amenities to please the fussiest guest: down pillows and comforters, hair dryers, refrigerators, coffeemakers and microwaves, robes, private phones, cable TV, and both DSL and wireless Internet service. Several rooms have gas fireplaces, mini-kitchens, whirlpool tubs, and handicapped access.

After a good night's rest, you are ready to explore Farmington before setting off to Crownpoint. **The Farmington Museum & Visitor Center at Gateway Park** is the best place to start. In addition to having a full selection of maps, brochures, and a 20-minute video titled *Totah: Land Where the Waters Meet,* it has exhibits detailing the history of the area from the heyday of the trading posts to the development of the oil and gas industry in the San Juan Basin. Adults and kids alike will love the Geovator, a simulated elevator ride to the bottom of an oil well, complete with sound, light, and vibrations. Another area traces Farmington history from its early days as an agricultural area to its immersion as a significant supplier of petroleum.

To compare the trading posts of old with today's diminished versions, check out the Three Waters Trading Post display in 200 Years of Change. It has a walk-through replica of a 1930s trading post with a bull pen stocked with period goods and artifacts, a pawn room, and an office showcasing jewelry and rugs.

If you're traveling with the small-fry, The **E^3 Children's Museum & Science Center** on North Orchard will pique the interest of your young Einsteins. Exhibits encourage learning the properties of sound, light, and magnetism, while the participatory activities of Tot's Turf are aimed at children under 6.

Or take them over to the **Riverside Nature Center of Animas Park** to work off some energy. The center was designed to overlook wetlands of one of the oxbows that once existed along the Animas River. In 2006 new wetlands were constructed, and wildlife is coming back. There are walking trails along the Animas River and through the woodlands, and visitors will enjoy checking out the science exhibits or browsing the gift shop's nature-themed gifts.

A large array of shops up and down Main and Broadway are a shopper's delight. For Indian art, truck over to **Fifth Generation Trading Company,** where Joe Tanner Jr. is carrying on the family tradition of traders, which had its roots in Gallup. The showroom overflows with Navajo, Hopi, and Zuni jewelry, Navajo and Pueblo pottery, sandpaintings, alabaster sculptures, carved Navajo and Hopi kachinas, old pawn, and more. Fifth Generation also carries a selection of Navajo folk art, including the work of Delbert Buck, famed carver of humorous figures from the reservation.

The buying room is where the Indian artists come to sell their work Monday, Tuesday, Friday, and Saturday. If you're lucky, you'll see them presenting their efforts to be evaluated. The vault is also in the buying room, and it's where the most important pieces are housed. If you would like to see some samples, like Maria Martinez pottery, ask permission.

Another portrayer of Navajo humor is well-known painter Anthony Chee Emerson. He and wife, Michele, have **The Emerson Gallery** on West Main, where he sells his original oils and acrylics, prints, and trademarked pillows, jewelry, table runners, and signature glassware. Michele categorizes his work as traditional with a contemporary flair—a type of folk art.

More than a dozen artists in a variety of media have studios and display their work for sale in an old lumberyard building. **Artifacts** is owned by Bev Taylor and daughter Tara Churchill, who have provided a home and working space for potters, painters, paper artisans, fiber artists, calligraphers, bookmakers, and glassworkers. The range of styles is eclectic, and the artists are happy to stop and chat with potential customers or browsers. There's an adjoining shop selling chile products.

Be sure to have a bite to eat before venturing down NM 371, a rather barren stretch void of restaurants. The primo lunch spot in Farmington is **Something Special Bakery and Tea Room** on North Auburn, just a block or two from Main. This attractive restaurant was started more than 20 years ago by Charliene Barns, and the bakery was added later by Charliene's son, Dean, who eventually took over the burgeoning business from his mother.

Housed in a tidy cottage with outdoor dining on an attached porch, the restaurant serves a different special every day. A month's menus are printed on cards so patrons will be sure not to miss their favorite dishes, which might include roast chicken with apricot stuffing, chile-seared tuna, or "good old meatloaf." There always is one meat and one vegetarian entrée. The ingredients are scrupulously fresh, and all the sauces and dressings are homemade. The desserts are a dieter's downfall. Dean's wife, Deci, bakes 12 old world breads daily in special steam-injection ovens, and delectable cookies and muffins round out the offerings.

Kolbjorn Lindland's **Andrea Kristina Bookstore and Kafé** is another lunch possibility. The Norwegian-born proprietor has a winning combination of books, good eats, and neighborhood gathering place. They stage open mike nights every Thursday and "Too Far Out Film Night" on Friday. Saturday evening brings live music and poetry readings. Lunch is popular and crowded. You order your salad, sandwich, and drink at the counter and then hunt up a table, where they bring your completed order. The most popular item is the Jane Austen Waldorf Tuna with tuna, apples, nuts, provolone cheese, and gourmet mustard on honey wheat bread. Delicious! If you're looking for a salad, perhaps you'd choose the Avocado Shrimp with spring greens, sprouts, shrimp, Roma tomatoes, red onions, and multigrain croutons.

Well fortified for your trip, you head south into the Navajo Nation. If you want to see one of the oldest and most authentic trading posts still in existence, take Navajo 48 ten miles to **Borrego Pass.** This remote post on a dirt road in the heart of the reservation is run by Josie Gonzales, who manages the place for the heirs of Don and Vern Smouse, the original owners. She does her best to keep the place running, although improvements are hampered by the property being tied up in probate. She sells the usual reservation necessities and some rugs, jewelry, and Navajo-carved kachinas at very reasonable prices.

The post is much as Don Smouse left it when he departed for a nursing home years ago. The stone warehouse is still stocked with full canning jars, dusty, outdated clothing, tires, and a Voss wringer washer, still in its carton. An Edsel and 1968 Cadillac rust in the back, and the orchard's plum, apple, and cherry trees are running wild.

If you are fortunate enough to be in the area on the third Friday of the month, you'll want to repair to **Crownpoint,** ideally arriving at the elementary school by 4 PM to watch the Navajo weavers check in their rugs. The women in their traditional multitiered skirts, velvet blouses, and massive turquoise jewelry line up patiently in a queue that stretches from the gymnasium through the hall and out the door. At last they arrive at the check-in table, where they register their weaving, receive an identifying number, and tell the helper the minimum price they will accept. All the rugs are tossed on tables, and eager prospective buyers dig right in, checking to see if the weaving is well done—squared sides with even weaving and a good texture. It's a bit of a riot, with wool flying in every direction and guarded comments from the buyers, who range from dealers to wealthy Santa Fe collectors.

At 6 PM the rugs are moved to the stage, where they will be auctioned. Simultaneously, food service begins. Crownpoint has no restaurant, so to fill a demand the school cafeteria serves a simple meal of Navajo tacos, fry bread, chile and beans, coffee, and punch. In the hall, artisans display jewelry, pottery, crafts, and other art.

The kitchen stops serving at 7, when auctioneer Wayne Conner promptly starts the auction. There is no set order of sale, and the bidding continues until the last rug is sold, whether that is 11 PM or 1 AM. The gym's 240 seats are generally packed with buyers. The weavers and their families sit and stand against the walls, hoping and praying for a good return on their effort. Each auction is different. Sometimes smaller pieces sell well, and other evenings special shapes bring in the big bucks. Prices can range from hundreds to thousands of dollars. Whether or not you buy, it's a wonderful show and one you'll remember.

Leaving Crownpoint, you continue south on NM 371, eventually meeting I-25 at Thoreau (pronounced "Throw"). Before hitting the highway you'll pass the **Rainbow Trading Company,** owned by David Hayes. He specializes in made-to-order rodeo jewelry, but also sells some Indian jewelry, a few rugs taken in trade, and some Navajo kachinas.

If you're searching for lodging after such a busy tour, you'll want to reserve a place at **Stauder's Navajo Lodge,** located 8 miles west of Thoreau at Coolidge, Exit 44. The lodge spent many years as a bar, restaurant, motel, and trading post catering to travelers on what is currently a fractured remnant of old Route 66. Times and owners changed, and in 1969 Sherwood and Roberta Stauder purchased the property and transformed it into a red-tile-roofed, Spanish-style hacienda with center courtyard. Two comfortable guest cottages line one side of this enclosure, where guests can relax amid shade trees and colorful flower beds.

A continual continental breakfast is served in the hacienda great room, which boasts a full wall of windows looking out on the grassed backyard with its full-size heated swimming pool and children's playhouse. In the distance, red rock bluffs shimmer in the clear light.

The Stauders have done an amazing job with the main building. The great room is strewn with exceptional pieces of Southwestern art, some accumulated by Sherwood and Roberta and others part of a collection left to Roberta by her father, an Indian trader who operated the Fort Defiance and Sawmill trading posts in Arizona.

The venerable pool table is draped with a collection of old and rare Navajo rugs, and a woolly sheep made by the Growler family guards the floor-to-ceiling stone fireplace. A collection of dolls of all lands looks out from the shelves of an oak server, and a terra-cotta fountain gurgles softly from a corner. Cozy conversational groupings of chairs and settees are scattered around the huge room, and breakfast tables are set with teal mats and pink napkins in sequined boot holders.

The Stauders encourage their guests to explore the area, and they are knowledgeable about the hiking trails, the trading posts, the rug auction, and the shops and special events at Gallup.

However, if you must be on your way and it's mealtime, head a short distance west on I-25 to Exit 39, to the **Pilot Travel Center and Grandma Max's Restaurant** at Ciniza. Like most truck stops, the food is good and plenty, even if the service can be a bit uneven, especially during off-hours. The restaurant is open from 6 AM to midnight and has a special noon buffet.

Breakfast might be an omelet, huevos rancheros, French toast, or the hearty Trucker's Special of three eggs with hash browns, toast, biscuits, or muffins. For lunch, you might order the hot buffet and salad bar, a burger, sandwich combo, Mexican platter, or a meal-in-a-bowl like the chef's special green chile stew. The dinner menu lists a selection of meat, fish, and poultry. There's chicken, prime rib, charbroiled salmon steak, grilled pork chops, and the obligatory chicken-fried steak.

Contacts:

Andrea Kristina Bookstore & Kafé, 318 W. Main Street, Farmington, 87401. Call 505-327-3313. Mon. through Sat. 7 AM–9 PM, Thurs. open mike 7–10 PM.

Artifacts Gallery, 302 E. Main Street, Farmington, 87401. Call 505-327-2907. Tues. through Sat. noon–6.

Aztec Chamber of Commerce, 110 N. Ash, Aztec, 87410. Call 1-888-838-9551 or 505-334-9551. Summer, Mon. through Fri. 8–5, Sat. 9–3; winter, Mon. through Fri. 8–3. Web site: www.aztecchamber.com.

Aztec Museum and Pioneer Village, 125 N. Main Avenue, Aztec, 87410. Call 505-334-9829. Summer, Mon. through Sat. 9–5; winter, Mon. through Sat. 10–4. Donation requested. Web site: www.nmculture.org/cgi-bin/instview.cgi?_recordnum=AZM.

Aztec Ruins National Monument, 84 Ruins Road, Aztec, 87410. Call 505-334-6174. Summer, daily 8–6; winter, daily 8–5. Fee. Web site: www.nps.gov/azru.

Blanco Trading Post, US 550 (28 miles south of Bloomfield), Bloomfield, 87413. Call 505-632-1597. Mon. through Sat. 8–6.

Borrego Pass Trading Post, 1601 County Road 19, P.O. Box 329, Prewitt, 87045. Call 505-786-5396. Mon. through Fri. 8–5, Sat. 8–1.

Casa Blanca Inn, 505 E. La Plata Street, Farmington, 87401. Call 1-800-550-6503 or 505-327-6503. Web site: www.4cornersbandb.com.

Chaco Culture National Historical Park, P.O. Box 220, Nageezi, 87037. Call 505-786-7014; 24-hour emergency number, 505-786-7060. Visitor's center, 8–5. Trails, sunrise to sunset. Camping limited to seven days. No trailers over 30 feet. Fee. Web site: www.nps.gov/chcu.

Counselor Trading Post, 9766 US 550, General Delivery, Counselor, 87018. Call 505-568-4453. Mon. through Fri. 8–5, Sat. 8–5:30, Sun. 10–6.

Crownpoint Rug Auction, Crownpoint Elementary School, contact: Crownpoint Rug Weavers Association, P.O. Box 1630, Crownpoint, 87313. Call 505-786-7386 or 505-786-5302. Third Friday of each month with some exceptions. Call to confirm. Inspection at 4:30, sale at 7. Web site: www.mttaylor.com/rug-auction.

Cuba Area Chamber of Commerce and Visitors Center, P.O. Box 1000, US 550, Cuba, 87013. Call 505-289-3514. Web site: www.cubanewmexico.com.

E^3 Children's Museum & Science Center, 302 N. Orchard, Farmington, 87401. Call 505-599-1425. Tues. through Sat. noon–5 and by appointment. Web site: www.farmingtonmuseum.org/childrens.html.

Emerson Gallery, 121 W. Main Street, Farmington, 87401. Call 505-599-8597. Open Mon. through Sat., but call first. Web site: www.emersongallery.com.

Farmington Convention & Visitors Bureau, 3041 E. Main Street, Farmington, 87402. Call 1-800-448-1240 or 505-326-7602. Mon. through Sat. 8–5. Web site: www.farmingtonnm.org.

Farmington Museum at Gateway Park, 3041 E. Main Street, Farmington, 87402. Call 505-599-1174. Mon. through Sat. 8–5. Donations welcome. Web site: www.farmingtonmuseum.org.

Fifth Generation Trading Company, 232 W. Broadway, Farmington, 87401. Call 505-326-3211. Mon. through Sat. 9–5:30.

Grandma Max's, Pilot Travel Center, I-25, Exit 39 (Ciniza), Jamestown, 87347. Call 505-863-7801. Daily 6 AM–midnight; Sat. breakfast buffet 7–11 AM.

Los Hermanitos, 3501 E. Main Street, Farmington, 87402, and 2400 W. Main Street, Farmington, 87401. Call 505-326-5664. Mon. through Sat. 6–9. Web site: www.loshermanitos.com.

Main Street Bistro, 122 N. Main Street, Aztec, 87410. Call 505-334-0109. Mon. through Fri. 7 AM–4 PM, Sat. 7 AM–noon. Web site: www.aztecmainstreetbistro.com.

Presciliano's Restaurant, 6478 US 550, Cuba, 87013. Call 505-289-3177. Tues. through Sun. 8–10.

Rainbow Trading Company, P.O. Box 395, NM 57 and Aspen, Thoreau, 87323. Call 505-862-7119. Mon. through Sat. 8–6.

Richard's, P.O. Box 97, US 550, Cuba, 87103. Call 505-289-3284. Daily 9–3.

Riverside Nature Center of Animas Park, Farmington, 87402. Call 505-599-1422. Summer, Tues. through Sat. 1–6, Sun. 1–5; winter, Tues. through Sat. 1–5. Web site: www.farmingtonmuseum.org/naturecenter.html.

Salmon Ruins, 6131 US 64, P.O. Box 125, Bloomfield, 87413. Call 505-632-2013. May through October, Mon. through Fri. 8–5, Sat. and Sun. 9–5; November through April, Mon. through Fri. 8–5, Sat. 9–5, Sun. noon–5. Web site: www.salmonruins.com.

Something Special Bakery & Tea Room, 116 N. Auburn, Farmington, 87401. Call 505-325-8183. Daily 7–2.

Stauder's Navajo Lodge, HC 32, Box 1 (Exit 44, I-40), Continental Divide, 87312. Call 505-862-7553.

Three Rivers Eatery and Brewhouse, 101 E. Main Street, Farmington, 87401. Call 505-324-2187. Restaurant, Mon. through Sat. 11–10, Sun. noon–9. Taproom, daily noon–midnight. Web site: www.threerivers brewery.com.

artifacts
ART GALLERY

CHAPTER

From the Mountains to the Plains

Getting there: From Albuquerque, take I-25 123 miles northeast to Las Vegas, Exit 345. From Las Vegas, take NM 518 for 31 miles north through Sapello and Buena Vista to Mora. In Mora, head north 37 miles on NM 434 through Guadalupita and Angel Fire. Where NM 434 connects with NM 64, go north 10 miles to Eagle Nest, then east 23 miles through Cimarrón Canyon and Ute Park to Cimarrón. In Cimarrón, go south, then east 35 miles on NM 21 through Rayado and Miami to Springer and Interstate 25.

Detour: To detour to **Pecos National Historical Park,** leave the interstate at Exit 307, Rowe, and take NM 64 4 miles north to the site. To detour to **Fort Union National Monument,** leave the interstate at Exit 366, Valmora, and take NM 161 8 miles north to the site.

Highlights: When you arrive in **Las Vegas,** you begin a journey into a New Mexico past attuned to Spanish colonial times and the heritage of the range and the railroad. You'll enjoy wandering the streets of this historic two-part town, half adobe, half Victorian. Take a detour to Pecos National Historical Park.

Head north through the small villages of **La Cueva** and **Mora,** and traverse the beautiful Mora and Moreno valleys. In Angel Fire stop at the

Vietnam Veterans Memorial State Park, or enjoy the area's opportunities for skiing in the winter and fishing, golfing, or hiking in summer. Leaving Angel Fire, steer northeast to **Eagle Nest,** a small town in the center of the valley along the shores of Eagle Nest Lake. Rimmed by peaks, including Wheeler on the west, the lake is a fisherman's haven in both summer and winter.

Bearing east, you navigate Cimarrón Canyon with its sheer walls and rushing mountain stream. The town of **Cimarrón** is known worldwide as home to **Philmont Boy Scout Ranch**, and the historic district's **St. James Hotel** boasts a boisterous history of gunfights, range wars, and badmen.

Let's Go: The two-hour journey between Albuquerque and Las Vegas is enhanced by the beauty and variety of the terrain. Leaving the valley of the Rio Grande, the highway climbs La Bajada Hill's steep escarpment, bypasses Santa Fe, and swings west around the foothills of the Sangre de Cristo Mountains. Joining the path of the old Santa Fe Trail, it crests Glorietta Mesa near the site of the 1862 Union-Confederate battle that crushed the South's attempts to control New Mexico and Colorado. Cutting through the tilted rocks of the hogbacks at the southern end of the range, it crosses steeply sloping beds of multicolored sandstone and shale, finally opening on the vast spaces of the Great Plains to the east.

Be sure to pause halfway north on your interstate journey, take the short detour at Rowe, and visit **Pecos National Historical Park.** This site has been the background for human habitation for more than 10,000 years, first for the Pueblo and Plains Indians, then for Spanish conquerors and missionaries, Mexican and Anglo armies, and ultimately for settlers crossing the Santa Fe Trail. Geographically located in a 30-mile-long corridor between mountains and mesa, Pecos was a crossroads for travel and commerce between the upper Rio Grande and the Plains.

Check in at the attractive visitor's center and museum, a gift of actress Greer Garson and her husband, Colonel E. E. "Buddy" Fogelson. Their donations of money, land from their Forked Lightning Ranch, and key ruins permitted the creation of the monument in 1965.

Walk the paths to the ancient pueblo of Cicuye, where in 1540 the Spanish discovered a city of 2,000 inhabitants, farmers who implemented their wealth with trade between the Apache and Comanche tribes of the Plains. Climb a ladder into a reconstructed kiva, a place of ritual and worship where the pueblo people performed ceremonies to ensure good hunting, plentiful crops, and cures for the sick. View the imposing walls of the

Stunning sights such as the mission Nuestra Señora de los Angeles de Porciuncula de los Pecos await visitors to Pecos National Historical Park.

great church built by the Franciscan priests arriving with the Spanish. The first church, completed in 1625 and destroyed during the Pueblo Revolt of 1680, was much larger than the second, built in 1717 on the foundations of the original. Look to the wide expanses north and east, where the scored ruts of wagon wheels still delineate the passage of the wagon trains along their 800-mile journey from Missouri to Santa Fe.

Leaving Pecos, continue your route to **Las Vegas,** named not for the Nevada gaming mecca whose birth the New Mexico town predates by more than 150 years, but for the region's "big meadows," part of the 1821 land grant to Luis Maria C. de Baca. Originally a farming and commercial center, the city became an important stop on the Santa Fe Trail and later, in 1879, on the Atchison, Topeka and Santa Fe Railway. The railroad builders bypassed the old town, or West Las Vegas, and routed the line east of the Rio Gallinas, creating the new Victorian area, East Las Vegas. Once separate communities, the two sections eventually incorporated, although each retains its distinct characteristics to this day—Old Town heavily Hispanic and East Las Vegas mainly Anglo.

Leaving the interstate at Exit 345, take East University Avenue to Grand Avenue. Seek out the **Railroad Avenue Historic District,** where you'll find the Las Vegas–San Miguel Visitor's Center. Pick up a city guide and copies of the excellent driving and walking guides. Las Vegas has nine historic districts, and the Citizens' Committee for Historic Preservation has designed easy-to-follow tour pamphlets that highlight the more than 900 buildings listed in the National Register of Historic Places. While in the vicinity, you might want to check out the **Castenada Hotel,** built in 1898 as one of Fred Harvey's chain of railroad hotels. It is in a state of decline, but an aura of better days still clings to the mission revival structure, and efforts may be made to restore the building. New shops are coming to the area, too. **Rough Rider Antiques,** formerly of Bridge Street, stocks a bounty of antiques, collectibles, linens, textiles, primitives, jewelry, rugs, and furniture.

After securing your maps and brochures, drive over to the **City of Las Vegas Museum and Rough Riders Collection.** The museum was founded after veterans of Teddy Roosevelt's Spanish-American war regiment named Las Vegas their official reunion home. Along with the Rough Riders collection, the museum acquired city and county domestic artifacts, from Rio Grande weaving to Spanish colonial furniture.

Cross the Rio Gallinas and proceed to the **Plaza,** the heart of Old Town and the residential historic district. Once a regular stop for ranchers, miners, bankers, bunko artists, cardsharps, women of ill repute and desperados, the Plaza hosted some of the West's most infamous characters—Billy the Kid, Doc Holliday, and Black Jack Ketchum among them.

The place to start your exploration and reserve your overnight is the **Plaza Hotel,** built in the Italianate bracketed style in 1882 and still site of convivial gatherings today. Restored to Victorian splendor, the second- and third-floor guest rooms are nicely appointed and inviting. The first floor hosts the public areas. The Landmark Grill has an attractive dining room featuring upscale American comfort food. Entrées might include an 8-ounce filet mignon with Gorgonzola mushroom sauce or the scampi campellini, black tiger shrimp sautéed in butter and garlic. If you have room for dessert, try the flan or chocolate raspberry torte. All soups, baked breads, and desserts are made on-premise.

If you're just looking for palaver, wander over to **Byron T's Saloon,** the local watering hole, where you can rub elbows with cowboys, local businesspeople, and visiting firemen.

Stroll the plaza. From the flat rooftop of the Dice apartments on the north side, Brigadier General Stephen Kearney, Commander of the Army of the West, proclaimed New Mexico for the United States. South and west of the plaza are the city's oldest homes, early adobe structures built in traditional Spanish style.

Stop in at **Tapetes de Lana Weaving Center** and watch the weavers craft beautiful rugs, blankets, runners, placemats, and silk scarves and shawls in the classic Rio Grande style. A nonprofit organization created to help rural residents by offering employment opportunities, the center has been a godsend to many who learn weaving and benefit from the sale of their creations, The plaza location is one of two; the larger facility in Mora houses a weaving gallery, culinary arts center, and a performing arts theater. A spinning mill specializes in the creation of yarns made from natural fiber.

Walk down Bridge Street, where you'll find clustered an interesting group of shops. There's Neita Fran Ward's **War Dancer Gallery** with its wide range of New Mexican art, including oil paintings by David Escudero; the Brian Billie collection of Native American jewelry; Arthur Court giftware; Pendleton clothing, blankets, and housewares; and leather designs by Buz Sickler. **Tito's Gallery** has a wide selection of art and craft items from New Mexican artists. **Tome on the Range** is Nancy Colalillo's cozy bookstore with a wide range of books on local topics. Across the street is its sister store, **Second Tome Around Used Bookstore,** which sells pre-owned books and has a spiffy little café with yummy pastries and specialty coffee drinks.

If it's getting on lunchtime, **Estella's** is a Bridge Street institution. Don't be put off by the restaurant's scruffy exterior. It once housed a hardware store, and evidence of its previous existence is apparent. The food, however, is superb and very authentic northern New Mexican. You'll find all the traditional dishes—flautas, tostadas, burritos, enchiladas, tacos, and combination plates. Their rellenos are a model of their kind. Lunch is extremely popular with locals, so plan accordingly. Dinners, which are served only on Thursday, Friday, and Saturday, might be huachinanago a la Veracruzana (red snapper) or camarones al Caribe (shrimp).

The afternoon is the perfect time for a stroll in the Victorian neighborhood of East Las Vegas, which contains many beautiful old homes and the **Carnegie Library,** one of the many steel king and philanthropist Andrew Carnegie built in small towns across America. Constructed in 1903 and modeled after Thomas Jefferson's home, Monticello, the library is one of a few Carnegie libraries still operating as a book repository.

In the late afternoon, drive out NM 65 to Montezuma, where the **United World College of the American West** was founded in 1982 by philanthropist Armand Hammer. The educational institution brings together young people from a range of nations, races, and social backgrounds to study in a two-year program and serve the community.

The **Montezuma Hotel,** the school's landmark, has been renovated and is being used for classrooms, dorms, faculty apartments, a cafeteria, the campus store, and the student activities center. Constructed by the Santa Fe Railroad in 1888 as a multistoried, balconied, 343-room grand spa hotel, it hosted luminaries such as U.S. Presidents Theodore Roosevelt, Ulysses S. Grant, and Rutherford B. Hayes. Kaiser Wilhelm and Japan's Emperor Hirohito also were guests.

When the railroad opened the El Tovar at the Grand Canyon, business for the Montezuma declined, and the railroad closed the property, eventually donating it to the YMCA. In following years, the structure served many uses, including a Baptist college and a monastery for Mexican priests.

If you look closely near the base of the hill leading to the campus, you will discover several rustic concrete basins. These modest baths contain hot springs, once used to restore health to soldiers from nearby Fort Union. Still in sporadic use, the springs have a rate of 325 gallons per minute and an average temperature of 130 degrees Fahrenheit.

While you're out this way, stop at tiny **Cristo Rey** church, approximately 2 miles beyond the college campus on NM 65. One of the most photographed buildings in the area, its facade is covered with colorful murals depicting the Ascension.

Your evening's repast might be at **Black Jack's Grill** at the Inn on the Santa Fe Trail. Rather than the expected Western motif, the restaurant has an old world atmosphere. The menu is divided into distinct categories. The grill listings concentrate on steaks, chicken, pork chops, and trout. Specialties list Southwestern dishes like old Mexico pork tenderloin, seafood enchiladas, and shrimp tacos. Owner Lavinia Fenzi's Italian heritage asserts itself in Mediterranean dishes like melanzane y spinaci or scaloppini de salmone.

After retiring to your quarters at the Plaza and a refreshing night's sleep, it's time to finish your tour of Las Vegas. You might start the day with breakfast at **Charlie's Spic & Span Bakery & Café,** where the tortillas arrive fresh off a machine that cranks out the dough, rolls it thin, and spits out the disks onto the griddle.

Charlie Sandoval serves up fresh tortillas and other treats at Charlie's Spic & Span Bakery & Café in Las Vegas.

Perhaps you want to drive through the campus of **New Mexico Highlands University,** or check out **Lincoln Park** and its great brownstone residences. Douglas Avenue, which runs through the district, is home to Ken Kimbrel's **20th Century Store,** located in the old Masonic Temple. It's chockablock with 25 years' worth of collected and traded pottery, glassware, furniture, and jewelry.

If antiquing is your thing, you'll want to range farther afield, checking out **Plaza Antiques,** a 4,000-square-foot, multidealer cooperative on the Plaza's west side. Specialties of the shop include quality antiques, collectibles, primitives, and fine furniture.

Stop at **Dick's Deli** and pick up a picnic to go. Don't be put off by the fact that the deli is housed in a liquor store cum bar. Their "deliciously different" sandwiches include such winners as the "Wild, Wild West," rare roast beef, green chile, pepper cheese, jalapeno relish, lettuce, and tomato on a tortilla, or "Cranky Turkey," oven-roasted turkey breast, cream cheese, and cranberry sauce on sourdough. Veggie lovers are accommodated with goodies like a mushroom melt or hummus, avocado, sprouts, and tomato on whole wheat.

Leaving Las Vegas, head north past **Storrie Lake State Park,** a nice place to picnic if you've taken your order "to go" from the deli. Storrie was created when the waters of the Gallinas River were dammed in 1916. If conditions are right, you'll see water-skiers, windsurfers, and sailboarders plowing the lake's surface.

Beyond Storrie Lake, a road sign designates a turnoff to Las Dispensas. Up this rural byway, astronomer Phil Mahon built his **Star Hill Inn** on 200 unspoiled acres in 1988. Since that time professional and amateur astronomers as well as seekers of a bucolic retreat have been drawn to the spot, where they can view nighttime skies without reflective light pollution from the ground. The eight guesthouses with full kitchens have their own telescopes and amenities like fireplaces, handcrafted furnishings, and covered porches. During the day, there are hiking trails, a meditation labyrinth, and meadows for bird-watching. When the sun goes down, Phil conducts nightly star tours using the inn's multiple telescopes.

Forging on along NM 518, you pass the small village of Sapello before arriving in **La Cueva,** once a supply ranch for Fort Union, now a National Historic District thanks to the intervention of Colonel William Salman, who purchased the land and buildings between 1942 and 1950. With its old roller mill, settler Vincente Romero's adobe home, San Rafael Mission Church, and the mercantile building, the village would be worth a stop in itself without the added attraction of the **Salman Raspberry Ranch.**

Open from May through mid- to late October, the ranch and its gardens are a showplace. The wildflower meadow is a wonder, thick with bachelor buttons, coreopsis, poppies, and lupine. Shoppers flock to the mercantile, now the ranch store, to stock up on raspberry products, fresh produce, dried flowers, New Mexico products, and unusual gifts.

Fresh raspberries are usually available in late August through the first frost, and throughout the growing season you'll find fresh asparagus, sweet corn, pumpkins, onions, garlic, apples, and other fruits as well as a selection of annuals and perennials.

The café serves a variety of excellent sandwiches and daily specials, but you really should try Theresa's tamales, made at the ranch and served with red chile. They are truly scrumptious! If you have room for dessert, a brownie sundae is a rich brownie topped with vanilla ice cream and raspberry topping.

Outside La Cueva, you head northwest to Mora, named for the wild berries found in the vicinity. The town rests at the foot of the beautiful Mora, once the breadbasket of the north, its valleys filled with wheat. Stretching the length of the Mora River watershed from the Sangre de Cristo Range in the west to the Canadian River in the east, the area is part of an 1835 land grant.

Following the valley north, you pass the village of El Turquillo and shadow Guadalupita Canyon as the road climbs to **Coyote Creek State Park,** a good place to get out and stretch your legs on a hike to the beaver ponds that dot the creek bed.

Between the park and the road's junction with NM 120, the roadway is narrow and winding, sometimes tapering to a single lane without a center stripe. Although driving commands your attention as you climb the pass between the Mora and Moreno valleys, do sneak a glance at the rushing mountain stream bordered by massive blue spruce and Douglas fir.

Once over the saddle you encounter a broad mountain meadow with marshes and two small lakes. Passing a group of vacation homes, you face a better highway as you approach **Angel Fire,** a four-season resort started in the mid-1970s as a ski area. At an elevation of 8,600 feet and with an average annual snowfall of 210 inches, the ski area's 67 slopes and trails attract in-state skiers as well as those from Texas, Arizona, and Oklahoma. A Nordic center sports a beginner's area and four different trails for a total distance of almost 14 miles. Rentals and lessons are available.

In summer Angel Fire attracts golfers, hikers, anglers, and folks who simply want to escape the heat and enjoy the many opportunities for outdoor recreation the region offers. There are summer chairlift rides, an 18-hole PGA-rated championship golf course, tennis courts, horseback riding, mountain biking, and fishing in nearby **Eagle Nest Lake.**

During any season, the **Vietnam Veterans Memorial State Park** is a stop not to be missed. Perched on a hillside and with soaring walls reminiscent of sails, the memorial pays homage to all who served in Southeast Asia. In the chapel, combat boots and notes from Vietnam veterans lie at the foot of a simple cross, and on the wall a list of states and the months scheduled for remembrance is posted. The visitor's center includes a history of the conflict with videos and memorabilia.

Originally designed and constructed by the family of Dr. Victor Westphall, whose son David was killed in a 1968 enemy ambush in Vietnam, the memorial was transferred to New Mexico State Parks in 2005, making it the only state park in the nation dedicated solely to Vietnam veterans.

From Angel Fire, it's a beautiful drive through the Moreno Valley to Agua Fria, where you join US 64 to **Eagle Nest,** a small community on the shores of Eagle Nest Lake. If the appearance of bait shops and marinas is any indication, the lake is fertile ground for anglers. The cold waters support a vigorous population of rainbow trout and kokanee and koho salmon. Ice fishing is popular in winter.

From Eagle Nest you head west through **Cimarrón Canyon,** which borders the 33,116-acre **Colin Neblett Wildlife Area.** A breathtaking drive any time of year; sandstone cliffs rise several hundred feet from the canyon floor as the Cimarrón River cuts a narrow outlet from the Moreno Valley through the mountains. The road parallels the stream, which is dotted with pullouts, picnic areas, and hiking trails.

Passing Ute Park, a small settlement within the canyon, you traverse the western portion of the expansive **Philmont Boy Scout Ranch** and arrive in Cimarrón, a name conjuring up images of the rootin', tootin', wild, wild West. The sleepy town at the crossroads of US 64, NM 21, and NM 58 comes as a bit of a surprise. The modern part of town, which stretches east to west, is unremarkable. There are several motels, a small city park with a statue of Lucien Maxwell, and **Heck's Hungry Traveler** restaurant, "Home of the Original Cimarrón Roll." Here you can get the aforementioned sticky bun, New Mexican dishes, or a "Heck of a Burger," a half pound of beef smothered with green chile, cheese, and avocado.

Turn down NM 21 and cross the Cimarrón River. In a block or two you're at the **St. James Hotel,** heart of the historic area. Although the stately hotel is quiet now, it once was the locus of activity for every cowboy, mountain man, and outlaw coming down the mountain branch of the Santa Fe Trail.

The land the St. James occupies, as well as the totality of town properties and beyond, was part of the 1841 Beaubien-Miranda Land Grant, later known as the Maxwell Grant for Lucien Maxwell, who married into the Beaubien family and bought out the other heirs. The Maxwell Grant encompassed 1.7 million acres and was the largest single land-holding in the Western Hemisphere.

Henri Lambert, once a personal chef to Presidents Abraham Lincoln and Ulysses S. Grant, bought land from Maxwell and in 1880 built the St. James, a gambling saloon with a reputation for violence. Notorious gunman Clay Allison is said to have danced naked on the bar, and it wasn't unusual for cowboys to ride their horses through the wide side door and shoot out the lamps. Twenty-six men were killed within the adobe walls, and when the tin ceiling was first replaced in 1902, there were more than 200 bullet holes imbedded in its surface.

The hotel was carefully restored from 1985 to 1993 by local resident Ed Sitzberger, a retired engineer from Los Alamos and Sandia Laboratories, and is currently owned by a corporation of New Mexico businesspeople. Originally the hotel had 30 rooms but now is reduced to a more spacious and comfortable 12, all named for the famous and infamous.

Room 18, which is never rented, is said to be haunted by the ghost of T. J. Wright, who in 1881 won the hotel in a poker game and was killed before he could collect his debt. Other ectoplasmic beings occasionally manifested include a short blond poltergeist with a pockmarked face who hides things, steals items, and knocks dishes from shelves, and Mary Lambert, the first wife of the original owner, a friendly ghost who leaves the faint scent of perfume.

The hotel's public rooms are a study in Victorian elegance. The lobby settee and chairs are original to the hotel, and many of the transoms and door panels were painted by Harry Miller, a Santa Fe artist who stayed at the St. James. Miller also painted the impressive portraits of the Conqueror Don Diego de Vargas and Father Sera. There are also the obligatory mounted heads of deer, elk, bison, pronghorn, mountain lion, and black bear, and the gambling saloon's original roulette wheel still stands in the downstairs hall.

The Carson-Maxwell Dining Room offers a varied menu of upscale American comfort food with homemade soups and house-baked breads and desserts. A selection of entrées might consist of grilled smoked pork chops, bison pot roast, and a 16-ounce prime rib eye steak. Dessert might be chocolate pecan pie or old-fashioned bread pudding. In addition, Vera's Café offers breakfast, lunch, and dinner in a more informal atmosphere. The two-story hotel annex provides an additional 10 rooms with a variety of sleeping options

Just down the road from the St. James, the **Aztec Mill,** built by Maxwell in 1864, houses a museum of artifacts from Cimarrón and Colfax County. The four floors are filled to the rafters with an eclectic collection, including a model of Maxwell's adobe mansion, a CS Ranch chuck wagon, Indian artifacts, beadwork, pottery, Philmont memorabilia, the Cimarrón Cowboy Hall of Fame, and much, much more. There's also a Will James corner with books inscribed and illustrated by the writer. James had a riding job on the CS Ranch in 1922 while awaiting a commission for his art. Local ranchers Frank Springer and his associates, Jack Nairn and Burton Twitchell, recognized the cowboy's talent and funded his education at Yale School of Art. James eventually dropped out but made important contacts in the East that led to publication of his books, including perennial favorites like "Smoky," "Scorpion," "The Dark Horse," and "The Lone Cowboy."

From Cimarrón, head south toward Rayado and pass the headquarters of **Philmont Boy Scout Ranch.** The largest camping operation in the world, it hosts more than 20,000 scouts every summer. The ranch's 137,493 acres

(214 square miles) were a gift of Waite Phillips, founder of Phillips Petroleum. Born in southwest Iowa in 1883, Phillips was a twin, one of 10 children from a poor family. At 16 he and his brother left home, trapped in Montana's Bitterroot Mountains, and worked in logging camps, in mines, on ranches, and on the railroad. When his twin, Wyiat, died of a burst appendix, Phillips was devastated, and to bring him out of his depression, his older brothers enrolled him in business school. A circuit preacher told him of oil opportunities in Oklahoma, and he began the exploration that eventually led to his fortune.

Phillips visited the Cimarrón area often to hunt, and in 1922 began acquiring land in the area. He never had a direct connection with the Scouts but had come to admire their spirit. In 1938 he donated about 35,000 acres and in 1941 another 90,000 acres of the ranch to the organization.

Visitors today may tour his mansion, the **Villa Philmonte,** and visit the **Philmont Museum and Seton Memorial Library.** The villa remains pretty much as it was in 1926. The gardens are lush with pools and fountains. The portal walls are decorated with tile from Spain, Italy, and Portugal, and the floor is covered with tiles representing various New Mexican icons—cowboys, Indians, and brands.

Inside the mansion, the formal entry has a Western motif with horno fireplace and hand-finished walls. Decorations include a 100-year-old Zia olla, painted santos, and a bead and quill–decorated tepee dew cloth. The living room, with its substantial chairs, painted ceiling beams, Knabe baby grand piano, and a massive fireplace, is opulent but comfortable. The formal dining room has a pullout table seating 16 to 18, Moroccan leather chairs, a fireplace, and a mural of an Indian hunting scene. There is a solarium with a small fountain where Phillips's daughter is said to have kept goldfish, a library, and a New Mexico room with depictions of Indian and colonial Spanish culture, and photographs of ranch visitors such as Will Rogers and Wiley Post. Forty-five-minute guided tours are available throughout the summer and early fall.

The library and museum are in a combined building. The library, named for Ernest Thompson Seton (1860–1946), artist, naturalist, author, and first Chief Scout of the Boy Scouts of America, embraces 5,000 volumes on the religion, culture, history, and natural science of the area. It is open to researchers.

The Aztec Mill, built in 1864, houses a museum of artifacts from Cimarrón and Colfax County.

The museum contains a variety of Seton and Phillips memorabilia. The Plains Room displays include a Sioux tepee and willow backrest, a pipe bag, a beaded woman's dress, a man's porcupine hair roach, leggings, and moccasins. You'll see Phillips's dress riding gear, a hand-tooled silver- and turquoise-trimmed saddle, and many reminders of the ranch days.

Rayado Rancho and the Kit Carson Museum are farther down NM 21. Here, from mid-June to mid-August, ranch personnel create living history reenactments of the earliest days of the area. The complex is a replica of Carson's home during the period he worked to secure the region from marauding Jicarilla Apaches.

If you have time for one more detour, make it **Fort Union National Monument.** Just a few miles off the interstate, the once proud garrison entrusted with guarding the Santa Fe Trail from Indian attacks is now an adobe shell, gradually melting into the earth. Only the walls and a few chimney stacks still stand from what was the largest military installation on the 19th-century Southwestern frontier. Stop at the visitor's center to get a map for the self-guided walking tour. As you trace the windblown paths and walk the grass-grown ruts of the old trail, you can understand the feelings of dismay of many of the women who followed their husbands to that lonely, barren, dusty plain.

Contacts:

Angel Fire Chamber of Commerce, NM 434 Centro Plaza, P.O. Box 547, Angel Fire, 87710. Call 1-800-446-8117 or 505-377-6661. Mon. through Fri., 9–5. Self-serve lobby with brochures and information open 24 hours daily.

Angel Fire Resort, P.O. Box 130, 10 Miller Lane, Angel Fire, 87710. Call 1-800-633-7463 or 505-377-6401. Web site: www.angelfireresort.com.

Armand Hammer United World College of the American West, P.O. Box 248 (NM 65), Montezuma, 87731. Call 505-454-4211. Web site: www.uwc-usa.org.

Aztec Mill, 220 W. 17th St., Cimarrón, 87714. No phone. Call Cimarrón Chamber of Commerce at 1-888-376-2417 or 505-376-2417. Memorial Day to Labor Day, Fri. through Tues. 9–5; May and September, Sat. 9–5, Sun. 1–5. Fee.

Black Jack's Grill, Inn on the Santa Fe Trail, 1133 N. Grand Avenue, Las Vegas, 87701. Call 1-888-448-8438 or 505-425-6791. Mon. through Sat. 5–8:30. Web site: www.innonthesantafetrail.com.

Charlie's Spic & Span Bakery & Café, 715 Douglas Avenue, Las Vegas, 87701. Call 505-426-1921. Mon. through Sat. 6:30–5:30, Sun. 7–3.

Cimarrón Chamber of Commerce and Visitors Center, P.O. Box 604, 104 N. Lincoln Avenue, Cimarrón, 87714. Call 1-888-376-2417 or 505-376-2417. November through April, Mon. through Sat. 10–3; May, September, and October, daily 10–4; June through August, daily 9–5. Web site: www.cimarronnm.com.

City of Las Vegas Museum and Rough Riders Collection, 727 Grand Avenue, Las Vegas, 87701. Call 505-454-1401, Ext. 283. May through September, Tues. through Sun. 10–4; October through April, Tues. through Sat. 10–4. Web site: www.lasvegasmuseum.org.

Dick's Deli, 705 Douglas Avenue, Las Vegas, 87701. Call 505-425-8261. Food to go Mon. through Sat. 10–7:30.

Eagle Nest Chamber of Commerce, P.O. Box 322, Eagle Nest, 87718. Call 1-800-494-9117 or 505-377-2420. Summer, Mon. through Fri. 10–4; winter, Mon. through Fri. 10–2. Web site: www.eaglenest.org.

Estella's Café, 154 Bridge Street, Las Vegas, 87701. Call 505-454-0048. Lunch, Mon. through Wed. 11–3; Thurs. and Fri. 11–8; Sat. 11–7.

Fort Union National Monument, P.O. Box 217, Watrous (8 miles north from I-25, Exit 366), 87753. Call 505-425-8025. Memorial Day through Labor Day, daily 8–6; winter, daily 8–4. Fee. Web site: www.nps.gov/foun.

Heck's Hungry Traveler, NM 64, Cimarrón, 87714. Call 505-376-2574. Summer, daily 6:30 AM–8 PM; winter, daily 7–2 and 5–8.

Ken Kimbrel's 20th Century Store, 514 Douglas Avenue, Las Vegas, 87701. Call 505-425-3180. Irregular hours.

Kit Carson Rayado Museum, NM 21, Cimarrón. June 1 through end of August, daily 8–5. Closed off-season. Web site: www.scouting.org/philmont/facilities/museums.html.

Las Vegas–San Miguel Visitor's Center, 500 Railroad Avenue, Las Vegas, 87701. Call 505-454-4101. Mon. through Fri. 9–4, Sat. and Sun. 10–2. Web site: www.lasvegasnm.org.

Pecos National Historical Park, P.O. Box 418, Pecos, 87552. Call 505-757-6414, Ext. 1. Visitor's Center, Memorial Day through Labor Day, daily 8–6; Labor Day through Memorial Day, daily 8–4:30. Fee. Web site: www.nps.gov/peco.

Philmont Museum and Seton Memorial Library, NM 21, Cimarrón. Summer, daily 8–5; winter, Mon. through Sat., 8–noon and 1–5. Web site: www.scouting.org/philmont/facilities/museums.html.

Philmont Boy Scout Ranch, 4 miles south of town on NM 21, Cimarrón, 87714. Call 505-376-2281, Ext. 257. Web site: www.scouting.org/philmont.

Plaza Antiques, 1801 Plaza, Las Vegas, 87701. Call 505-454-9447. Thurs. through Mon. 10–6; Sun. 9–4. Web site: newmexicolasvegas.com/mall/plaza_antiques.html.

Plaza Hotel, 230 N. Plaza, Las Vegas, 87701. Call 1-800-328-1882 or 505-425-3591. Landmark Grill, daily 7–2 and 5–9; Byron T's Saloon, daily noon–midnight. Web site: www.plazahotel-nm.com.

Rough Rider Antiques, moving from 158 Bridge Street, Las Vegas, 87701, to the Railroad District in 2007. Call 505-454-8063 for verification. Mon. through Sat. 10–5.

St. James Hotel, 617 S. Collinson, Cimarrón, 87714. Call 1-866-472-5019 or 505-376-2664. Vera's Café, daily 7 AM–9 PM; Carson-Maxwell Dining Room, daily 5–9; Lambert's Saloon, daily noon–closing. Web site: www.stjamescimarron.com.

Salman Raspberry Ranch and La Cueva National Historic Site, junction NM 518 and NM 442, La Cueva (P.O Box 156, Buena Vista, 87712). Call 505-387-2900. Store, May through October, daily 9–5. Café, Tues. through Fri. 11–4, Sat. and Sun. 11–5. Abbreviated schedule November through April. Web site: www.salmanraspberryranch.com.

Second Tome Around Used Bookstore and Café, 131 Bridge Street, Las Vegas, 87701. Call 505-454-8511. Mon. through Fri. 8:30–5:30, Sat. 8:30–4. Web site: www.tomeontherange.com.

Star Hill Inn, P.O. Box 707, Sapello, 87745. Call 505-425-5605. Web site: www.starhillinn.com.

Tapetes de Lana Weaving Center, 1814 Plaza, Las Vegas, 87701. Call 505-426-8638. Mon. through Fri. 8–5, Sat. 10–5. Web site: www.tapetes delana.com.

Tapetes de Lana Weaving Center, Junction NM 518 and NM 434, Main Street, Mora, 87732. Call 505-387-2247. Hours and Web site, see Las Vegas center above.

Tito's Gallery, 157 Bridge Street, Las Vegas, 87701. Call 505-425-3745. Mon. through Sat. 10–5 or by appointment. Web site: newmexicolas vegas.com/mall/tito.html.

Tome on the Range, 116 Bridge Street, Las Vegas, 87701. Call 505-454-9944. Mon. through Fri. 9:30–5:30; Sat. 10–5. Web site: www.tomeontherange.com.

Vietnam Veterans Memorial State Park, County Road B-4, Angel Fire, 87710. Call 505-377-6900. Gate hours, daily 9–5; chapel 24 hours daily. Web site: www.emnrd.state.nm.us/emnrd/parks/VietnamVets.htm.

Villa Philmonte, NM 21, Cimarrón, 87714. Call 505-376-2281, Ext. 257. Tours, first week in June through end of August, daily 8–4:30, every 30 minutes; May, September, and first week of October, Mon. through Fri. 10:30 and 2:30; tickets available at museum. Maximum 25 people. Web site: www.scouting.org/philmont/facilities/museums.html.

CHAPTER

The Turquoise Trail

Getting there: From Albuquerque, take I-40 east to Exit 175, Cedar Crest/Tijeras. From the interstate, take NM 14 northeast 6 miles through Cedar Crest to San Antonito, where Sandia Crest Scenic Byway, NM 536, detours approximately 8 miles through Sandia Park to Sandia Ski Area and Sandia Crest. If you continue on NM 14, you travel 12 miles to Golden. Madrid is 11 miles beyond Golden, and Cerrillos is 3 miles beyond Madrid. Cerrillos to the NM 586 turnoff west is 7 miles. Head west on NM 586 8 miles and cross the interstate at Exit 271. Turn right onto the Frontage Road, and go approximately 4 miles, passing Santa Fe Downs Racetrack. Turn left onto Los Pinos Road. El Rancho de las Golondrinas is 3 miles from the intersection.

Highlights: Although the interstate route from Albuquerque to Santa Fe is fast and fairly scenic, the Turquoise Trail, a National Scenic Byway, does so much more than just get you there. Cedar Crest is home to eccentric **Tinkertown Museum,** and San Antonito provides a gateway to the wooded eastern slopes of the Sandia Mountains. The Turquoise Trail leads northeast through the old gold-mining town of Golden and coal producer Madrid, now an artists' enclave and village of shops. South of San Marcos, you intersect the Cerrillos hills, cross the interstate, and stop at **El Rancho de las Golondrinas,** a living history museum of rural Spanish colonial culture.

Let's Go: For Albuquerque visitors accustomed to the view of the Sandia ("Watermelon") Mountains from the west, a trip up the **Turquoise Trail** is a revelation. The Sandias run approximately 20 miles between Tijeras Canyon and the northern foothills. The western edge of the range is a precipitous array of Precambrian granite peaks and canyons, transformed nightly by alpenglow into the mellow rose tints that gave the pinnacles their name.

With its gradual wooded slopes of Pennsylvania limestone, the eastern side presents a different story. Here the desert falls away, and you're faced with a change not only of altitude but also of climate. "East Mountain," as it is dubbed by Albuquerque residents, often is colder, rainier, and snowier than the city or West Mesa areas. Although this can mean treacherous road conditions in winter, the weather is a blessing in summer for residents seeking to escape the desert heat.

As you leave boulder-ridden Tijeras Canyon and begin your ascent, you pass through Cedar Crest, a typical mountain community with small shops and stores providing essential services to residents not wanting to trek into Albuquerque. For a great selection from both local and international craftspeople, stop at the **Gallery of the Sandias** in the Turquoise Trail Shopping Center, "Where Crafts Become Art." Dragons in wood and hemp, masks from New Guinea and Bali, Gary Parker's stunning ceramics, Yixing teapots from China, and Philip Green's funky raku clocks are but a few of the possibilities.

Next to the gallery, Linda Lundgren's **Wooby Coffee Bistro** is a great place to take a break. Very dog-friendly and named for Linda's pug, the bistro serves up all homemade soups, salads, quiches, and pastries. If you dare, order a cinnamon bun. They are saucer-sized and definitely delicious. All of Linda's confections are made with butter and are exceedingly rich.

High on a ridge, **Elaine's Bed and Breakfast** provides a montane retreat for travelers. Elaine O'Neil's cozy stone and log chalet sits on 4 acres overlooking the Ortiz and Manzano mountains. If you wander out on the balcony in the morning, you're likely to see mule deer or a raccoon making an early foray through the cherry, plum, and peach trees. A great getaway for those shunning the city life, Elaine's location still provides an easy commute to Albuquerque or Santa Fe.

If your interests include the region's prehistory, you should visit the **Museum of Archeology and Material Culture,** a small gem tucked into the Cedar Crest hills. Funded in part by the Federal Highway Administration, its exhibits detail a 12,000-year Native American timeline with information on the nearby Sandia Cave and Clovis points as well as the local Cerrillos turquoise.

The fascinating Tinkertown Museum in Cedar Crest includes more than 1,000 carved figures and 20,000 miniatures along with other collections.

Continuing up the Trail, you pass Cañoncito, a small settlement, and arrive at the outskirts of San Antonito, where you connect with Sandia Crest Scenic Byway.

In the era of Disney, just another roadside attraction might elicit gigantic ho-hums. These generally eccentric creations of a fertile imagination can neither compete with Space Mountain, nor is that their design. Most originated with a hobby, a dream, or an obsession. **Tinkertown Museum** on the Sandia Crest Highway is a perfect illustration. Creator Ross Ward placed a prominent sign saying:

TINKERTOWN BEGAN AS A HOBBY MORE THAN 30 YEARS AGO AND SLOWLY EVOLVED INTO THE MUSEUM COLLECTION YOU WILL ENJOY. NO TAXPAYER'S MONEY, NO GOVERNMENT FUNDS AND NO PUBLIC GRANTS HAVE BEEN USED IN BUILDING OR MAINTAINING THIS DISPLAY. WE STILL BELIEVE IN FREE ENTERPRISE AND DETERMINATION. YOU CAN DO IT, TOO, NO MATTER WHAT YOUR PROJECT MAY BE.

Back in the 1940s and '50s, Ross was growing up in the Midwest and learning to carve from a Boy Scout handbook. His first opus was a miniature circus, which he set up in his garage for the amusement of his buddies. His diminutive world was the casualty of a fire, but his drive to create did not abate. In the 1960s he began to develop his Western town, which today consists of 23 buildings peopled by all sorts of characters, from the politician hopping out of the bed of a woman of ill repute to the blacksmith at his forge.

During the mid- to late '60s, Tinkertown was housed in a medicine show wagon parked in front of the New Mexico State Fair's Indian Arts Building, and Ross dressed as the slick hustler. When the collection grew to greater proportions, Ross and his wife, Carla, decided to find it a permanent home, and Tinkertown was born. In February 1998, at age 57, Ross was diagnosed with Alzheimer's disease. He passed away on November 13, 2002, but the Ward family continues his legacy by maintaining and running Tinkertown in his memory.

Tinkertown's walls are a combination of stone, cement, wood scrounged from old buildings, and bottles—more than 40,000 of them. Before recycling was fashionable, Ross met Simi Valley's Grandma Prisby, who had created a bottle village from discards. Her philosophy was:

"I took the things you threw away
And put them together night and day;
A million pieces all in one,
Washed by the rain and dried by the sun."

Take time to really inspect the scenes when you stop at this remarkable one-man creation, which includes more than 1,000 figures and 20,000 miniatures. The detail in both the village and the equally impressive circus—complete with a sideshow, menagerie tent, and three-ring big top—is hard to comprehend. Buttons animate certain figures, like the aerial acrobats or the town elder in a rocker.

In addition to the circus and Western town, Tinkertown houses a variety of collections such as wedding cake couples, antique tools, dolls, toys, bullet pencils, and the *Queen Theodora,* a full-size, 42-foot English sailing ship Ross's brother-in-law employed to traverse the Seven Seas. You'll discover two animated music machines, "Rusty Wyer and the Turquoise Trail Riders" and the amazing "Otto, the One-Man Band," a 6-foot contraption that consists of a fully functioning accordion, drums, and xylophone—all controlled by a music box roll. Perhaps you'll see what the future holds by dropping a coin in the "Esmeralda Fortune Telling Machine," made in 1940 by the Munves Company, New York, and for years a feature at Riverview Park in Chicago.

After leaving Tinkertown, continue on the Crest Highway. You'll pass **Sandia Peak Ski Area,** where 25 slopes and trails tempt downhill and cross-country skiers and snowboarders from mid-December to mid-March. On summer weekends the scenic chairlift ride transports sightseers or mountain bikers to the summit, where both hiking and biking trails await.

The drive terminates at 10,678 feet. From the observation deck, the city of Albuquerque is spread like a blanket below, and on most days you can see well beyond the escarpment containing **Petroglyph National Monument** and West Mesa's five volcanic cones to Mount Taylor, 60 miles to the west. Sandia Crest House, a gift shop and snack bar, is open daily.

If you want to see more, portions of the **Crest Trail** (TR 130) provide a short but bracing hike. Remember, it's not the distance, it's the altitude. This 1.3-mile, one-way scenic path begins at the south end of the parking lot. Meandering through aspen glades and across flowering meadows, it leads to the Rock House at Vista Point, built by the Kiwanis, once used to house weather forecasting teams, and now vacant. Continuing at a gradual downhill angle, your walk ends at the terminal of the **Sandia Peak Aerial Tramway,** which climbs 2.7 miles up the western face of the mountains. The tram summit houses a visitor's center for Cibola National Forest in addition to the **High Finance Restaurant and Tavern,** which has a varied lunch and dinner menu and a fantastic view. On days when the winds are right, you're likely to see hang gliders soaring like colorful, wide-winged birds after launching into thermals rising off the Rio Grande Valley.

Descending from the crest, you again join NM 14 as it winds northeast. Continuing down the Trail through grasslands dotted with juniper and piñon, you approach Golden. Aptly named, Golden sprang up as the result of a short-lived gold rush. The deposits proved scanty, and a shortage of water made mining attempts difficult. Today a few homes, a church, and Beatriz Galaviz's La Casita Gift Shop make up the town. **La Casita** ("Little House") is a rewarding stop. Beatriz's family has lived in Golden for generations, and the shop once was her aunt's home. She stocks an eclectic assortment of Indian crafts, including storyteller necklaces from Santa Domingo's Marie Coriz, jewelry by Navajo smiths Jefferson James and Robert Largo, and unusual bone carvings of Navajo maidens by Dwayne and Ron Upshaw.

From Golden, it's a scant 11 miles to Madrid (pronounced MAD-rid), once a vigorous coal-mining town, and currently undergoing a rebirth as colony for artists and craftspeople. Tucked in a valley on the north side of the Ortiz Mountains, Madrid's anthracite fueled area gold smelters as early as 1835. With the arrival of the railroad in New Mexico in the 1880s, demand for this high-quality coal increased, and a short branch of the Santa Fe Railroad was built into town. At one time the municipality produced 250,000 tons of coal yearly and was larger than Albuquerque.

The company built rows of houses, some of which have been restored. A golf course and tennis courts entertained the workers, and the town's Christmas light displays were so famous that TWA made detours to fly over the town. With the advent of diesel, coal demand dropped and the mines closed, as they did all over the country. Its economic base destroyed, the town went into decline, and in 1975 the owners sold the whole town—residences, shops, and all.

As you arrive in town, you will see everywhere evidence of Madrid's past—the weathered residences, the culm heaps, the mine ruins. As depressed as the town was in the 1970s, it is on more secure footing today. Many old buildings have been converted into galleries, shops, and restaurants. Hollywood has discovered the setting, and Disney's *Wild Hogs* with John Travolta and Tim Allen was filmed here in 2006, sending the tiny village into a frenzy of blocked streets, curious bystanders, and buildings retrofitted to accommodate the script's demands.

If you'd like to learn more about the town, stop at the **Old Coal Mine Museum, Engine House Theatre, and Mine Shaft Tavern.** You can browse the museum, which has an actual seam of coal and a 1900 steam locomotive, then attend a melodrama or have a bite to eat.

Getting a parking place on weekends can be an exercise in patience. Shops run the gamut from souvenir joints to fine art galleries, but several deserve special mention. The Company Stores Building with the shaded porch houses **Jezebel Gallery,** where the artist of the same name displays her glasswork as well as art from more than 25 other painters, sculptors, jewelers, and workers in bronze. Three other storefronts have varied histories. When you go, you might find them filled with new treasures or up for rent. There's a big turnover among Madrid's shopkeepers.

The Gifted Hand has some longevity. It handles several outstanding artists: Spirit Sullivan's designs in metal, John P. Saunders's Western scenes, Gary Scerveny's photos of New Mexico landscapes and traditional pueblo buildings, and Michelle Chisolm's pottery. Both Judy Mohr, the owner, and Alexandria Szeman, the gallery director, are very knowledgeable and can help you select the perfect piece for your collection.

For a fabulous selection of Indian jewelry, don't miss the **Great Madrid Gift Emporium** and its sister shop across the street, **The Ghost Town Trading Post.** Their selection of Native American silver jewelry is wide-ranging and includes representations from the Navajo, Santo Domingo, and Zuni tribes.

If your tummy is rumbling, head to Linda Dunnill's **Java Junction** for a home-baked pastry and a cup of latte or to shop her encyclopedic selection of hot sauces and unusual T-shirts. Or stop at **Tocororo** in the old Western frame building across the street from the Mine Shaft Tavern. Jules Mendel and Olga Deulofeu specialize in Cuban cuisine such as island-style roast pork, arroz con pollo (chicken and rice), and carne con papas (beef and potatoes). Try the Cuban coffee or their granitas and fruit shakes. Olga also creates vibrant artwork, and the colorful café tables are her design. The adjoining Santa Fe red boxcar contains a gallery displaying her paintings and those of other local artists.

If you hit a day when **Mama Lisa's** (aka the No Pity Café, Ghost Town Kitchen, or Lulu's Lard Bucket) is open, carpe diem and chow down on one of their homemade soups, salads, sandwiches, or enchiladas. The author heartily recommends the red chile cowboy smoked brisket enchiladas, perhaps followed by the red chile chocolate cake if you have room.

Java Junction in Madrid serves more than coffee and pastries—be sure to check out its collection of hot sauces and unusual T-shirts, too.

For a total change of pace, head on up the road to Cerrillos ("Little Hills"). Before 1680, Indians mined the beautiful blue turquoise that streaks the nearby peaks, and when the Spanish arrived they continued to work the mines. In fact, turquoise from Cerrillos was part of the crown jewels of Spain. In 1893 turquoise was worth, carat for carat, more than gold, and 63 percent of all the turquoise produced in the United States came from these mines. Gold and silver were discovered in 1879, and when the supply of precious metals was depleted, the town still had its veins of coal needed by the Atchison, Topeka and Santa Fe Railway. At its prime in the 1880s, Cerrillos supported 21 saloons and four hotels catering to miners and railroad workers.

Head out of the village and take the dirt road to **Cerrillos Hills Historic Park.** Today the mines are mainly played out, but by hiking, biking, or riding the trails in the park, you can experience much of the same terrain encountered by early miners. You'll find a 1,000-year-old turquoise pit, fossil worm tracks in 70-million-year-old shale, and a variety of flora and fauna.

The sleepy, picturesque town of Cerrillos has retained none of its boisterous past, but the dusty streets have a really timeless quality. Several movie companies have elected to film here because of this ambiance. You may be surprised to see "Wortley Hotel" and other reminders of the Lincoln County War painted on the two-story structure housing the Simonis store. This aberration was created during the filming of *Young Guns.* Walt Disney also filmed *The Nine Lives of Elfego Baca* here in 1968.

The What Not Shop has seen many guises—a grocery, post office, pool hall, and meat market, to name a few. However, for 45 years the 1892 quarry stone building served as repository and sales center for E. J. Mitchell's love of the deal. Originally from North Carolina, this former schoolteacher was as weathered and crusty as his building's exterior. From a chair down by the iron stove, he presided over his collection of minerals, Navajo rugs, Indian jewelry, Zuni fetishes, and American antiques. Carnival, cut, and pressed glass, old campaign buttons, and other curios keep company with the native crafts. Although E. J. died in 1999, Marge and Janet Mitchell still preside over the eclectic jumble guaranteed to keep you poking in corners for longer than you'd anticipated.

For a change of pace, visit **Tom Morin's Studio and Gallery** on First Street. Tom has had an illustrious career both as a sculptor and in teaching and administrative positions at Rochester Institute of Technology, Minneapolis College of Art, West Virginia University, and Ohio State University. He has exhibited everywhere from the Whitney Museum in New York City to the Kaywon Gallery of Art in Seoul, South Korea. His early work was in cast bronze, aluminum, and iron, but his current efforts are in a unique material—plastic-backed sanding belts and disks veneered onto wooden armature. The subject matter is mountains, mesas, and tribal designs. The concept may sound outré, but the results are exceedingly beautiful.

If you have kids clamoring for action, Todd and Patricia Brown's **Casa Grande Trading Post, Mining Museum, and Petting Zoo** is the place to let them wear off some energy. The well-tended petting zoo houses a supercilious white llama, several goats, and a bevy of fancy fowl. Food for the animals is available in the post. Adults will enjoy poking through the post and museum of local memorabilia, which occupies 31 rooms, all constructed by Todd over the years.

Leaving Cerrillos, you head east and north to San Marcos. This area was home to a large Tano pueblo at the time of the Spanish Entrada. There is a folktale that an Indian of San Marcos warned the Spanish in Santa Fe when the Rio Grande pueblos rose in revolt in 1680. This so greatly enraged the collaborating pueblos that they destroyed the town, sending some to live with the Hopis and others to exile with different tribes.

The ruins are there still, with nothing else to designate the district but a large feed and supply store fronted by the **San Marcos Café,** Tom and Susan MacDonell's creation and a favorite among the Trail cognoscenti. Open for breakfast and lunch, the café serves an eclectic cuisine. Its New Mexican offerings include the popular green chile chicken lasagna and roast beef burrito. Daily specials such as osso bucco, pork and spätzle, and catfish jambalaya add a bit of international flavor. There's always a couple of made-from-scratch soups, a quiche of the day, and a fiery green chile stew,

The Casa Grande Trading Post, Mining Museum, and Petting Zoo is a popular family spot in Cerrillos.

too. Save room for dessert. The selection is extensive, but the bourbon apple pie is a sellout favorite.

Just south of the café, your route swings west on NM 586, traverses the Cerrillos hills, and crosses the interstate. After a short stint on the frontage road you pass the Downs at Santa Fe and head toward La Cienega ("The Marsh") and **El Rancho de las Golondrinas** ("The Ranch of the Swallows").

A major paraje (stopping place) on El Camino Real, Las Golondrinas was acquired by Miguel Vega y Coca about 1710 and is one of the most historic ranches in the Southwest. The family intermarried with the Bacas and the property was passed to their descendants, who in turn sold it to the Curtin family in 1932.

In 1939 Leonora Curtin visited the New York World's Fair and met Finnish diplomat Y. A. Paloheimo. They married and developed a vision to restore the old ranch as a living history museum dedicated to the language, culture, and history of Spanish colonial New Mexico. They restored the remaining buildings, erected authentic structures on existing foundations, and brought in related buildings from other sites. The museum was opened in 1972, and in 1982 title was transferred to a charitable trust.

The sprawling 200-acre site is a town unto itself, with an 18th-century placita house, a 19th-century home replete with outbuildings, a molasses mill, a threshing ground, several early water mills, a blacksmith shop, a wheelwright shop, a winery, and vineyards. A separate section portraying a mountain village accommodates a descanso (resting place) with hilltop crosses; a campo santo, or cemetery; and a morada, the meetinghouse of Los Hermanos de Nuestro Padre Jesus Nazareno, or Los Penitentes. Dedicated to Our Lady of Peace, it is a copy of the south morada at Abiquiu.

If you can plan your trip to Las Golondrinas to include one of its special events, so much the better. A Civil War weekend starts off the season, followed by the Spring Festival and Animal Fair, Santa Fe Wine Festival, Summer Festival and Frontier Days, and Harvest Festival. Theme weekends such as "Celebrating New Mexico Music and Dance," "Food, Art, and Adobe" and "Fiesta de los Niños" are scattered throughout summer and early fall. Costumed villagers portray life in the village, operating the mills and doing the farm and domestic chores. Entertainers perform the old music, dances, and plays, and craftspeople demonstrate and sell their traditional art. It is a colorful, entertaining experience.

Don't neglect the gift shop, which stocks a wonderful assortment of Spanish colonial crafts. You'll find retablos (figures of saints painted on a flat surface), bultos (three-dimensional carvings of saints), tinwork, jewelry, and other items, all very reasonably priced.

Several caveats if you plan to visit: General admission for self-guided tours is only June through September, 10 AM to 4 PM Wednesday through Sunday. In April, May, and October, you may phone for an appointment for a guided tour. Since you will be visiting during the warm months, it is important that you bring sunscreen, a hat, water, and sturdy shoes. The paths are a bit rough, and you will be covering a lot of territory.

As you leave Las Golondrinas and return to the interstate for your journey to Albuquerque or Santa Fe, you reenter today's New Mexico, a land shaped by the many elements encountered on your sortie up the Turquoise Trail. Perhaps you feel a bit of nostalgia for those earlier days. Not to fear. The Trail awaits further exploration another day.

Contacts:

Casa Grande Trading Post, Mining Museum, and Petting Zoo, Waldo Street, Box 131, Cerrillos, 87010. Call 505-438-3008. Open daily. Fee for museum.

Cerrillos Hills Historic Park, Santa Fe County Projects & Facilities Management Department, P.O. Box 276, Santa Fe, 87504. Call 505-992-9860. Park access through village of Cerrillos. Directions and trail map on Web site: www.cerrilloshills.org.

Elaine's: A Bed and Breakfast, P.O. Box 444, 72 Snowline Estates, Cedar Crest, 87008. Call 1-800-821-3092 or 505-281-2467. Web site: www.elainesbnb.com.

El Rancho de las Golondrinas, 334 Los Pinos Road, Santa Fe, 87505. Call 505-471-2261. Self-guided tours June through September, Wed. through Sun. 10–4. Fee. Web site: www.golondrinas.org.

Gallery of the Sandias, 12220 NM 14, Cedar Crest, 87008. Call 505-281-4333. Mon. through Fri. 10–6, Sat. and Sun. 10–8.

The Gifted Hand Gallery, 2851 NM 14, Madrid, 87010. Call 1-800-471-5943 or 505-471-5943. Daily 9:30–5:30.

Great Madrid Gift Emporium and **Ghost Town Trading Post,** NM 14, Madrid, 87010. Gift emporium call 505-471-7605; trading post call 505-438-0094. Daily 10–6. Web site: www.ghosttowntradingpost.com.

High Finance Restaurant, Sandia Tram summit. Call 505-243-9742. Daily 11–3 and 4:30–8:30. Reservations requested. Web site: www.highfinancerestaurant.com.

Java Junction, 2855 NM 14, Madrid, 87010. Call 505-438-2772. Summer, daily 7–6; winter, daily 8–5. Web site: www.java-junction.com.

Jezebel Gallery, 2860 NM 14, Madrid, 87010. Call 505-471-3795. Daily 10–5. Web site: www.jezebelgallery.com.

La Casita, 1759 N. NM 14, Sandia Park (Golden), 87047. Call 505-281-3896. Mon. through Sat. 10–4.

Mama Lisa's, Main Street, Madrid, 87010. Call 505-471-5769. Hours vary. Call to confirm.

Old Coal Mine Museum, Engine House Theatre, and Mine Shaft Tavern, 2846 NM 14, Madrid, 87010. Museum and theater, call 505-438-3780; tavern, call 505-473-0743. Melodrama, Memorial Day through Columbus Day, Sat., Sun., and holidays 3 PM. Museum, Tues. through Sun. 10–5. Tavern, summer, Mon., Tues., and Thurs. 11–6, Wed. 11–7, Fri. and Sat. 11–8, Sun. 11–7; winter, open until 4 Mon., Tues., and Thurs. Web sites: mineshafttavern.com and www.madridmelodrama.com.

Sandia Peak Aerial Tramway, 10 Tramway Loop N.E., Albuquerque, 87122. Call 505-856-7325. Tram, Labor Day through Memorial Day, Wed. through Mon. 9–8, Tues. 5–8. Call for winter ski tram hours. Fee. Web site: www.sandiapeak.com.

Sandia Peak Ski Area, 10 Tramway Loop N.E., Albuquerque, 87122. Call 505-242-9133 or 505-856-6419. Skiing mid-December through mid-March. Summer chairlift rides Memorial Day weekend through Labor Day, Thurs. through Sun. 10–4; winter skiing, Wed. through Mon. 9–8, Tues. 5–8. Fee. Web site: www.sandiapeak.com.

San Marcos Café, 3877 NM 14 (San Marcos), Santa Fe, 87505. Call 505-471-9298. Daily 8 AM–2 PM.

Tinkertown Museum, P.O. Box 303, 121 Sandia Crest Road, Sandia Park, 87047. Call 505-281-5233. April 1 through November 1, daily 9–6. Fee. Web site: www.tinkertown.com.

Tocororo Restaurant, 2849 NM 14, Madrid, 87010. Call 505-471-2285. Thurs. through Mon. 11:30–3 and 5–9.

Tom Morin Studio and Gallery, 8 First Street, P.O. Box 322, Cerrillos, 87010. Call 1-800-484-3147 (PIN 3798) or 505-474-3147. April through November 1, daily 10–5 or by appointment. Web site: www.diamondt hacienda.com/artiststudio/artiststudio.html.

Turquoise Trail Association, Cedar Crest, 87008. Call 1-888-263-0003. Web site: www.turquoisetrail.org.

What Not Shop, P.O. Box 38, Cerrillos, 87010. Call 505-471-2744. Thurs. through Sun. 10:30–4.

CHAPTER

6

Savoring the Salt Missions Trail

Getting there: From Albuquerque's I-40/I-25 interchange, take I-25 south 9.8 miles to Exit 220, Rio Bravo. Take Rio Bravo west 4.2 miles to Coors Boulevard/NM 45. Go south on Coors 8.8 miles to NM 314. A short dog-leg to the left onto NM 314 is followed by a quick right onto NM 147. Isleta Pueblo is 1.3 miles over a dirt road.

Leaving the pueblo, retrace your steps to return to NM 314 south for 6.7 miles until you reach NM 6 in Los Lunas. Turn right for Luna Mansion or Teofilo's, or left to continue. Follow NM 6 for 3 miles to NM 47 south. After 8.5 miles, turn right on NM 309 and follow the route across the river (1.9 miles).

Turn left onto Belen's Main Street, then left after 0.2 mile onto Becker Street. Follow Becker to the end. Pete's Café is on the right. Turn left onto First Street. Harvey House Museum is straight ahead.

From the museum, take First Street to Dalies and follow Dalies to Main. Turn right onto Main and right onto NM 309. Follow NM 309 for 0.7 mile. Take a right onto NM 109 (Jarales Road). Continue on Jarales Road 3.5 miles, and turn left onto NM 346, crossing the river. Turn right onto NM 304 after 1.5 miles and continue south through Veguita, Las Nutrias, and Boys Ranch, 9 miles.

Take US 60 east to Abó, 29 miles, and Mountainair, 9 miles. Detour south on NM 55, 25 miles to Gran Quivera. Retracing your route to

Mountainair, continue on NM 55 north to Punta de Agua and Quarai, 8 miles. Follow NM 55 north 16 miles to NM 337 through Manzano, Torreon, and Tajique. Go north 30 miles through Chilili to Escobosa, Ponderosa, Cedro, and Tijeras. Exit Tijeras at I-40.

Highlights: If you're in Albuquerque for several days, do the unexpected and head south. You'll visit **Isleta Pueblo** and its ancient church; dine at historic **Luna Mansion** or **Teofilo's** in Los Lunas; visit the **Harvey House Museum,** a working roller mill between Belen and Jarales; follow the Rio Grande through the old Hispanic villages of Veguita and Las Nutrias; and roam the ruins of the great Indian pueblo and Spanish mission complexes of **Abó, Quarai,** and **Gran Quivera.**

Let's Go: For visitors to New Mexico, a sojourn in Albuquerque may be brief before heading north to the charisma of Santa Fe or the celebrated mountains of the Taos. These locales exert a siren call, hard to ignore, but for the traveler seeking the uncommon, the path less taken, a venture south along the great river will transport the voyager to a land steeped in history, its roots deep in the bosque soil of the Rio Grande.

As you leave the city on I-25, take a minute to look around you. The **Sandia Mountains** rise 10,000 feet to the east, a tilted fault block of 1.4 billion-year-old granite topped with 300 million-year-old sedimentary rock.

To the west of the city, the land rises to the mesa, the Llano de Albuquerque, about 5,800 to 6,000 feet above sea level. Extinct for 250,000 years, five small volcanic cones define the horizon along a north–south fault. Few cities in the world have as many extinct volcanoes nearby as Albuquerque—about 275 within 65 miles!

Dividing the city proper from West Mesa, the Rio Grande flows along, yearly adding to the layer of sediment that through the ages has filled the great rift containing the river. A muddy torrent when spring snow melt courses from the northern mountains, the river seems placid enough during the balance of the year as it winds its way from its source in Colorado to its mouth in the Gulf of Mexico.

Leaving the hustle and bustle of the state's largest city, you head south on Coors Boulevard, which runs parallel to the river through gradually diminishing commercial development. Approaching the **Isleta Reservation,** you enter a wetland where hawks patrol the sky and sandhill cranes browse for forage in the fields. Your route passes under the interstate, intersecting Black Mesa, a basalt lava flow.

Unlike some pueblos, Isleta has never been forced to relocate. It has occupied the same location since Captain Hernando de Alvarado, a soldier in Coronado's expedition, came through in 1540. The Spaniards named the place after their word for a small delta or island, but the Indians named their village Tsugwevaga, or "kick flint," after a popular kicking race played with a piece of obsidian. Because Isleta is located so near to Albuquerque, many of today's residents work in the city, but this brush with modern life seems hardly to have affected the pueblo's guardians. Once within the dusty plaza, the centuries fall away.

St. Augustine Mission Church was built about 1613, and although it was almost completely destroyed in the Pueblo Revolt of 1680, it was rebuilt when the Spanish returned. It is one of the oldest churches in New Mexico, and its stained-glass windows portray various scenes of pueblo life. The altar is crowned with a carved image of the crucified Christ, encrypted with the credo "I Am the Bread of Life." The church gardens are scented islands of meditation, and a special grotto celebrates Kateri Tekakwitha, the "Lily of the Mohawks," the only beatified Native American.

Several entrepreneurs have small gift shops on the plaza's perimeter, and frequently you can purchase crusty loaves of pueblo bread fresh from the beehive-shaped adobe ovens called hornos.

To forestall disappointment, call the tribal office prior to visiting Isleta. During times of sacred ceremonies, non-Indians are prohibited from entering the pueblo. And remember, this is home to the residents, not a tourist attraction. Courtesy and respect go a long way toward making your visit memorable.

Not long after leaving Isleta, you arrive in Los Lunas, named for the Luna family, early settlers who laid claim to the San Clemente Grant of 1716 originally awarded to Don Felix Candelaria. The union of the Luna and Otero families created a powerful political force in Valencia County, and in 1880, when the Santa Fe Railway approached Don Antonio José Luna to purchase a right-of-way that included the family hacienda, he agreed with the stipulation that a new home would be built to his specifications. What emerged is a curious but gracious estate, Southern Colonial in style but built of adobe—a stately Southwestern Tara.

Today the elegant white columns and expansive bay windows house a fine restaurant, the **Luna Mansion.** Restored to the 1920s opulence created by doyenne Josefita Manderfield Otero and designated a State Historic Site, the facility is owned by Danny and Penny Griego. The various rooms of the house have been converted into charming dining quarters graced with many family treasures and photos from years gone by. The menu is classic with a Southwest touch. Their Mansion Steak, a hand-cut 8-ounce filet topped with crabmeat and béarnaise sauce, is a 25-year tradition. The variety extends from the red chile linguini to grilled salmon in a lemon caper cream sauce.

Although the Luna Mansion is open for dinner only, you won't go hungry if you arrive in the area for lunch. Across the street from the mansion's iron gates, **Teofilo's** offers classic New Mexican cooking with some of the finest red chile in the state. The restaurant, a Registered State Landmark, is housed in the home of an early Los Lunas doctor. Acclaimed by local businesspeople and visitors alike, the restaurant really hums at noon as plates of carne adovada and tamales fly out of the kitchen. Owners Pete T. (Teofile) and Tenci Torres use many of the family recipes developed by Pete's mother, Eligia, who runs a well-known café in Belen. Do try any-

Luna Mansion in Los Lunas is both a State Historic Site and an opulent restaurant.

thing with the "red," a sauce with the complex blend of flavors found in the best chile. With a sufficient bite to satisfy chile-heads, it is mellow enough for the tourist, too.

A serendipitous means of sampling the specialties is ordering the combination platter: a chile relleno, beef taco, and cheese enchilada. Be sure to leave room for dessert. The natillas are what angels would have for pudding—rich, light-as-air, and flavored with vanilla, cinnamon, and nutmeg.

Thoroughly sated, you may not be thinking of food again until, say, the dinner hour. However, do stop a short distance out of town at **Sunset Foods,** purveyors of truly great jerky. Thinly sliced round of beef is dried and flavored with a variety of seasonings: red chile, green chile, pepper, teriyaki, mesquite, hickory, country style, and natural. If you can't decide, ask for a sample. Then just try to eat just one piece.

Continuing south through fields watered by irrigation ditches called acequias, you pass many small farms and the small village of Tome. To the northeast, **El Cerro de Tome,** a hill crowned with three crosses, is visible. This dormant volcano is the scene of an annual Good Friday pilgrimage climb for many locals. A small park is located at the base with an entrada arch and iron sculptures of the region's three founding races: Indian, Spanish, and Anglo.

Your next destination, Belen, originally was a sleepy Spanish farming community. The town, recipient of an economic boost when the Santa Fe Railway came through in 1880, was touted as the "Hub City." The convergence of the north–south line and the Belen cutoff from the east relays both freight and Amtrak cars northwest toward Gallup and Los Angeles.

Located next to the still-busy railroad yards, the **Valencia County Historical Society Museum** is situated in an original Harvey House, one of a series of elegant railside hotels built by Fred Harvey throughout the Southwest. The museum houses a permanent collection of material on the Santa Fe Railway and serves as a repository of memorabilia and mementos of Valencia County history. There is a representative Harvey Girl's room with a white iron bed, a steamer trunk, washstand, and primitive rocker. Recruited for a year's contract by Harvey to work as waitresses, these women of good reputation discovered the West while serving the traveling public.

Before leaving Belen, you might want to visit **Pete's Café** across the street from the museum. Owned by Eligia Torres, this restaurant is the gastronomic incubator for many of the fine New Mexican dishes served at Teofilo's in Los Lunas.

Heading out of town toward Jarales, you will discover the **Valencia Flour Mill,** where Jose and Kathy Cordova operate the last family-owned steel-roller mills in the state. This commercial operation, which is additionally certified organic, turns out tortilla and sopapilla mixes and low-gluten pastry flour from New Mexico red winter wheat.

Although Jose comes from an old Valencia County family, both he and Kathy were working in Minnesota when a visit to New Mexico took them to El Rancho de las Golondrinas, a re-creation of an early Spanish settlement south of Santa Fe. The museum's restored mills captivated them, and when they discovered the mill Jose's grandfather established was for sale, they purchased it from the family estate and set about becoming millers. Actually, they are reviving a tradition. Before flood control changed the nature of the area, Belen was a wheat-growing and milling center. Now the Cordovas must purchase most of their supplies from the northern and eastern part of the state.

There are no tours as such, but if you come at a slack time, Kathy might break away from her books to show you the 1920 Decatur milling machine, beautifully restored to working condition by Jose.

The next miles of your journey take you through the tiny Hispanic river towns of Veguita ("Little Meadow") and Las Nutrias ("The Beavers"). Before joining US 60, you pass the gates of New Mexico Boys Ranch, a residential facility for boys 8 to 18 operated by a Christian nonprofit organization. The property, a working cattle ranch with 2,400 acres, occupies a site that was once a watering hole and salt reservoir on the old Camino Real.

You now are heading north into the Estancia Basin. In prehistory, the area was covered by a vast lake, which gradually dried up as the climate became more arid. The salts left behind condensed into salt flats and salt "lakes" a few inches deep. The Spanish named the place Salinas Jurisdiction. They used Indian labor to carry the salt down to the Rio Grande, where it was transported to the silver mines in Chihuahua, Mexico. Salt was a necessary part of the "patio" process of smelting silver.

Even before the Entrada, however, there were settlements in the Estancia Basin. Archaeologists differ as to the exact date early Indians occupied the region, but estimates range anywhere from 19,000 years ago to between 10,000 and 12,000 years ago. At first, the people were nomads, hunter-gatherers. Later two great ancient cultural traditions overlapped in the Salinas: the Ancestral Puebloan and Mogollon. They produced settled societies that at first built clusters of pit houses and eventually mastered the art of above-ground masonry structures. Villages grew up and flourished, and the area became a major trade center between the Rio Grande pueblos and the plains tribes to the east.

Today the once prosperous villages and the missions the Spanish built to serve them are in ruins. The winds sweep through both pueblo and church, piling little drifts of sand against walls that witnessed the comings and goings of gray-robed friars and the everyday life of area residents. Now the only sign of life is the whip-tailed lizard warming itself in the sun or the voice of the occasional visitor.

What happened? A clash of cultures was partly to blame. The Spanish brought a new set of values and a new religion to the pueblos. Famine and European diseases also played roles.

Compounding these elements was the dependence of a very large population upon rainfall for agriculture, more than usual reliance on hunting, and high exposure to the depredations of the Apaches. Over a period of time these factors led to a gradual migration of the people to join other native groups along the edge of the Rio Grande. The final disintegration occurred during the 1680 Pueblo Revolt, when the remnants of the Salinas people fled with the Spanish to the El Paso area.

Today **Salinas Pueblo Missions National Monument** consists of the ruins of three separate pueblos/missions: **Abó** and **Quarai** to the north and **Gran Quivera** to the south. Your first stop is Abó, which is the favorite of many for its splendid isolation and the ruins of the San Gregorio de Abó mission church. Built between 1629 and 1659, the church and convento have a design that combines European form with Indian construction materials and techniques. The walls are of sandstone rock and mud mortar with two exterior buttresses and a bell tower supporting the west wall to a height of 40 feet. The convento walls act as east side buttresses, and the crenellated roof gives a fortress-like appearance to the church and mission compound. In the morning sun the buildings glow with an almost incandescent light. The unexcavated Tampiro Indian pueblo lies to the south of the mission and is connected to it by a half-mile, handicapped-accessible trail. There is a small visitor's center with a display area, books for sale, and restroom facilities.

To reach the second of the missions, you must detour south 25 miles to Gran Quivera, a modern designation for the village known originally as Cueloze. The Spanish renamed it Pueblo de las Humanas, which means "a town of Indians with stripes painted or tattooed over their noses," a characteristic of Plains Indians appearing in many pictographs in this region.

The Abó ruins, part of Salinas Pueblo Missions National Monument, are home to the remains of San Gregorio de Abó mission church.

The site encompasses the excavation of a large pueblo with plazas, homes, storage rooms, and ceremonial kivas; the ruins of the old mission church, San Buenaventura; and the Chapel of San Isidro, the first Christian church built on the site by Father Letrado, who was later killed at Zuni during the Pueblo Revolt. A half-mile trail wanders among the ruins, and a visitor's center houses exhibit space, books for sale, and restrooms.

The farming and ranching town of **Mountainair** is the headquarters for Salinas Pueblo Missions National Monument, where you may secure additional information or view *Breath of Life,* a 27-minute film that interprets the cultural clash between the pueblo people of the Estancia Valley and the Spanish Colonial Empire in 17th-century New Mexico.

Mountainair is the place to pause for a meal or overnight stay. Founded in 1903 by three Kansas men in anticipation of the construction of the Santa Fe Railway's Belen cutoff, the town is at the highest point on the railroad's southern transcontinental route. Once known as the "Pinto Bean Capital of the World," the area was hit by a severe drought in the 1950s that forced a change in economic focus to ranching.

Mountainair struggles to maintain its presence, its vitality sapped by the main street's many boarded-up storefronts. A notable exception is **Cibola Arts,** a 14-artist cooperative founded in 1995. There you will find works by local and regional artists in oil, glass, jewelry, pottery, tinwork, quilting, weaving, alabaster sculpture, and basketry, as well as cards and scented soaps.

Although not vying for the title of gastronomical capital of New Mexico, Mountainair's eateries handle the basic Southwestern cuisine adequately. Try the **Firehouse Restaurant** or the **Mountainair Chuck Wagon,** a dine-in, carryout, or drive-through operation. Or check out the restaurant in the Shaffer Hotel, if it's operational. It's been an on-again, off-again proposition in the past.

One of the early settlers, Clem "Pop" Shaffer, was the counterpart of the hippies of the 1960s. An acclaimed merchant, horse trader, land speculator, philanthropist, and folk artist, he built his idiosyncratic hotel over his hardware and implement store in 1923. You'll be happy to learn that owner Joel Marks, who discovered the relic while riding his Harley through the Manzano Mountains, has kept Pop's eccentric decor while accomplishing needed modernization of the guest rooms. The Shaffer features 19 antiques-furnished rooms, from a simple cowboy room with community bath to an elegant wedding suite with two claw-foot tubs and a wet bar. Pop's Curio Shop is an added attraction with its jumble of Southwestern jewelry, musical instruments, and gifts from all over the Southwest.

A variety of art, particularly folk art, can be found in the galleries and shops of Mountainair.

Even if you don't dine at the Shaffer, the hotel restaurant is a must-see thanks to its 1920s Pueblo Deco ceilings and oddball chandeliers. Every possible surface is painted or carved with a combination of whimsical forms and Native American symbols. The chairs alone are painted in five colors.

Both the hotel and Rancho Bonito, where Pop grew much of the produce for the dining room, are on the National and

State Registers of Historic Places. Pop's eccentric art forms, his wooden zoo at the ranch and his hotel decor, are formally classified as Folk Art Environmentalist, a style in which "expression often takes the form of a lifetime, single project . . . guided by the desire to form an environment over which the artist has complete control."

Eight miles beyond Mountainair, the red walls of Quarai's church, La Purísima Concepción de Cuarac, rise above the small valley. The smallest of the three missions, it is thought to have been constructed around 1630 under Fray Juan Gutierrez de la Chica, who came to minister to the Tiwa-speaking Indian pueblo. Like the others, it was abandoned in the late 1600s. The visitor's center contains a museum with a model of the original mission as well as Indian and missionary artifacts.

Heading north, you pass a series of small Hispanic towns. Manzano was named for the apples grown in orchards thought to have been planted by Franciscan friars in the 17th century. Torreon, Tajique, and Chilili were all built on the sites of Indian pueblos. Torreon was named for the fortified towers the Spanish built to the south, and Tajique is a corruption of the Tiwa pueblo name. Chilili is from a Pueblo word for "very weak spring" or "sound of water barely trickling." It is one of the oldest place-names in New Mexico, having been recorded as the site of a pueblo in 1581. The present Hispanic settlement was established as part of a land grant in 1841.

Your last stop on the Salt Mission Trail is the Sandia Ranger Station in Tijeras. To the rear of the station, the ruins of another old pueblo lie under the sighing grasses. In the mid-1300s it was a settlement with 200 rooms, a dozen or so smaller buildings, and a great kiva. Although a second phase of growth occurred in 1390, by 1425 the people had moved on. Today a large mound of earth marks the remnants of the pueblo, but illustrated trail signs and a scale model bring the scene to life. If you are resourceful and imaginative, you may be able to pierce the veil of time and hear in the wind the whisper of the past—the spirits of a departed but not forgotten people.

Contacts:

Firehouse Restaurant, Broadway at Ripley Street, Mountainair, 87036. Call 505-847-2374. Tues. through Sat. 11–3 and 5–8, Sun. 7–5.

Greater Belen Chamber of Commerce, 712 Dailes, Belen, 87002. Call 505-864-8091. Mon. through Fri. 9–5. Web site: www.belennm.com.

Historic Harvey House, Valencia County Historical Society, 104 N. First Street, Belen, 87002. Call 505-861-0581. Tues. through Sat. 12:30–3:30. Web site: www.nmculture.org/cgi-bin/instview.cgi?_recordnum=HARV.

Isleta Pueblo, P.O. Box 1270, Isleta, 87022. Call 505-869-3111 or 505-869-6333. Mon. through Fri. 8–4:30. Web site: www.isletapueblo.com.

The Luna Mansion, P.O. Box 789, 110 Main Street, Los Lunas, 87031. Call 505-865-7333. Thurs. through Sat. 5–9:30, Sun. 4:30–8:30. Web site: www.thelunamansion.com.

Mountainair Chamber of Commerce, 217 Broadway, P.O. Box 595, Mountainair, 87036. Call 505-384-9767. Call for hours. Web site: www.mountainairchamber.com.

Mountainair Chuck Wagon, 305 W. Broadway, Mountainair, 87063, Call 505-847-0046. Daily 8–10.

Pete's Café, 105 N. First Street, Belen, 87002. Call 505-864-4811. Mon. through Thurs. 11–8, Fri. and Sat. 11–8:30.

Salinas Pueblo Missions National Monument, P.O. Box 517, Ripley and Broadway, Mountainair, 87036. Headquarters, call 505-847-2585; Gran Quivera, 505-847-2770; Abó, 505-847-2400; Quarai, 505-847-2290. Monument headquarters, Memorial Day through Labor Day, daily 9–6; winter, 9–5. Web site: www.nps.gov/sapu.

Shaffer Hotel and Dining Room, 103 W. Main Street, Mountainair, 87036. Call 1-888-595-2888 or 505-847-2888. Call for restaurant information. Web site: www.shafferhotel.com.

Sunset Foods Beef Jerky, 3072 NM 47, Los Lunas, 87031. Call 505-865-9202. Tues. through Sat. 10–6, Sun. 11–5.

Teofilo's Restaurant, 144 Main Street, Los Lunas, 87301. Call 505-865-5511. Tues. through Thurs. 11–8:30, Fri. and Sat. 11–9, Sun. 9–8:30.

Tijeras Pueblo Archaeological Site, Sandia Ranger District, Cibola National Forest, 11776 NM 337, Tijeras, 87059. Call 505-281-3304. Trail, weekdays 8–5, weekends 8:30–5. Web site: www.fs.fed.us/r3/cibola/districts/sandia.

Valencia County Chamber of Commerce and Visitor's Center, 3447 Lambros, P.O. Box 13, Los Lunas, 87031. Call 505-352-3596. Mon. through Fri. 9–5. Web site: www.loslunasnm.gov/chamber.

Valencia Flour Mill, P.O. Box 210, 74 Mill Road, Jarales, 87023. Call 505-864-0305. No formal tours.

St. Augustine Mission Church

St. Augustine

CHAPTER

Billy the Kid Territory

Getting there: From Albuquerque, take I-25 south to San Acacia, Exit 163. From San Acacia, take NM 408, which runs 10 miles through the villages of Chamizal and Palvadera to the outskirts of Lemitar. Your option here is to continue on to San Antonio on NM 408 or leave the pavement and drive Quebradas Back Country Byway, a well-maintained dirt and gravel road that is navigable by touring car in dry weather. The road leaves Lemitar and traces east and south approximately 27 miles before joining US 380 11 miles east of San Antonio.

To visit Bosque del Apache Refuge, drive south from San Antonio 8 miles on NM 1. Retracing the route on your return, go north to US 380. The exit to Trinity Site, location of the first atomic explosion, is 12 miles beyond San Antonio; Carrizozo, 53 miles.

Continue east on US 380. The distance between Carrizozo and Capitan is 20 miles; Capitan and Lincoln, 12 miles; and Lincoln and Hondo, 10 miles. Turn west on US 70 at Hondo, passing through San Patricio and Glencoe. Take the Hollywood exit to detour into Ruidoso, 24 miles from Hondo.

Leaving Ruidoso, resume the journey southwest 12 miles on US 70 through Apache Summit to the junction of NM 244, which winds 29 miles to Cloudcroft. From Cloudcroft, take US 82 west through Mountain Park and High Rolls to US 70/54, 20 miles south to Alamogordo. The turnoff to White Sands National Monument is 14 miles southwest of Alamogordo on US 70.

Returning to Alamogordo, drive north 30 miles to Three Rivers and take Forest Service Road 579 about 5 miles to the Three Rivers Petroglyph Site. Carrizozo is 28 miles beyond Three Rivers on US 54.

Highlights: While in the Rio Grande Valley, visit **Bosque del Apache National Wildlife Refuge,** home of thousands of wintering waterfowl and sandhill cranes. From the green of the riverine environment, cross the notorious Jornada del Muerto and pass the Trinity Site (open to the public on the first Saturdays of April and October only).

Explore deep into the Sacramento Mountains, stopping at the tiny towns of **Capitan,** home of Smokey Bear, and **Lincoln,** site of the infamous Lincoln County War. Drop into the beautiful **Hondo Valley,** made famous by the Hurd-Wyeth family of artists. Stop for a while in the busy four-season resort of **Ruidoso** before ascending to the lofty heights at **Cloudcroft** with its shops and restaurants.

Leaving the mountains, descend into the Tularosa Valley, where a short detour will take you to the gleaming gypsum dunes of White Sands National Monument. Heading north and passing the ridge containing thousands of petroglyphs near Three Rivers, you end your tour in Carrizozo.

Let's Go: Many small farming and ranching communities doze in relative obscurity between the interstate and the Rio Grande River, where the soil is rich and water for irrigation is plentiful. **San Acacia** is one such place. Named for a Roman soldier martyred for his Christian faith, the community once boasted a fine church and a school. The original mission—a proud structure of adobe three times the size of the current building—was built in the 1800s and contained massive vigas, wooden pews, and hand-carved santos. The land on which it stood was donated by a rancher, and the village provided the construction labor. Before the era of dams, dikes, and levees, the region was susceptible to occasional rampages of the Rio Grande, and in 1929 a flood claimed the church. Some material was saved, and the parishioners rebuilt the current sanctuary on a smaller scale. Through the years the building has fallen into disrepair and only a shell remains.

Leaving San Acacia, you pass through the small villages of Chamizal and Palvadera, arriving in Lemitar, where **Quebradas Back Country Byway** originates. Quebradas means "breaks" in Spanish, and the drama of the land's desolation, broken here and there with the green punctuation of juniper, creates a haunting beauty. The journey is one that internationally known Taos artist Doug West has portrayed many times in his exquisite serigraphs.

Head back west on the highway to **San Antonio,** now just a crossroads but once a bustling town and popular stop on the Atchison, Topeka and Santa Fe Railway. Conrad Hilton, famed hotelier, was born here in 1887 and got his start in the family business hustling bags and directing travelers from the train station to his father's store and hotel.

Currently, you'll find a store and gas station there and the venerable **Owl Bar and Café,** where Adolfo and Rowena Baca are celebrated for serving scrumptious green chile cheeseburgers. Although best known for its cheeseburgers (between 400 and 500 are served each day on busy weekends), the restaurant also features steak dinners. Decor is minimal, with the walls of the dimly lit interior plastered with dollar bills and business cards. There's a rumor that the expansive front bar originally came from the Hiltons' store.

After a good solid burger chased down with chile cheese fries, take the south road to **Bosque del Apache National Wildlife Refuge.** The "Woods of the Apache" is managed and maintained by the U.S. Fish and Wildlife Service and is one of the nation's most successful wildlife refuges. Stretching 9 miles along the Rio Grande, land for the 57,191-acre refuge was purchased by the government beginning in 1936, and the refuge was formally established in 1939. Even with years of heavy grazing, it still supported a rich wildlife population. This changed in 1941, when a river flood destroyed the cottonwood savannah and buried the marshlands in more than 30 feet of silt.

The following years were ones of rebuilding. Dikes were constructed and water diverted to develop forests and marshes. Today there are 325 species of birds: 15,000 sandhill cranes, 40,000 snow geese, 400 Canada geese, and 60,000 ducks make the refuge their fall and winter home, flying in from nesting grounds 1,000 miles away. Mornings and evenings are the most spectacular viewing times, when the immense population takes to the sky, creating a whirling, wheeling, honking snowstorm of birds sometimes stretching a mile in length.

During the third week of November, the refuge, Friends of the Bosque del Apache, the city of Socorro, and the Socorro County Chamber of Commerce sponsor the immensely popular **Festival of the Cranes.** Visitors may choose from seminars, workshops, and tours to birding sites, including some not generally open to the public. In addition, there are other featured events like concerts, an arts and crafts show, and special exhibits.

Events fill up fast, so if you're planning to visit at this time, try to preregister by October 31. You can buy tickets from the Friends of the Bosque through mid-November or at the refuge front desk on a first-come, first-served basis after November 15.

If you're not anticipating an in-depth experience, you can visit the refuge anytime. The site is at its prime in the winter, with thousands of snow geese, waterfowl, eagles, and sandhill cranes. During spring and fall, you can see migrant warblers, flycatchers, and shorebirds. The summer months are prime for nesting songbirds, waders, shorebirds, and ducks. Year-round residents are mule deer, coyote, muskrat, Canada goose, coot, pheasant, turkey, quail, and roadrunner.

Your first stop should be the visitor's center, where you can pick up a brochure with a map of the hiking and self-guided 15-mile auto tour routes. There are displays, videos, a bookstore, and current information on sightings. A limited number of binoculars are available for rent in case you've forgotten yours. Picnic tables wait under shade trees for visitors savvy enough to have packed their lunch, an especially good move on busy fall and winter weekends when local restaurants are so busy. Don't forget a water bottle, and bring insect repellent if you come during warm months. Remember, these wetlands are marshes, and that means mosquitoes!

Leaving the refuge, you retrace your steps to San Antonio and head east through the **Jornada del Muerto** ("Journey of the Dead Man"). This expanse of sun and sand was named not for its inhospitable nature but for Bernardo Gruber, who escaped from the local arm of the Inquisition and attempted to cross the desert. His desiccated corpse was discovered at a place called El Alemán ("The German"), and the waterless waste came to be called Jornada del Muerto.

A short distance into the region you pass Range Road 7, which is the northern entrance to the **Trinity Site** and is open to the public only on the first Saturdays of April and October. If you've timed your visit to coincide with these dates, you may visit the site of the first atomic test operation, known as Project Trinity. Here, on July 16, 1945, U.S. scientists successfully detonated the device that would power the bombs dropped on Hiroshima on August 6 and Nagasaki on August 9.

Today the site bears little evidence of that massive explosion, which shattered windows 120 miles away. You enter the restricted area from the north by way of the Stallion Gate or from the south on a tour departing from the Otero County Fair Grounds in Alamogordo. The surrounding landscape is otherworldly, with the Oscura–San Andres Mountains to the east and a series of hills rising like the backbone of some prehistoric beast to the south. Checking through security, you join a line of cars directed to a parking site, where a festive atmosphere prevails thanks to food vendors selling "Atomic Burgers" and souvenir stands purveying T-shirts, books, and knickknacks.

You must walk a quarter mile to ground zero, where a large fenced enclosure contains a monument, historical photos fastened to the wire barrier, a shelter protecting a portion of the original crater, a replica of the "Fatman" bomb casing, and a sample of the footing from the test tower.

If you wish to visit the McDonald Ranch, where the plutonium core of the bomb was assembled, you must return to the parking lot and use the army tour buses provided. The ranch house was built in 1913 by Franz Schmidt, a German immigrant, and an addition was constructed on the north side in the 1930s by the McDonald family. Abandoned in 1942, when the Alamogordo Bombing and Gunnery Range took over the land to use in training World War II bombing crews, the house stood empty until the Manhattan Project support personnel arrived in early 1945. Working with the National Park Service, the army restored the building in 1984, and the exterior appears as it did in 1945. The interior is empty except for photos of the era, which line the walls.

A monument marks the spot where the nation's first atomic test operation, known as Project Trinity, was held.

Leaving the Missile Range, US 380 crosses the foothills of the Oscura Mountains and climbs the edge of Chupadera Mesa. On the outskirts of **Carrizozo** you encounter the massive lava flow that dominates the views of the Tularosa Valley. Originating from a small,

The Carrizozo visitor's center is housed in a train caboose, fitting for a town with such a rich railroading history.

extinct volcano to the north named Little Black Peak, this flow covers more than 125 square miles. Amazing as it seems, plants and animal life make the region home. Mule deer, a small band of Barbary sheep, coyotes, kit foxes, bobcats, and ringtail cats prowl its expanse. Pockets of soil harbor the white waxy spire of yucca flowers and the scarlet bloom of hedgehog cactuses.

The portion of the lava flow that frames the highway and borders the town is a national recreational area named **Valley of Fires.** The U.S. Bureau of Land Management maintains campground sites, a pavilion, a three-quarter-mile nature trail, and a visitor information station. If you decide to explore the trail, wear sturdy shoes, carry water, and try to hike in early morning or late afternoon to beat the heat.

Carrizozo is just 4 miles to the southeast. Named for the abundance of reeds (carrizos) growing at springs north of town, Carrizozo grew to a city of respectable size when the El Paso and Northeastern Railroad built a roundhouse and repair yards there, bypassing the mining town of White Oaks. With the decline of railroading, the need for maintenance yards diminished and Carrizozo's economy suffered.

As the seat of Lincoln County, the town still is a regional hub, complete with a few stores, county offices, and a library. **The Outpost** restaurant is a good example of the old Western saloon, with an expansive bar, mounted animal heads, jukebox, pool table, and small dance floor. The menu is predictable, running heavily to staples like burgers and chicken-fried steak

If you have an interest in old ghost towns, take a detour north to **White Oaks,** where three prospectors discovered gold in 1879. By 1884 White Oaks had 1,000 residents, but the mines played out and most of the population departed. A few buildings from the 1890s remain standing, and the town is still home to a handful of residents and artists.

East of Carrizozo, you enter the Sacramento Mountains, the road running between Nogal Peak to the south and Vera Cruz Mountain to the north. As you ascend into Lincoln National Forest, you pass through different climatic zones: the lower Sonoran at 3,000 to 5,000 feet with its grama grass, mesquite, creosote bush, opuntia, and yucca; the upper Sonoran at 5,000 to 7,000 feet with its piñon pine and buffalo grass; the transition zone with forests of ponderosa pine and hardwoods; and finally, in the upper elevations of 8,000 to 10,000 feet, the Canadian zone with Douglas fir and quaking aspen. You can actually pinpoint your elevation with a fair degree of accuracy just by looking out the window.

Arriving in **Capitan,** you can't miss the town's best-known attraction, **Smokey Bear Historical Park.** It was in the nearby mountains on May 9, 1950, that a crew fighting the Los Tablos forest fire found a badly singed black bear cub clinging tenaciously to the side of a burned pine tree.

While most people believe this was the start of the Smokey Bear fire prevention program, the truth is that artist Albert Staehle produced a bear wearing Levis and a ranger hat for an original poster in 1944. The bear was called "Smokey" after New York City Fire Chief Joe Martin. The little cub became the embodiment of the artist's concept.

As the real Smokey grew, he was moved to quarters at the National Zoo in Washington, D.C. Upon his death his body was returned to Capitan and buried there, where a whole complex is devoted to his memory. You can visit his grave in a pretty garden at the park, or you can spend time at the visitor's center, where there are exhibits about forest health, forest fires, wildland/urban interface issues, fire ecology, and the history of the Cooperative Forest Fire Prevention Program, as well as a theater that shows a 10-minute film discussing today's fire and forest health issues. An outdoor exhibit features six of the vegetative life zones found in New Mexico, and an outdoor amphitheater is used for educational programs for school groups. Also located at the park are a playground, a picnic area with group shelters, and the original train depot for the village of Capitan. A small log cabin next to the park was built by volunteers with local funds and serves as a museum and gift shop.

Capitan's second big attraction is **The Greenhouse Café** in the old Hotel Chango. Here chef Tom Histen and his wife, Gail, serve what Tom classifies as groundbreaking and eclectic cuisine. "Like a musician, a chef needs inspiration," he says. The standard menu might include an appetizer of heirloom tomatoes caprese or shrimp cocktail with avocado salsa. A selection of main courses ranges from Greek-style roast pork tenderloin on a roasted eggplant base with tzatziki sauce, New Zealand orange roughy sautéed in chardonnay with a fresh nectarine and peach compote, or a 6-ounce pan-seared beef filet in merlot demi-glace on a giant portobello mushroom. Dinners always include a vegan entrée, a rare item in these parts. Lunch, served only in the summer months, is prix fixe and includes a selection of three soups, fresh breads, a build-your-own salad based on fresh greens grown on premise (supplemented with shrimp, chicken, or fish if you wish), and a fresh fruit dessert.

When William Bonney first came to the little town of **Lincoln** in the Rio Bonito Valley, two factions were trying to wrest political and economic control of the region. Englishman John Tunstall and his partners, Alexander McSween and cattle baron John Chisum, took on the established powers led by James Dolan and L. G. Murphy. The 1878 murder of Tunstall was the fuse that ignited the hostilities and led to the creation of "The Regulators," a vigilante group vowed to avenge the murder. The climactic gun battle between the two sides lasted five days, but hostilities continued for nearly a year.

One of the Regulators was teenage ranch hand William Bonney, also known as "Kid" Antrim and later as Billy the Kid. Billy eventually was captured near Fort Sumner by Sheriff Pat Garrett, but not before he shot his way out of the Lincoln jail, where he was to hang for the murder of Sheriff William Brady. During his escape, he killed Deputy Robert Ollinger, and a marker outside the courthouse designates where he fell.

Lincoln's place in history does not depend on its association with Bonney. Other famous players were part of its legacy: New Mexico Governor Lew Wallace (author of *Ben Hur*), Black Jack Pershing and the

Buffalo Soldiers, Indian scout Kit Carson, Pat Garrett, and Apache Chief Victorio.

Today the properties on both sides of the road look much as they did in the late 1800s. When you tour the courthouse, you can still see the bullet hole from Billy the Kid's escape. The building has been restored and is now operated by New Mexico State Monuments, which also owns other historic buildings in Lincoln. You may visit the Tunstall Store, the José Montaño Store, San Juan Mission Church, the Convento, the Dr. Woods House, the Torreon, and the Anderson-Freeman Visitors Center, where you can watch a video capturing Lincoln's tumultuous past or examine exhibits highlighting the various forces influencing its history. A gift shop is in the planning stages.

Currently, Lincoln's closest eatery is **Tinnie Silver Dollar Saloon and Restaurant.** Tinnie's, located just a couple of miles beyond the intersection of US 380 and US 70, is well worth the trip. The building is an old mercantile and post office built in the 1870s. Purchased by Robert Anderson of Roswell in 1959, it was renovated and its landmark tower and

The Dr. Woods House is one of several historic buildings open to visitors in Lincoln.

pavilion added. Photographs from Tinnie's past as well as 13 paintings by artist Peter Hurd grace the walls, while the elegant decor is a legacy from San Patricio artist John Meigs, who scoured the countryside for the ornate doors, stained-glass windows, furniture, and artwork. The old store houses the banquet room, stables, and a gift shop.

Owned by New Mexico's Cattle Baron chain, the Silver Dollar has an upscale chophouse menu with a variety of appetizers like fresh oysters on the half shell, jumbo lump crab cakes, and coconut shrimp. French onion soup and classic New England clam chowder are always on the menu along with a variety of salads. Entrées run from the filet Oscar, a 9-ounce filet mignon topped with jumbo lump crab, asparagus spears, and green chile béarnaise, to a mixed grill of rack of lamb, a hefty pork chop, and a 12-ounce top sirloin. If beef isn't your dish, try the roast chicken with lemon, garlic, and rosemary or the king crab legs.

From the Rio Bonito ("beautiful river") Valley, you head southeast into the **Hondo Valley.** With its river, fruit orchards, and small farms, the Hondo is one of New Mexico's most beautiful places. It's no wonder that through the years famous people have settled there—actress Helen Hayes, author Paul Horgan, artist John Meigs, sculptor Luis Jimenez, and the Wyeth/Hurd family.

The village of **San Patricio** is the locus of present-day artistic activity. In its confines is the **Hurd La Rinconada Gallery,** which exhibits major pieces by Peter Hurd and Henriette Wyeth Hurd, as well as work by other notable family members Michael Hurd, Jamie Wyeth, and Carol Hurd Rogers.

La Rinconada is located on Sentinel Ranch property, the New Mexico home of Peter Hurd and his wife, Henriette, daughter of famous illustrator N. C. Wyeth. The gallery is an opus unto itself. Designed by Michael Hurd, its steeply pitched copper roof, dormers, and tiered brick terrace complement the pastoral surroundings.

For those wanting more than a brief visit, the **Hurd Ranch Guest Homes** on the property provide an in-depth San Patricio experience. The gallery's guest wing has a large bedroom, kitchen, bath, and living area opening onto the terrace. Orchard House and Apple House are cozy, renovated old adobes.

With the Rio Ruidoso to your left, you travel southeast toward **Ruidoso Downs,** home of **Ruidoso Downs Race Track, Billy the Kid Casino,** and the **Hubbard Museum of the American West.** If you like to watch the ponies run, Ruidoso Downs schedules thoroughbred and quarter horse races from Memorial Day to Labor Day weekend.

Hubbard Museum of the American West in Ruidoso Downs is filled with horse-related artifacts, fine art, and historical pieces.

Track fan or not, be sure to stop at the museum, where you'll find not only exhibits on horse lore but also a special collection of art, sculpture, and historical pieces. The core of the collection came as a legacy from Anne C. Stradling, who started her accumulation of horse-related artifacts at age 6, when she hung a bit and worn-out stirrup on the wall of the family's New Jersey barn. Her encyclopedic accumulation grew to more than 10,000 horse-related items: carriages, wagons, saddles, bits, and bridles. Fine art, furniture, and silver came from her family estate, and a distinguished group of Indian artifacts is the result of her Arizona days. The museum complements the permanent assembly with changing exhibits.

An imposing sculpture fronts the museum. Ruidoso's well-known master of bronze, Dave McGary, created *Free Spirits at Noisy Water,* a grouping of eight larger-than-life-size horses depicting the seven classic breeds. The scope of the project is monumental—three stories tall at its highest point and stretching nearly the length of a football field. A thoroughbred leads the procession, followed by the quarter horse, the Appaloosa, the paint mare and her foal, the Arabian, the Morgan, and the standardbred.

Ruidoso evenings are enhanced by a visit to the $20-million **Spencer Theater for the Performing Arts.** A short distance northeast of town near the Sierra Blanca Regional Airport, the center was designed by Albuquerque architect Antoine Predock, who created an architectural work of art reflecting the shape of the surrounding mountain peaks. Faced in 450 tons of Spanish mica-flecked limestone, the theater features a waterfall gently

The sand at White Sands National Monument, which is actually fine particles of gypsum, not sand as we know it, is best explored in the early morning or evening.

cascading from the core of the white wedge-shaped structure and a crystal lobby jutting from the north side. The heart of the Spencer is its 514-seat hall, which has outstanding acoustics and intimate seating. The theater houses the largest private collection of Seattle glass sculptor Dale Chihuly's work in the Southwest. Installations include the *Glowing Sunset Tower,* a 14-foot glass tower in squiggles of red and orange; *Indian Paint Brushes,* a 177-piece sculpture inspired by New Mexico's wildflowers; *The Persians,* a massive fireworks burst; *Cobalt Blue Baskets,* six bowl-like baskets held within the womb of an 18-inch-wide, cobalt blue mother basket; and *Ruby Sea Garden & Chandelier,* constructions of ruby glass tentacles. The complex opened in 1997 and is a gift to the region by Alto resident Jackie Spencer and her husband, Ron. The cultural center books musicals, drama, concerts, dance, and children's programs.

When you venture into the village of **Ruidoso,** you'll find a variety of restaurants and shops along Sudderth Drive. Becki Knight-Zarndt's **Galleria West** has Native American jewelry in gold and silver, artifacts, and occasionally old estate jewelry. Her helpful sales force is a bonus. Shirley Kostka's **White Dove Gallery** carries downtown's best assortment of Indian crafts, while **White Mountain Pottery**'s focus is on the work of seven local artists producing stoneware crockery, lamps, and accessories. Shopping for unusual creations? Check out sisters Leslie Belcher and Shelley Harper's art glass jewelry at **accessoreez—the gallery.**

If you enjoyed Dave McGary's *Free Spirits at Noisy Water,* you'll be dazzled by his gallery on Sudderth, **McGary Studios: Expressions in Bronze.** Considered the master of realism depicting Native Americans of the past, McGary showcases two decades of his sculpture in his gallery.

Take a lunch break at **The Village Buttery,** where the husband-and-wife team of Becky and Frank Walston fixes gourmet sandwiches, salads, homemade soups, and rich dessert pies. A local favorite is their buttermilk pie, which is known to sell out early. Or try **Café Rio,** a pizza parlor full of surprises. Owner John Terrell serves up all the traditional Italian favorites, pizza, and calzones; but good as these are, it's the Portuguese-Mediterranean café menu that shines. A head of garlic slow roasted in olive oil or Portuguese kale soup are robust starters. Entrées include delectables like Cajun jambalaya; herbed polenta with Portuguese molho sauce; and finally Greek spanakopita, the spinach and feta cheese pie baked in flaky phyllo dough. If you've room for dessert, their double-layer chocolate cake with chocolate espresso frosting is superb.

For dining with a French flair, try **Le Bistro.** Chef Richard Girot prepares classic dishes like Coquille St. Jacques and Filet de Canard au Poivre Vert in his snug restaurant with its outdoor patio and Euro-style interior. His wine list is extensive and prices are reasonable.

Heading south from Ruidoso, you pass through the **Mescalero Apache Indian Reservation** en route to Cloudcroft. The reservation, established in 1872, consists of 460,177 acres between the Sacramento and White mountains. The tribe manages hunting and fishing preserves, the **Inn of the Mountain Gods,** a luxury resort and casino, and **Ski Apache,** a downhill area on the slopes of Sierra Blanca.

Cloudcroft can leave you breathless, literally. At 8,640 feet, the little town often tops the cumulus. Founded in 1898, when a group of surveyors for the railroad reached the summit of the Sacramento Mountains and established a camp for logging operations, Cloudcroft's cool summer weather made it a popular retreat for Alamogordo and El Paso residents. The main street, Burro Avenue, is filled with the usual tourist lures—knickknack shops, restaurants, and a small archive, the **Sacramento Mountains Historical Society Museum,** which is loaded with artifacts and photographs of early days.

Cloudcroft's most distinguished destination is **The Lodge.** Constructed of logs in 1899, the original structure burned in 1909, but by 1911 the new building had been completed on its current, more scenic site. The Lodge is a complete four-season resort. Warm-season guests enjoy an 18-hole Scottish links golf course, an outdoor pool, a hot tub, and sauna. Winter visitors downhill ski at nearby Ski Cloudcroft or cross-country ski, inner tube, or snowmobile at The Lodge.

The Lodge's public rooms are adorned in turn-of-the-20th-century furniture, antique fixtures, mounted game, and paddle fans. Breakfast, lunch, and dinner are served in the Fireside Room Terrace and the Conservatory of Rebecca's Restaurant, named for the resident ghost, a red-headed chambermaid who met her end at the hand of a jealous lover. The 59 guest rooms and suites have been completely renovated and each is individually decorated.

As you leave Cloudcroft and descend from its lofty summit, watch for the old railroad trestle on your left. The road twists and turns as it plunges down through the peach, pear, cherry, and apple orchards of High Rolls and Mountain Park. By the time you reach the Tularosa Basin and US 54, you will have gone from the fir and aspen of the high mountains to the mesquite and creosote of the Chihuahuan desert.

No journey to this area is complete without a visit to **Alamogordo** and **White Sands National Monument,** 15 miles southwest of the city. This quirk of nature is not comprised of sand particles as we commonly recognize them, but of fine particles of gypsum, a hydrous form of calcium sulfate.

It's not too far beyond human ken to imagine the shallow sea that covered this area 250 million years ago. The gypsum-bearing marine deposits that form the sands were deposited at the bottom of this body of water, and the whole area was uplifted into a giant dome 70 million years ago. The dome collapsed approximately 10 million years ago, creating the Tularosa Basin. The sides of the original dome now comprise the San Andres and Sacramento mountain ranges.

The dunes develop when mountain rains dissolve gypsum from the rocks and carry it into the basin. Since the area has no outlet for drainage, water and its sediments are trapped. As the fluids evaporate, the crystalline gypsum is deposited on the surface. Winds blowing across the low-lying depressions carry gypsum particles downwind. These accumulate, creating dunes.

If you plan to visit, be prepared for road delays en route. White Sands National Monument's 275 square miles are completely surrounded by the White Sands Missile Range. When tests are conducted on the range, US 70 between the park and Las Cruces may be closed. These closures occur about twice a week and last from one to two hours.

Upon arrival, your first stop at the monument should be the visitor's center, a historic adobe building with geology exhibits and a diorama explaining the formation of the dunes. Rangers can help you plan the best use of your time, whether you expect to hike the 1-mile, self-guided Big Dune nature trail or drive the 8-mile scenic road into the heart of the dunes. At the center, you also can browse the book selections or check out the adjoining gift shop.

There is a science to experiencing this land so inhospitable to all but a few plants and animals. The glistening, highly reflective sands become downright uncomfortable during the heat of the day, so plan your explorations for early morning or evening. If you're hiking, carry water, wear a hat, and use sunscreen.

After the majesty of those eye-dazzling dunes, almost anything else is an anticlimax. However, if you have space fans in your entourage (perhaps if you're old enough to remember Sputnik), you'll enjoy stopping at the **New Mexico Museum of Space History's International Space Hall of Fame,** the **IMAX Dome Theater and Planetarium,** the **Stapp Air & Space Park,** and the **Astronaut Memorial Garden.**

The Hall of Fame's 28,111 square feet contain artifacts, models, memorabilia, and biographical material on space pioneers. Neil Armstrong, the first man to walk on the moon, is there along with Soviet Alexei Leonov, the first man to walk in space. In addition to the always popular moon rock, the Hall of Fame's exhibits include the primate capsule and space suit for Ham, first chimpanzee in space; models of a Mercury capsule, a Gemini spacecraft, and a lunar module; and many other items of interest.

The popular ViewSpace exhibit gently guides the viewer to a deeper understanding of astronomy through an Internet-fed, self-updating, permanent exhibit from the Space Telescope Science Institute, home of NASA's Hubble Space Telescope and its successor, The James Webb Space Telescope.

At the Clyde W. Tombaugh IMAX Dome Theater, IMAX films are featured along with a selection of star shows, special multimedia presentations, and laser light concerts.

Outside inspect the Air and Space Park's Sonic Wind I rocket sled and the Little Joe II rocket, which tested the Apollo Launch Escape System. Explore the Daisy Decelerator, an air-powered sled track used to study the effects of acceleration, deceleration, and impact on the human body and various equipment systems. A memorial garden commemorates the seven American astronauts who died in the January 28, 1986, explosion of the *Challenger* space shuttle.

As you head north leaving Alamogordo, you pass the outskirts of **Tularosa,** named for the red reeds that grew along the banks of Tularosa Creek when settlers first arrived in the area. The town was established in 1863 with the mapping of the 49 original blocks and the recording of water rights. Those 49 blocks are now on the National Register of Historic Places, and the original ditch irrigation continues to water the town's lush gardens, yards, and tree-lined streets. The valley surrounding the city is a major growing area for pecans, pistachios, and alfalfa.

Tularosa celebrates two major yearly festivals: the **Rose Festival** during the first weekend in May, complete with an old-timer's picnic, carnival, arts and crafts festival, and crowning of the Rose Queen; and, on the following weekend, the **St. Francis de Paula Fiesta,** which features Spanish dancers, a carnival, and regional foods.

The route to Three Rivers and Carrizozo is typical of the Chihuahuan desert, with expanses of creosote bushes, cholla and prickly pear cacti, yucca, and sotol. Before heading out to the interstate, take a detour on County Road B30 to **Three Rivers Petroglyph Site.** A rocky ridge of basalt is the stage for this parade of more than 23,000 human figures, animals, and esoteric symbols scratched in the rock by generations of prehistoric Jornada Mogollon Indians. Positioned on an open plain with the San Andres Mountains on the eastern horizon, it is a lonely place where the wind whips through the scrub and howls over the boulders. In such a great enormity, man needed the reassurance of his gods and totems to keep the wild spirits at bay. At the same place today, the weight of the wilderness is intense, the road and car a modern assurance.

Contacts:

accessoreez—the gallery, 2306 Sudderth, Ruidoso, 88345. Call 505-257-0740. Summer, Wed. through Sat. 11–4; winter, call for hours. Web site: www.accessoreez.com.

Alamogordo Chamber of Commerce, 1301 N. White Sands Boulevard, Alamogordo, 88310. Call 1-800-826-0294 or 505-437-6120. Mon. through Fri. 8–5, Sat. and Sun. 9–5. Web site: www.alamogordo.com.

Bosque del Apache National Wildlife Refuge, P.O. Box 1246, Socorro, 87801. Call 505-835-1828. Visitor's center, Mon. through Fri. 7:30–4; Sat. and Sun. 8–4:30. Tour route open one hour before sunrise to one hour after sunset. Seasonal tour road open April through September. Web site: www.fws.gov/southwest/refuges/newmex/bosque/index.html.

Café Rio, 2547 Sudderth, P.O. Box 1004, Ruidoso, 88345. Call 505-257-7746. Daily 11:30–8.

Capitan Chamber of Commerce, 433 Smokey Bear Boulevard, P.O. Box 441, Capitan, 88316. Call 505-354-2273. Mon. through Fri. 8–5.

Carrizozo Chamber of Commerce (train caboose, US 54 and US 380), P.O. Box 567, Carrizozo, 88301. Call 505-648-2732. Irregular hours.

Cloudcroft Chamber of Commerce, 1001 James Canyon Highway, P.O. Box 1290, Cloudcroft, 88317. Call 505-682-2733. Mon. through Sat. 10–5. Web site: www.cloudcroft.net.

Festival of the Cranes, see Friends of the Bosque del Apache. Web site: www.friendsofthebosque.org/crane.

Friends of the Bosque del Apache, P.O. Box 340, San Antonio, 87832. Call 505-838-2120. Web site: www.friendsofthebosque.org.

Galleria West, 2538 Sudderth, Ruidoso, 88345. Call 505-257-4560. Daily 10–5.

The Greenhouse Café, 103 S. Lincoln Avenue, Capitan, 88316. Call 505-354-0373. Lunch, Wed. through Sat. 11–2; dinner, Wed. through Sat. 5–9; Sun. brunch 10–1. Closed first two weeks of November. Reservations suggested.

Hubbard Museum of the American West, 841 US 70 W., Ruidoso Downs, 88346. Call 505-378-4142. Daily 9–5. Fee. Web site: www.hubbard museum.org.

Hurd La Rinconada Gallery and Guest Homes, 105 La Rinconada Lane, P.O. Box 100, San Patricio, 88348. Call 1-800-658-6912 or 505-653-4331. Gallery, Mon. through Sat. 9–5. Web site: www.wyeth artists.com.

Inn of the Mountain Gods, 287 Carrizo Canyon Road, Mescalero, 88340. Call 1-800-545-9011 or 505-464-7777. Web site: www.innofthe mountaingods.com.

Le Bistro, 2800 Sudderth Drive, Ruidoso, 88345. Call 505-257-0132. Mon. through Sat. 11–2 and 5–9.

Lincoln State Monument, US 380, P.O. Box 36, Lincoln, 88338. Call 505-653-4372. Daily 8:30–4:30. Fee. Web site: www.nmstate monuments.org.

The Lodge, One Corona Place, P.O. Box 497, Cloudcroft, 88317. Call 1-800-395-6343 or 505-682-2566. Breakfast, Mon. through Sat. 7–10:30, Sun. 7–10. Memorial Day through Labor Day, lunch, daily 11:30–2; dinner, Sun. through Thurs. 5:30–9, Fri. and Sat. 5:30–10. Spring, winter, and fall, lunch, daily 11:30–2, dinner, daily 5:30–9. Web site: www.thelodge resort.com.

McGary Studios: Expressions in Bronze, 2002 Sudderth, Ruidoso, 88345. Call 1-800-687-3424 or 505-257-1000. Summer, Mon. through Sat. 10–5; winter, Mon. through Fri. 10–5. Web site: www.dave mcgary.com.

New Mexico Museum of Space History, NM 2001, P.O. Box 5430, Alamogordo, 88311. Call 1-800-545-4021 or 505-437-2840. Daily 9–5. Tombaugh IMAX Dome Theater: Mon. through Sun., multiple screenings from 10 AM. Fee for both museum and IMAX theater. Web site: www.spacefame.org.

The Outpost, 415 Central Avenue, P.O. Box 811, Carrizozo, 88301. Call 505-648-9994. Sun. through Thurs. 10–10, Fri. and Sat. 10–11.

Owl Bar and Café, Main and Second streets, P.O. Box 215, San Antonio, 87832. Call 505-835-9946. Mon. through Sat. 8–9:30. Web site: www.owlbarandcafe.com.

Quebradas Back Country Byway, Bureau of Land Management, Socorro Field Office, 901 S. NM 85, Socorro, 87801. Call 505-835-0412. Web site: www.publiclands.org/explore/site.php?search=YES&back=Search%20Results&id=263.

Ruidoso Downs and Billy the Kid Casino, 1461 US 70 W., P.O. Box 449, Ruidoso Downs, 88346. Call 505-378-4431. Racing Memorial Day through Labor Day, Thurs. through Sun. (Fri. through Mon. on holiday weekends). Casino, Sun. through Thurs. 10 AM–midnight, Fri. and Sat. 10 AM–2 AM. Web site: ruidosodownsracing.com.

Ruidoso Valley Chamber of Commerce and Visitors Center, 720 Sudderth Drive, Ruidoso, 88455. Call 1-800-253-2255 or 505-257-7395. Mon. through Fri. 8:30–5, Sat. 9–3, Sun. 9–1. Web site: www.ruidosonow.com.

Sacramento Mountains Historical Society Museum and Pioneer Village, P.O. Box 435, Cloudcroft, 88317. Call 505-682-2932. Mon., Tues., Fri., and Sat. 10–4, Sun. 1–4. Web site: www.cloudcroft museum.com.

Ski Apache, P.O. Box 220, Ruidoso, 88355. Call 505-464-3400. Web site: www.skiapache.com.

Smokey Bear Historical Park, 118 Smokey Bear Boulevard, Capitan, 88316. Call 505-354-2748. Daily 9–5. Fee. Web site: www.smokey-bearpark.com.

Smokey Bear Museum, 102 Smokey Bear Boulevard, Box 729, Capitan, 88316. Memorial Day through Labor Day, daily 9–5; winter, daily 9–4.

Socorro County Chamber of Commerce, 101 Plaza, Socorro, 87801. Call 505-835-0424. Mon. through Fri. 9–5, Sat. 9–noon. Web site: www.socorro.com.

Spencer Theater for the Performing Arts, 108 Spencer Road, Box 140, Alto, 88312. Information, tours, and tickets, call 1-888-818-7872 or 505-336-4800. Mon. through Fri. 9–5. Web site: www.spencertheater.com.

Three Rivers Petroglyph National Recreation Site, County Road B30 (5 miles off NM 54, 17 miles north of Tularosa), Bureau of Land Management, Caballo Resource Area, 1800 Marquess Street, Las Cruces, 88005. Call 505-525-4300. Campsites, picnic shelters, and interpretive trail open year-round. Fee. Web site: www.nm.blm.gov/recreation/las_cruces/three_rivers.htm.

Tinnie Silver Dollar Saloon and Restaurant, US 70 E., Tinnie, 88351. Call 505-653-4425. Mon. through Thurs. 4–9, Fri. and Sat. 4–10, Sun. brunch 10–3.

Trinity Site (see Alamogordo Chamber of Commerce for tour information), Public Affairs Office, Building 122, White Sands Missile Range, 88002. Call 505-678-1134. Site open first Sat. of April and October 8–2; caravan from Alamogordo departs at 8 AM. Web site: www.wsmr.army.mil/pao/TrinitySite/trinst.htm.

Valley of Fires (4 miles northwest of Carrizozo on US 380), Bureau of Land Management, Roswell Field Office, 2909 W. Second Street, Roswell, 88292. Call 505-627-0272. Visitor's center, daily 8–3:30. Fee. Web site: www.nm.blm.gov.

The Village Buttery, 2107 Sudderth, Ruidoso, 88345. Call 505-257-9251. Mon. through Sat. 10:30–2:30.

White Dove Gallery, 2828 Sudderth, Suite A, Ruidoso, 88345. Call 505-257-6609. Daily 10–5.

White Mountain Pottery, 2328 Sudderth, Ruidoso, 88345. Call 505-257-3644. Summer, daily 10:30–5:30; winter, call for hours. Web site: www.whitemountainpottery.com.

White Oaks, see Carrizozo Chamber of Commerce.

White Sands National Monument, off US 70, P.O. Box 1086, Holloman AFB, 88330. Call 505-479-6124. Visitor's center, January through Memorial Day, daily 8–5; Memorial Day through Labor Day, daily 9–7; Labor Day through December, daily 8–5. Dunes Drive entrance, January through Memorial Day, daily 7–sunset; Memorial Day through Labor Day, daily 7–9; Labor Day through December, daily 7–sunset. Fee. Web site: www.nps.gov/whsa.

Ruidoso Time Square

CHAPTER

8

Mining Towns and Mountains

Getting there: From Albuquerque, take I-25 south 77 miles to Socorro, Exit 150. From Socorro, follow US 60 west 27 miles to Magdalena, where you take a marked road south 3 miles to the ghost town of Kelly. Retrace your steps to Magdalena, and continue west on US 60 for 23 miles to NM 166, the turnoff for the Very Large Array radio telescope's visitor's center. Leaving the center, return to US 60 and drive 11 miles to Datil, where you turn south onto NM 12. Staying on NM 12 through Old and New Horse Springs, Aragon, Apache Creek, and Reserve, go south on US 180 for 29 miles to Glenwood.

If the weather has been dry, you're feeling adventurous, and you've secured an excellent map showing U.S. Forest Service roads, you can leave civilization in Reserve and head south on NM 435, which joins Forest Service Road 141 before turning to gravel at Negrito Fire Base. From here you follow dirt and gravel roads—Forest Service Roads 28 and 159—to the mining ghost town of Mogollon. This is definitely the long way around and should not be attempted in the rain or late in the day.

From Glenwood, retrace your steps 29 miles on US 180 to its junction with NM 12 north, which passes Reserve and joins NM 32 at Apache Creek. Stay on NM 32 north 41 miles to Quemado, where you take NM 36 for 74 miles to NM 53. Zuni Pueblo is 10 miles west on NM 53. East of the junction of NM 36 and 53, El Morro is 25 miles, Bandera Volcano and Ice Caves, 41 miles, and Grants a total of 75 miles.

Highlights: After exploring old **Socorro** with its mission church and leafy plaza, you head into the neighboring peaks, where you investigate the dusty little town of **Magdalena** and explore the nearby ghost town of **Kelly,** once center for silver and zinc mining. The vast open Plains of San Augustin beckon, and coasting along through this sea of grass, you spy the multiple antennae of the **Very Large Array** radio telescope marching in formation to the horizon.

Taking a southerly turn through **Apache Creek,** you wend your way to **Glenwood.** After a foray into Whitewater Canyon and its famous **Catwalk National Recreational Trail,** retrace your steps north through Reserve and Quemado, finally arriving at **Zuni Pueblo** for a visit to the old mission church to see its murals depicting the pueblo kachinas and the cycle of the seasons. Browse the shops for inlay jewelry in turquoise, jet, and shell, or check out the fetish carvings.

Leaving Zuni, you range east through the Zuni Mountains, pausing at the **Ramah Navajo Reservation** to observe the native weavers. Farther on you scale the heights of **El Morro National Monument** and stop at the **Bandera Volcano and Ice Caves.** Journey's end is Grants, crowned by Mount Taylor.

Let's Go: Long before the Europeans came to New Mexico, the Piro, early ancestors of today's pueblo people, built the town of Pilabo, where fertile fields stretched east to the Rio Grande and an evergreen spring provided water for drinking and agriculture. In 1598, the weary explorers of the Juan de Oñate expedition arrived at the Piro village on their way to establishing a colony near Santa Fe. The villagers gave the wanderers food and shelter, and the Spanish left behind two Franciscan priests who established the mission of San Miguel and named the place Nuestra Señora de Perpetuo Socorro. Later it was simplified to Socorro, which means "help" or "aid" in Spanish.

During the Pueblo Revolt of 1680, the Piros were one of the few Rio Grande tribes to side with the Spanish. To escape the wrath of their brethren, the tribe fled south, where its descendants still reside near El Paso.

Socorro lay in ruins for many years. By the late 18th century, officials in Santa Fe began to see the wisdom of resettling the area to protect wayfarers on the El Camino Real, which ran right through the old plaza. However, it wasn't until 1815 that the governor of New Mexico ordered the area resettled.

The Atchison, Topeka and Santa Fe Railway arrived in 1880, and what followed was an explosion in both population and mining activity. The nearby mountains were rich in ore, which was ferried to Socorro for smelting. In 1889 the New Mexico School of Mines (currently the **New Mexico Institute of Mining and Technology**) was established.

In the 1890s the price of silver and other metals declined, ending the mining boom, and Socorro's economy once more became dependent on agriculture. During World War II, the village played host to many of the scientists from nearby **White Sands Missile Range,** and today scientists and astronomers from the Very Large Array (VLA) radio telescope make Socorro their post in civilization.

Do not be dismayed by the commercial strip that greets you as you exit the interstate. This amalgam of fast-food joints and motels serves the needs of busy travelers. To see the heart of Socorro, you must traverse California Street's commercial district, turn right at the Manzanares light, and go one block west. The **San Miguel Historic Area** is crowned by **Kittrel Park,** or the Plaza, as it is more commonly known. Kittrel is a green oasis highlighted by a copper-roofed bandstand and ornate cast-iron benches, where the town's viejos (senior citizens) gather to discuss politics or the weather.

An army field in the 1850s and one of the village's original six Spanish colonial plazas, the park was named for Dr. L. W. Kittrel, a local dentist. Kittrel was instrumental in beautifying the area, and he is buried there.

Surrounding the square is a scattering of shops and many historic buildings. The Abeytia Building houses the chamber of commerce, once the Hilton Drugstore, which was opened in the 1890s by relatives of Conrad Hilton. If you wish to further investigate the town, the chamber has a free walking tour brochure which details the various quarters and their historic structures.

On the plaza's south side, the historic (some say notorious) Capitol Saloon sits cheek by jowl with Carl Frisch's Spoke N' Word Cycles. Around the corner, Carl's wife, Patty, runs the **Manzanares Street Coffeehouse,** dispensing java, pastries, panini sandwiches, and real Italian gelato.

From the plaza you'll want to head down Bernard Street toward the Old San Miguel Mission. The current church was constructed between 1819 and 1821 and is thought to have been built on the ruins of the earlier mission, which burned during the Pueblo Revolt. A legend says that when the priests heard of the impending trouble, they had the Indians disassemble the solid silver communion rail, which was buried along with other valuables. Many have searched for the treasure, but none have met with success.

Another legend concerns the name of the church. It is said that during a raid by Apaches around 1880, the Indians withdrew when they saw a man with wings and a shining sword poised above the door to the church. The parishioners sent a petition to their bishop in Durango, Mexico, requesting the name of the church be changed to San Miguel in honor of St. Michael, God's warrior archangel. The church has borne his name ever since.

The church has undergone several restorations since then, and its current adobe bell towers are typical of California mission style. The main doors are generally open, but if you wish to see the interior, a courtesy stop at the parish office would be seemly.

Socorro's **Hammel Brewery and Museum** houses exhibits on the brewing industry, but is open only on the first Saturday of each month. Built by the Hammel Brothers during the boom years, the brewery produced Illinois Beer until shut down by Prohibition. The plant operated as an icehouse and soft drink bottling plant until it closed in the 1950s.

Anyone with more than a passing interest in geology will enjoy visiting the **New Mexico Bureau of Mines and Mineral Resources Museum** on the second floor of the Workman Addition (Gold Building). The collection of more than 10,000 specimens began with an assortment from the New Mexico Institute of Mining and Technology and was augmented by contributions from prominent mining speculator C. T. Brown and others. Perhaps the most interesting samples are the fluorescent minerals illuminated by ultraviolet light or the minerals from New Mexico—aquamarine smithsonite from Kelly, copper from Silver City, gold from White Oaks, and uranium from Grants.

Some of the best chow in Socorro is dished up at Mic and Molley Heynekamp's **Socorro Springs Brewing Company** on California. The menu is typical pub food, with daily specials, soups, salads, sandwiches, and wood-oven-fired pizzas, lasagna, and calzones. Try the salmon with a creamy red bell pepper sauce or the fire-grilled rib eye on a rosemary cheddar batard loaf topped with Gorgonzola. Their beers and ales run the gamut from Pick Axe India Pale Ale to Prohibition Stout, a version of the classic dry Irish Stout.

If you have your heart set on classic New Mexican food, go where the locals go, **La Pasadita** at 230 Garfield. Probably not found on any list of officially recommended restaurants, this tiny café would not be out of place in a Mexican border town. You'll find oil-cloth-topped tables, families with children chattering away in Spanish, and basic corn, beans, and chile cooking. The enchilada plate is especially recommended, its red or green chile topping crowned with a poached egg.

Leaving Socorro, you head out into the Magdalena Mountains, clothed in the greens of mesquite and creosote bush. Soon the vegetation changes to tracts of grass, Apache plume, and juniper. Eventually, you arrive at the old mining town of **Magdalena.** It's hard to believe that this quiet village once was one of the largest cattle-shipping centers in the Southwest. With the demise of mining and the abandonment of the railroad spur that hauled both ore and livestock, the town settled into its current somnolent state.

If you stop at Village Hall, you can pick up the key for a self-guided tour of the **Box Car Museum,** which contains artifacts of Magdalena's glory days. The old railroad car sits on a section of track to the rear of the building that houses both the government and the library.

Magdalena Café is a good place to eat in town. Owner Alanna Van Winkle boasts "home-cooked meals since 1986." The usual fare runs to hot roast beef sandwiches, chicken-fried steak, burritos, and homemade pies and cakes. You'll be dining with the locals, who on any day could include a state trooper, high school students, Indians from the Alamo Chapter of the Navajo Reservation, or bona fide cowboys.

From Magdalena it's 3.5 miles on a part-paved, part-gravel road to the ghost town of **Kelly.** Kelly was an active silver and zinc mining area that had a population of 3,000 at one time. The ore played out, the people departed, and what remains are ruins, a cemetery, and St. John the Baptist Church.

The old mine up the hill operates from mid-May to mid-October for rock hounds who pay an entrance fee to prospect for any of the 80 minerals found on the site. Five shafts lead to 24 tunnels with a total length of 42 miles. Traylor Shaft still sports its famous head frame, designed by Alexander Eiffel of Paris fame and constructed by Gustav Billing in the 1880s. Many of the tunnels are flooded and all are closed, but the four stockpiles contain a wealth of malachite, smithsonite, fossils, pyrite, quartz, and other minerals.

Departing Magdalena, you climb out of the mountain valley and enter the **Plains of San Augustin,** a prehistoric lake basin 45 miles long and 12 miles wide. Juniper and piñon punctuate the vast grasslands as the road scribes a straight line to the horizon. Finally, the **Very Large Array** dishes

The 27 dishes of the Very Large Array radio telescope collect faint radio waves emitted by celestial objects.

materialize. The 27 giant antennae, which capture radio photographs of the heavens, appear like white sails upon an ocean of brush. A railroad track consisting of three 13-mile-long arms provides a movable base. When packed together, the dishes operate like a wide-angle lens on a camera. When far apart, they function like a zoom lens.

Radio waves are a form of low-frequency light. The VLA collects these faint waves emitted by celestial objects and sends the data to the control building, where the byproducts are combined to form a single image. In truth, all of the dishes function as one giant radio telescope.

The VLA Visitor Center has displays that help the public understand both the nature of radio waves and the functioning of the telescope. A 20-minute slide show, *Star Trails,* further explains the work done here.

A short walking tour takes you outside to get up-close and personal with the 94-foot dishes, each measuring 82 feet in diameter. Standing by one of these behemoths, you may be startled to discover it's moving, constantly focusing on those beams from space.

Leaving the VLA, you head toward the far distant foothills of the Mangas Mountains. Reaching New Horse Springs, you exit the Plains of San Augustin and, crossing the Continental Divide, approach the Apache and Gila national forests. At Reserve, determine whether you want to follow NM 12 west or brave the dirt and gravel Forest Service roads.

If you take the latter, you will go through the ghost town of **Mogollon,** not truly deserted but home for a scattering of artisans. You should have no problem negotiating this route in a touring car as long as weather has been dry and you have a good, detailed map. Your reward for valor is a beautiful drive and the possibility of sighting an elk herd. The drawback is the extra time it takes and the possibility of chancy road conditions.

If you choose the highway, you will head south near Rancho Grande Estates and follow US 180 south through Alma to Glenwood, where you'll encounter **Whitewater Canyon,** site of one of the most unique hikes in New Mexico: the **Catwalk National Recreation Trail.**

During the mining era of the late 1890s, deposits of gold and silver were discovered in the mountains high above the canyon. The Helen Mining Company had 13 claims in this area. To process the ore, John T. Graham built a mill at the head of the wash in 1893, and eventually the town of Graham, or Whitewater, grew up around the works. The mill could not have been constructed closer to the mines due to the rough, narrow canyon.

Water was not always available in the town, although the creek ran almost continuously farther up. To remedy the situation, a 4-inch pipeline was built along the west wall of the canyon. Eventually a larger amount of water was needed to power a new generator, and an 18-inch pipeline was built parallel to the old line in 1897.

It was quite a feat of construction. Brace holes were drilled into the solid rock walls to hold the timbers and iron bars supporting the water line along its course. Repairs often were necessary, and the workmen who had to walk the line to repair damage dubbed it "The Catwalk."

When the Graham mill closed in 1913, most of the construction material, including the pipelines, was salvaged and sold. Today all that remains of the mill is a section of wall near the Catwalk's entrance.

In the 1930s the Civilian Conservation Corps was assigned the task of rebuilding the catwalk as an attraction in Gila National Forest. The CCC catwalk served until 1961, when the current metal structure was constructed by the Forest Service. Floods roaring down the canyon wreaked havoc with the trail, and in 1986 the portion past the steel span was relocated out of the flood path. Recent improvements include a metal walkway and interpretive panels. There is also a universally accessible trail.

To visit the Catwalk, take NM 174 (Catwalk Road) about 5 miles to the paved road's end at the Whitewater picnic ground. A short uphill walk takes you to the start of the steel walkway, which hangs 20 to 30 feet above the waters of the creek. This section is easily negotiated and less than a mile in length. More ambitious hikers can continue on Trail 207, a strenuous journey to the junction of Whitewater and South Fork creeks. Here ruins of the power plant that supplied electricity for the mines and Mogollon can still be seen.

After your foray into the wilds, depart Glenwood, passing the expansive WS Ranch, where Butch Cassidy and his Wild Bunch were employed as honest wranglers. You'll drive through Alma, site of many raids by Indians and Mexicans, and follow your earlier route to **Apache Creek,** an excellent place to stop, gas up, and get a cold drink or a snack. There's not much in the way of civilization between here and Zuni.

The one exception is **Quemado,** where Jim and Irene Jaramillo run **El Serape Café,** a snug little eatery decorated with multicolored Mexican serapes, deer and antelope heads, and an original tin ceiling. Irene prepares daily specials and "authentic New Mexican food," and her taco salad may be the best you'll find anywhere.

After the long haul between Glenwood and the junction of NM 53 and 30, you'll welcome the short western detour to **Zuni.** If you've visited Acoma's Sky City or the Taos Pueblo, your first impression of Zuni might be less than propitious. Although there's the beautiful Corn Mesa, a silver stream, and acres of green fields, Zuni is not located on a soaring mesa, nor are its stone buildings comparable to Taos's twin adobe apartments. The highway cuts through the modern village, and the route to the old plaza and its mission church is not readily apparent. However, Zuni is very old and its history is intrinsically woven with the Southwest. It was in the old village of Háwikuh that the Spanish first encountered the pueblo people.

In the spring of 1536 four survivors of a shipwreck near present-day Galveston arrived in Culicán, Mexico, after five years of Indian captivity and a weary foot journey through western Texas and northern Mexico. En route they heard tales of the incredible riches to be found in the "Seven Cities of Cibola," somewhere to the north.

Eventually arriving in Mexico City, they petitioned the viceroy, Antonio de Mendoza, to mount an expedition to these unknown lands. Mendoza was unwilling to commit a large force, but agreed to dispatch a Franciscan friar, Marcos de Niza, along with Estevan, a black Moorish slave and shipwreck survivor, as guide. They traveled north through Arizona, and Estevan was sent ahead to scout the terrain. Instead of discovering the seven gold cities, he came upon the Zuni village of Háwikuh. Zuni history relates that when Estevan arrived, he demanded women and turquoise. This did not sit well with the Zuni, and he was summarily executed. Good Fray Marcos fled back to Mexico City, where he compounded the "cities of gold" fiction to defend his participation in the unsuccessful venture.

Responding to these wild tales, the young Francisco Vásques de Coronado, governor of Nueva Galicia, led 300 soldiers and 800 Indians from Compostela to Háwikuh in 1540. Coronado was deeply disappointed to find only a simple agricultural community instead of a golden hoard. The Zuni did not welcome his presence, either. Initially, they defended their city with vigor, but compared to the Spanish force of arms, they were badly outclassed and forced to surrender.

Throughout the remainder of the 16th and early 17th centuries, the Spanish were a periodic manifestation in the Zuni villages. In 1629 the first Catholic mission was established in Háwikuh, and the priests were well received at first.

Unrest followed as the Spanish made more and more excessive demands on the pueblos for food and slaves. This culminated in the 1680 Pueblo Revolt, when all the priests were killed and the mission at Hálona was burned. The Spanish were absent for 12 years thereafter, until Don Diego de Vargas led an army out of Mexico to negotiate peace with the pueblos in 1692.

With a population of about 8,500, Zuni today is the largest of the New Mexico pueblos and has all the conveniences of a modern town—restaurants, grocery stores, gas stations, and especially jewelry stores. Zuni jewelers are known worldwide for their exuberant use of colored stones in their inlay jewelry, while Zuni carvers craft fetish stone animals with meticulous attention to detail. Beadworkers make koshares (clowns), turkeys, and dancers in sizes ranging from 1 to 6 inches. It seems as if the whole community is one gigantic band of artists.

Your first stop should be the **Pueblo of Zuni Visitor and Arts Center** to plan your time in the village. You'll want to visit the **A:shiwi A:wan Museum and Heritage Center,** which has rotating exhibits on Zuni history and culture. Adjoining the museum, **Pueblo of Zuni Arts & Crafts** stocks a wide array of jewelry, paintings, fetishes, and pottery.

If you're searching for beadwork, the **Pueblo Trading Post** has one of the best selections in town. In addition, the post has an exhaustive line of pottery, fetishes, and jewelry. Stop by and watch the silversmiths at work.

Of course, if the piece you seek isn't available in either of these locations, you surely will find it at one of the many other shops and trading posts along the highway.

You should not leave Zuni before visiting its old mission church, noted not just for its beauty and historic value, but especially for the spectacular murals decorating its walls. The mission has a long history. After the Pueblo Revolt, all outlying Zuni villages were abandoned and most of the inhabitants moved into the old village of Hálona on the banks of the Zuni River. Hálona became modern Zuni. Although a church existed there since about 1629, there are no ruins or descriptions of the building, which was destroyed during the insurrection.

Over the remnants of the old structure, in 1706 Fray Juan Alvarez constructed a new church, which was dedicated to **Our Lady of Guadalupe.** After Mexico achieved independence in 1821, many Franciscans returned to Spain, leaving only a handful of priests to serve the missions of northern New Mexico. By the 1840s, when the region came under control of the United States, missionary work ceased and the buildings fell into ruins.

In 1966 and 1967 the National Park Service excavated the mission and parts of the convento for the tribe and the Roman Catholic Diocese of Gallup. A Gallup contractor and stonemason undertook the reconstruction, which was completed in 1970.

During the restoration, several elders spoke of the murals that adorned the interior walls before the mission was abandoned. The parish pastor contacted Alex Seowtewa, a noted local artist, and asked him if he would take on the project of re-creating those murals. The project began in 1970 and involved not only Alex but also his sons Gerald and Kenneth.

Creating a stunning dramatic impact, 24 life-size kachinas, or kokos, run the length of the two side walls. These images portray the supernatural beings that the Zuni believe bring rain, successful hunting, prosperity, and all good things. In traditional ceremonies they are impersonated by village men, and their actions are directed by the elders at specific times of the year. The Zuni believe that the spirit of the kachina actually enters the form of the dancer, transforming him into the being he represents.

The figures on the south wall of the nave represent kachinas associated with summer ceremonies, while the northern wall displays kachinas seen in winter rituals. Traditional plants and local wildlife accompany the dancers, and even the sky mirrors the seasonal change. Seowtewa warrants the figures are authentic in every detail down to the clacking bill of the great Sha'lako kachina and the antic figure of the Mudhead. What makes this masterpiece so extraordinary is both its location, tucked away in a dusty little New Mexico town, and its accepted presence in a Catholic mission.

Heading east out of the village, you pass Towayálane, the sacred Corn Mesa, rising 1,000 feet above the valley floor. The Zuni Mountains in colorful striations of buff, ochre, and gray crest to the north. The next hamlet is **Ramah** (RAY-mah), a town settled by Mormons in 1876.

Before reaching El Morro, you'll pass the cutoff to the Ramah Chapter of the Navajo Reservation. Pine Hill is headquarters of the **Ramah Navajo Weavers Association,** a grassroots cooperative made up of more than 40 traditional weavers. These artisans work to increase family self-reliance using indigenous resources and native skills. Leaders in restoring churro stock, a traditional breed believed to be the ancestral sheep of the Navajo people, the association operates in four areas: improving weaving techniques, breeding better wool sheep, restoring and protecting the land, and developing leadership.

Each weaver raises his or her own sheep, cards and spins the wool, hand-dyes the yarn exploiting native plants, and weaves on the traditional upright loom. If you phone ahead, a weaver will meet you at the cooperative. There you can view or purchase the weavings, which range in size from miniatures to full-size rugs.

Just down the highway from the Ramah turnoff, **El Morro National Monument** rises from the valley floor like some great gray ship. The technical term for the formation is a cuesta, a long formation with a gentle upward slope that drops off abruptly at one end.

El Morro is a historic registry of those who passed by. The Zuni gave it the name A'ts'ina, or "place of writings on the rock"; the Spaniards called it El Morro, "the headland"; and Anglo-Americans dubbed it Inscription Rock because of the generations of travelers who carved symbols, names, dates, and fragments of their histories there. Here in one place are Anasazi petroglyphs keeping company with the scratching of explorer Don Juan de Oñate. Farther on you'll find the inscriptions "Beale" and "Breckinridge," two soldiers in the army's 1857 camel corps.

The walk to Inscription Rock is agreeable, passing the evergreen spring where travelers through the ages knew they could secure water. The trail covers about a half mile and takes 45 minutes to an hour, depending on how long you linger to decipher the imprints.

The ruins of two Anasazi pueblos top the cuesta, one cloaked in sand and vegetation, the other, A'ts'ina, partially unearthed and stabilized by archeologists in the 1950s. The path to the top is a 2-mile loop with an increase in elevation of 250 feet. Allow 90 minutes to two hours for the trip, and be sure to take water, which is available at the visitor's center, the origin of all trails. The center also stocks books, posters, slides, tapes, and CDs. A small but comprehensive museum deals with the El Morro region from prehistoric times, and a 15-minute video is screened regularly.

When searching for accommodations, you have two alternatives. Twelve miles east of El Morro and 3 miles west of the Ice Caves, Sheri McWethy Kennedy operates **Cimarron Rose Bed and Breakfast** on 20 ponderosa pine–covered acres. Cimarron Suite is reminiscent of a mountain cabin with its pine plank floor, wood-burning parlor stove, and claw-foot tub in the bathroom. Bandera Suite is decorated in traditional Southwestern style and has a private patio. Zuni Mountain Suite is commodious, offering guests two bedrooms and two patios. All suites have their own entrances and full kitchens. Sheri's breakfasts of homemade foodstuffs are delivered to guests' doorsteps to consume at their leisure. On any day you might expect blue-corn pancakes, "mountain" crepes, vegetable quiches, genuine, long-simmered Irish or Scottish oatmeal, multigrain cereal, breads, berry muffins, biscuits, fresh fruit, or hot compote over creamy yogurt with juice and French-press coffee.

If Cimarron Rose is full, you won't go wrong stopping at **Ancient Way Café and El Morro RV Park and Cabins** near the national monument. If the idea of cabins in a RV park conjures up images of a dilapidated, unheated tourist court, have no fear. Owner Sharron Dishongh's six cottages are heated, clean, and comfortable, and all have refrigerators and wireless Internet access for guests' convenience. The café is open for breakfast, lunch, and dinner, and features New Mexican food, burgers, soup, and sandwiches.

While you're in the vicinity, check out **Inscription Rock Trading and Coffee Company,** where you can browse art from the Eight Northern Indian Pueblos and grab a good cup of joe or a fruit smoothie at the coffee bar.

As you head east, you enter **El Malpais National Monument,** a mammoth lava flow originating from several volcanoes between 2,000 and 113,000 years ago. El Malpais means "badlands" in Spanish, and the area

El Morro National Monument is a cuesta, a long formation with a gentle upward slope that drops off abruptly at one end.

NEW·MEXICAN FOOD
CAFE
AMERICAN FOO
OLD·FASHION·BURGERS
FISH·AND·FRIES
SHAKES AND HOT
STEAKS CAKES
NATIVE
FOODS
CAFE
OPEN
El Sarape
CAFE
OPEN
NO SHIRT
SHOES
SERVICE

features jagged spatter cones, a lava tube cave system extending at least 17 miles, and fragile ice caves.

On the highway you skirt the northern section of the monument. There are two trailheads accessible from the road: the 1.5-mile round-trip Junction Cave Trail in the Calderon area and the Zuni-Acoma Trail, which is 7 miles one-way. These are not casual hikes, and should not be attempted without proper preparation. The lava is rugged, sharp, and exceedingly hot in warm weather. Wear very sturdy hiking boots, a hat, and leather work gloves, and carry a ration of 1 gallon of water per person per day. Trails are marked with rock cairns, which may be elusive.

If you want a kinder, gentler introduction to the region's geography, take the turnoff to **Bandera Volcano and the Ice Caves.** This small area is privately owned and more accessible to the casual visitor. The cave is a collapsed lava tube where the year-round temperature never rises above 31 degrees Fahrenheit.

As you approach **Grants,** you will be popping in and out of monument land. Before exiting onto I-40, you might want to spend an hour or two

Above: Grants Fountain.
Opposite: El Sarape Café

in Grants, originally settled in 1872 when Don Jesus Blea homesteaded on the south side of San Jose Creek. The advent of the railroad, lumber from the Zuni Mountains, and mining for copper, fluorspar, and pumice all contributed to the city's early growth. After the completion of the Bluewater Dam in 1929, the nearby fertile valley was a utopia for truck gardens, and the quality of the vegetables earned the town the title of "Carrot Capital."

All these economic bases waxed and waned with the times. Grants's greatest boom occurred during the 1950s, when Paddy Martinez discovered uranium at Ambrosia Lake. Five mills were built, and Grants's population jumped from 2,200 in 1950 to 10,000 in 1960. New stores, banks, a hospital, library, and schools rode the construction wave, and a branch of New Mexico State University was awarded the town. However, prosperity was short-lived. By the 1980s the demand for uranium dried up, and the mines and mills closed one by one.

Today Grants is still struggling, depending more and more on the development of its visitor services. Most motel chains have located off the interstate, and more players make their appearance every year. Among the many restaurants, three stand out: the **Uranium Café** across from the New Mexico Museum of Mining, **El Cafecito** on East Santa Fe Avenue, and **La Ventana Steakhouse,** hidden away on Geis Street a block off Santa Fe.

The Uranium Café serves breakfast, lunch, and dinner with a funky

The lower level of the New Mexico Mining Museum in Grants simulates an actual uranium mine.

1950s flair. The Stewart family has used neon and old mining pictures to bring back Grants's glory days, and half a 1955 Chevy is the restaurant's centerpiece. The menu sports New Mexican flair along with daily blackboard specials.

Angie and Larry Baca run El Cafecito, where you'll find they live up to their motto of "authentic New Mexico cuisine." Whether it's a morning order of huevos rancheros, a lunch of a stuffed sopapilla with beans and meat, or a dinner combo plate of tacos, enchiladas, and chimichangas, the emphasis is on chile in its many and varied forms.

True carnivores will love La Ventana. For 30 years this hideaway has served some of the best beef in the state in addition to seafood and an occasional New Mexican dish. The restaurant is a trifle difficult to locate, though; it's directly in back of the New Mexico Labor Department building and next to Checker Auto Parts.

If you have time, stop in the **New Mexico Mining Museum.** The first level traces the history of Grants from prehistoric times to the present, but it's the lower level, which simulates an actual uranium mine, that's special. You are led to the "mine shaft," where you take a simulated ride in the "cage" 900 feet below the surface. Here you trek through dim caverns, visit the assignment station, and enter an open stope, an expanse stripped of ore. Kids, in particular, will enjoy this unusual museum.

Lastly, Grants provides access to 11,301-foot **Mount Taylor,** one of the four mountains sacred to the Navajos. Once an active volcano, Taylor now is popular among hikers, anglers, campers, and photographers. Lobo Canyon and Coal Mine Canyon have campsites and picnic areas, and in winter cross-country ski trails lace the area. On cloudless days the scenic drive to the summit is well worth the effort.

Contacts:

Ancient Way Café and El Morro RV Park and Cabins, NM 53, HC 61, Box 44, Ramah, 87321. Call 505-783-4612. Café daily 9–5.

A:shiwi A:wan Museum and Heritage Center, P.O. Box 1009, Zuni, 87327. Call 505-782-4403. Mon. through Fri. 8:30–6. Web site: www.experiencezuni.org.

Bandera Volcano and Ice Caves, 12000 Ice Caves Road, Grants, 87020. Call 1-888-423-2283 or 505-783-4303. Summer, daily 8–7; winter, daily 8–4:30. Fee. Web site: www.icecaves.com.

The Catwalk National Recreation Trail, Glenwood Ranger District, U.S. Forest Service, Glenwood, 88039. Call 505-539-2481. Office, Mon. through Sat. 8–4:30. Trail open daily. Parking fee. Web site: www2.srs.fs.fed.us/r3/gila/recreation/attractions.asp?attid=1.

Cimarron Rose Bed and Breakfast, 689 Oso Ridge Route, Grants, 87020. Call 505-783-4770. Web site: www.cimarronrose.com.

El Cafecito, 820 E. Santa Fe Avenue, Grants, 87020. Call 505-285-6229. Mon. through Fri. 7–9, Sat. 7–8.

El Malpais National Monument, National Park Service, P.O. Box 939, Grants, 87020. Call 505-783-4774. Access NM 53 and 117. Monument always open except Sandstone Bluffs Overlook, which closes at dusk. El Malpais Information Center, daily 8:30–4:30. Web site: www.nps.gov/elma. See also Northwest New Mexico Visitor Center.

El Morro National Monument, NM 53, Route 2, Box 43, Ramah, 87321. Call 505-783-4226. Memorial Day through October 1: visitor's center, daily 8–7; trails, daily 8–6. October 2–29: visitor's center, daily 8–6; trails, daily 8–5. Winter: visitor's center, daily 9–5; trails, daily 9–4. Upper trail may close in bad weather. Fee. Web site: www.nps.gov/elmo.

El Serape Café, P.O. Box 132, Quemado, 87829. Call 505-773-4620. Summer, Mon. through Fri. 6:30–7, Sat. 7–2; winter, Mon. through Fri. 7–7, Sat. 7–2.

Grants/Cibola Chamber of Commerce, 100 N. Iron Avenue. (Mining Museum Building), Grants, 87020. Call 1-800-748-2142 or 505-287-4802. Mon. through Fri. 9–5, Sat. 9–4. Web site: www.discovergrants.org.

Hammel Brewery and Museum, Sixth Street; contact the Socorro Historic Society, P.O. Box 923, Socorro, 87801. First Sat. of the month 9–1.

Inscription Rock Trading and Coffee Company, HC 61, Box 5026, Ramah, 87321. Call 505-783-4706. Summer, Tues. through Sat. 9–6, Sun. 10–5; winter, Thurs. through Sun. 9–6.

Kelly Mine, Magdalena, 87825. May 15 through October 15, Tues. through Sat. 9–4. Fee.

La Pasadita Café, 230 Garfield, Socorro, 87802. Call 505-835-3696. Mon. through Fri. 8–8.

La Ventana Steakhouse, 110-½ Geis Street, Grants, 87020. Call 505-287-9393. Mon. through Sat. 11–11.

Magdalena Café, NM 60, P.O. Box 294, Magdalena, 87825. Call 505-835-2696. Mon. through Sat. 6 AM–1 PM, Thurs. 5–7 PM, Sun. 8 AM–1 PM.

Magdalena Village Hall, Library, and Box Car Museum, 108 Main Street, Magdalena, 87825. Call 505-854-2261. Village Hall, Mon. through Fri. 8–5; library and museum, Mon., Tues., and Fri. 11–4, Wed. and Thurs. 11–9, Sat. 9–2. Web site: www.magdalena-nm.com.

Manzanares Street Coffeehouse, 110 Manzanares, Socorro, 87801. Call 505-263-7192.

New Mexico Bureau of Mines and Mineral Resources Museum, Workman Addition, 801 Leroy Place, Socorro 87801. Call 505-835-5420. Mon. through Fri. 8–5, Sat. and Sun. 10–3. Closed college vacations and holidays. Web site: www.geoinfo.nmt.edu/museum.

New Mexico Mining Museum and Visitor Center, 100 N. Iron Avenue, Grants, 87020. Call 1-800-748-2142 or 505-287-4802. Mon. through Sat. 9–4. Museum fee. Web site: www.discovergrants.org.

Northwest New Mexico Visitor Center, 1900 E. San Francisco Avenue, Grants, 87020. Call 505-876-2783. Daily 9–6 during Mountain Daylight Time, 8–5 during Mountain Standard Time. Web site: www.nps.gov/archive/elma/NNMVC.htm.

Our Lady of Guadalupe, Old Zuni Mission. Call Pueblo of Zuni Visitor Center at 505-782-7238 for an appointment or to set up a tour. Web site: www.experiencezuni.com.

Pueblo Trading Post, 1192 NM 53, P.O. Box 1115, Zuni, 87327. Call 505-782-2296. Mon. through Sat. 9–6, Sun. 9–5. Web site: www.pueblotrading.com.

Pueblo of Zuni, 1203 B NM 53, P.O. Box 1029, Zuni, 87327. Call 505-782-7022. Web site: www.ashiwi.org.

Pueblo of Zuni Arts & Crafts, 1222 NM 53, P.O. Box 425, Zuni, 87327. Call 505-782-5531. Summer, Mon. through Fri. 9–6, Sat. 9–5; winter, Mon. through Fri. 9–5. Web site: www.ashiwi.org.

Pueblo of Zuni Visitor and Arts Center, 1239 NM 53, Zuni, 87327. Call 505-782-7238. Mon. through Fri. 8:30–5:30, Sat. 10–4. Sun. noon–4. Web site: www.experiencezuni.com.

Ramah Navajo Weavers Association, P.O. Box 153, Pine Hill, 87357. Call 505-775-3254. By appointment.

San Miguel Church, Otero Street, Socorro, 87801. Call 505-835-1620. Mon. through Fri. 9–noon and 1–4.

Socorro Chamber of Commerce, 101 Plaza, Socorro, 87801. Call 505-835-0424. Mon. through Fri. 9–5, Sat. 9–1. Web site: www.socorro-nm.com.

Socorro Springs Brewing Company, 1012 California Street, Socorro, 87801. Call 505-838-0650. Mon. through Fri. 6:30 AM–10 PM, Sat. and Sun. 8 AM–10 PM. Breakfast service ends at 11 AM daily. Web site: www.socorrosprings.com.

Uranium Café, 519 W. Santa Fe Avenue, Grants, 87020. Call 505-285-4550. Tues. through Thurs. 7–8, Fri. and Sat. 7–9, Sun. 7–3.

Very Large Array, National Radio Astronomy Observatory, Public Information Office, P.O. Box O, Socorro, 87801. Call 505-835-7000. Daily 8:30–dusk. Web site: www.vla.nrao.edu/genpub/tours.

Our Lady of Guadalupe in Zuni

MICKIE M.

CHAPTER

9

The Silvered South

Getting there: From Albuquerque take I-25 south to Exit 115, which is 30 miles south of Socorro. Turn east and go 1.5 miles south on NM 1 (Frontage Road) to County Road 1598 and El Camino Real International Heritage Center. Retrace you route back to I-25 and continue south to Truth or Consequences, Exit 79. Take NM 187 south from Truth or Consequences 17 miles through the suburb of Williamsburg and along the western edge of Caballo Reservoir. Cross the interstate south of the town of Caballo and head west on NM 152 for 51 miles through the towns of Hillsboro and Kingston, over Emory Pass to San Lorenzo. Here you may continue on NM 152 for 14 miles to its junction with US 180, the direct road to Silver City.

Alternately, you may take NM 35 northwest 27 miles to Lake Roberts, where you connect with NM 15 north, which winds 19 miles to Gila Hot Springs and dead-ends at Gila Cliff Dwellings National Monument. Returning south, you stay on NM 15 at Lake Roberts and traverse 18 miles of extremely narrow, winding roadway to Pinos Altos, eventually connecting with US 180 outside Silver City. Heading south from Silver City, take NM 90 southwest 44 miles to Lordsburg, where you join I-10. Deming is 60 miles east on the interstate.

Detour: For the Columbus detour, you head south from Deming 32 miles on NM 11.

Las Cruces is 59 miles east of Deming, and if you continue to Fort Selden, it's 19 miles north of Las Cruces, off I-25.

Highlights: A loop around southwestern New Mexico begins at the visitor's center for the fabled **Camino Real,** continues through **Truth or Consequences** with its mineral hot springs, and ends in **Las Cruces,** home of New Mexico State University and historic Old Mesilla. The route winds through the **Black Mountains,** ranges into the **Gila Wilderness,** site of ancient cliff dwellings, and pauses in **Silver City,** once an old mining town and now a thriving retirement community.

This is your starting point for a foray into the southern plains and the communities of **Lordsburg,** including its ghost towns of **Shakespeare** and **Steins,** and **Deming,** which has an exceptional community museum.

Detour south to Columbus, a Mexican border crossing and home to Pancho Villa State Park, commemorating the general's infamous 1916 raid on the United States. After a stint in Las Cruces and old Mesilla, hit the highway north to Fort Selden State Monument, where Douglas MacArthur spent his boyhood years.

Let's Go: Traveling south on I-25 from Socorro, the landscape is a pastiche of aridity and chaparral, interspersed with ancient arroyos. To the west, the Jornada del Muerto sands raise heat mirages in the sun. Settled in this unkind landscape, the **El Camino Real International Heritage Center** takes visitors back in time to journey down the historic trail that affected all aspects of Mexican–U.S. history. The oldest and for years the longest of the great roads leading into North America, the Camino Real extended from Mexico City to the pueblo of O'ke Owingeh outside Santa Fe. Architecturally splendid and in perfect harmony with its desert setting, the building contains a floor of permanent and temporary exhibits. Special sections with photographs, artifacts, and recorded sound displays are devoted to the main towns along the route.

A small gift shop encourages browsing, and an outdoor amphitheater is the site of special presentations. If the day is not too scorching, take time to walk the grounds, stroll the native plant and healing herb gardens, and stare out into the miles and miles of scrub rimmed by ghostly mountains. As you return to the interstate, you have a better understanding of the hearty pioneers who traveled this hard road.

Western towns have a look about them, a kinship with the lay of the land. The false-fronted stores define a strip called Main Street, or some variation thereof, and development extends only a block or two in supplemental parallel roads. What defines the individual communities, what makes the chambers of commerce sit up and "point with pride," is not immediately obvious to the casual visitor. **Truth or Consequences** is a good example. Other than its unusual and puzzling name, there appears not much to intrigue the traveler. However, there's more than initially meets the eye in this town situated 5 miles from the recreational boating and fishing haven of **Elephant Butte Lake.**

Recreational opportunities abound on Elephant Butte Lake.

T or C, as New Mexicans call it, was well known for its healing thermal waters long before Europeans settled the area. Native Americans frequently visited the site and bathed in its natural springs. It is said it was a place of peace where all tribes could gather without rancor.

The Spanish settlers called the place Alamocitos, or "little cottonwoods," and the spot was sparsely populated until the checking of the Rio Grande from 1912 to 1916 and the construction of Elephant Butte Dam. During this phase of its existence, the town was known as Hot Springs in honor of the mineral waters. Although the stream of visitors coming to the spas continued through the early decades of the 1900s, that stream gradually became a trickle by the 1950s.

In 1951 *Truth or Consequences,* hosted by Ralph Edwards, was one of television's most popular game shows. As a promotional tool, Edwards promised to broadcast his show from any town willing to change its name to that of the program. Hot Springs jumped at the chance. Not only would it give the town national prominence, it would eliminate the confusion with the many other U.S. towns called Hot Springs. In a special election, the conversion was approved 1,294 to 295. A protest was held, resulting in another vote. This time the outcome was 4-to-1 in favor of the alteration. Through the years the town has tested its residents to determine if they wish to continue under their quirky name, and the response always has been a firm "yes."

In addition to that first big year when Edwards beamed his program from the small burg on the Rio Grande, Edwards returned every year for the May fiesta as long as his health permitted (he died in 2005) and brought his Hollywood friends. In honor of his unstinting support, the town named Ralph Edwards Park after him.

The first thing you notice as you turn off the interstate is the city's utilitarian water tower, a fixture in much of the Southwest. The formerly unaesthetic structure is gloriously decorated by Las Cruces artist Tony Pennock in a rendition of Native Americans journeying to the sacred spring. Two other examples of his work may be viewed on the towers of his hometown.

Passing the tower, you discover your route branching, creating two main arteries. Date Street, which exits the interstate from the north, swings down the hill and becomes Main, a one-way east–west thoroughfare. Broadway meets Main west of town and travels east to its junction with Main. It's a bit confusing at first, but you get the lay of the land rather quickly.

Natural and organic ingredients take center stage on the menu at White Coyote Café in Truth or Consequences.

As you descend the hill and before the roads diverge, you pass one of T or C's top restaurants, **Los Arcos.** Opened in 1969 and owned by Bob Middleton, proprietor of the popular Monte Vista Fire Station and Owl Restaurant in Albuquerque, Los Arcos is always busy. The manifold arches, crimson carpeting, and massive wood inlay tables and chairs might strike some as a bit labored, but there is no question about the artistry of the consistently good food. Basically a steak house with seafood and chicken alternatives, the restaurant prides itself on prime beef, cooked as ordered. The service is outstanding.

Other choices include **White Coyote Café, Cuchillo Café,** and the **Happy Belly Deli.** The White Coyote Café is housed in a colorful adobe building with murals of mischievous canines. It's where owner Eunice C. Hundseth turns out a delicious selection of dishes with an emphasis on the use of natural and organic ingredients. Although entrées like her frittata with artichokes, zucchini, mushrooms, onions, and cheddar may tempt, save room for desserts like apple bread pudding with caramel sauce or chocolate pot au crème.

For fine New Mexican food with a long legacy, trot on down to Cuchillo Café on Broadway. The café's history goes back to the 1940s, when current owner Orland Romero's grandfather, Felix Sanchez, opened a small dirt-floored adobe restaurant in a tiny town a few miles from T or C. Felix's daughter, Hermila Romero, took over from her father and operated the modest café for 20 years before passing the torch to her son, Orlando, who brought the restaurant to T or C. Specializing in blue corn and red chile, Orlando's offerings are spanking fresh and delicious. Hermila still comes in every other day to make the masa for the sopapillas, and their salsa and chile sauces are assembled from scratch every day.

For a light bite, the Happy Belly Deli on Broadway is a popular spot for breakfast and lunch. The small, seven-table restaurant specializes in homemade soups, bagels, and overstuffed sandwiches.

If it's just a cup of java you're wanting, you won't go wrong at **Coffee, Tea or C** on Main. In an old building constructed in 1917 by Conrad Hilton and once used as a bank, David and Paula Packard roast their own organic specialty-grade coffees "with a large helping of love." The outcome is truly exceptional.

The Black Cat Books and Coffee is another place to get your caffeine fix and browse through a fine selection of used and remaindered books. Town regulars stop by every morning to chat with owner Rhonda Brittan and give the resident cat, Mr. Poe, a pat on his shiny pelt. The store is bright and cheerful, not a musty repository of ancient tomes.

Fully fortified, you are ready to take on the sights. **Geronimo Springs Museum** on Main Street traces the history of the area from frontier days to the present. Built beside the hot spring that gives the museum its name, the structure is laid out in multiple rooms devoted to varying aspects of town culture—ranching, farming, the rise and fall of mining and cattle towns, and the construction of Elephant Butte Dam. The Ralph Edwards Wing relates the tradition of the annual fiesta, and the Heritage Wing displays artwork by local artist Delmas Howe and Hivana Leyendecker, a Las Cruces sculptor and artist. The murals and bronze busts depict four historic figures important to area history: Juan de Oñate, Spanish explorer; Geronimo, Chiricahua Apache leader; Eugene Manlove Rhodes, cowboy author; and Pancho Villa, Mexican revolutionary.

Students and admirers of prehistoric Indian pottery should be sure to see the outstanding Fairs Watson Chestnut Indian Heritage Collection. The exhibit highlights artifacts from the Casa Grande, El Paso, Tularosa, Mesa Verde, Hohokam, White Mountain, and Mimbres Mogollon cultures. A reconstructed settler's log cabin is bound to please the children, and there is a compact gift shop specializing in books on the Southwest.

T or C's wide choice of mineral baths offers travel-fatigued road warriors soothing respite. Most are registered and licensed by the state, and their temperatures range from about 98 to 115 degrees. There is no odor to the waters, and the pH is about seven, or neutral. An analysis by the Los Alamos National Laboratory revealed 38 different minerals.

Your selection of a spa should be determined by the proffered method of the soak. Some baths provide tubs and private or semiprivate rooms, while others offer natural flowing pools. All are enclosed against the weather, and most furnish massage or other therapies. If you like the experience of a natural pool, make a reservation at **Hay-Yo-Kay** on Austin, or drop by **Indian Springs Pools** on Pershing. Other spas run the gamut from the popular **Artesian Bath House,** with five individual and three double-occupancy tubs, to the funky **Riverbend Hot Springs Hostel,** whose pool is a converted minnow tank from the oldest live bait store in New Mexico and whose deck overlooks the placidly flowing Rio Grande.

If you're searching for T or C's top-of-the-line accommodations with a full-facility spa, **Sierra Grande Lodge and Spa** is the ticket. Another good choice might be downtown at the **Firewater Lodge Bed & Breakfast.** Economy-minded individuals should look into the **Charles Motel and Spa** on Broadway. Built in the late 1930s, it has been refurbished by Kathy Clark. There are 20 motel-style units, 18 with kitchens and two without, all individually and simply decorated. The Charles's spa boasts the hottest water in town—110 to 112 degrees—and its immaculate facilities include nine individual tubs, a sauna, and a massage room.

For those interested in shopping, there's a plethora of art galleries and shops. **Rio Bravo Fine Art** has the greatest longevity, having been founded by the late H. Joe Waldrum. Now run by Eduardo Alicea, it showcases more than 15 artists, including Margaret Davenport, Olin West, and T or C's own Delmas Howe. **Main Street, Grapes,** and **When** galleries form a triumvirate owned by businessman and collector Sid Bryan. Each features exhibits that change every six to eight weeks.

Long noted as a mecca for vintage clothing and retro gear, T or C has three stores specializing in preworn boutique wear: **Dust and Glitter, MIAO,** and **Second Hand Rose,** which stocks a variety of gifts from around the world in the front section with secondhand duds in the rear.

As you leave T or C and continue your journey south on Broadway, stop at **Buffalo Bill's Exotic Cactus Ranch.** Dave Lamb and Maryann "George" Lambert have assembled an astonishing variety of cacti and succulents for sale. In addition to the garden variety of prickly pear and hedgehog cactus, you'll find exotics like Wrinkled Blue Myrtle, Elkhorn, and Black Rose Tree. You might even be tempted to buy a rare Golden Saguaro, no small investment. A gift shop stocking pots, garden implements, and Dave's photography complements the greenhouse.

Broadway winds south and becomes NM 187 after passing the suburb of Williamsburg. You skirt the village of Las Palomas and flank Caballo Reservoir, another dammed waterway on the Rio Grande. In the town of Caballo you turn west, cross the interstate, and head toward the Black Mountains.

Not much remains of the Hillsboro of the 1800s, when it was a gold and silver mining town.

The first 10 miles or so are an arrow-straight, two-lane road with roller-coaster dips, but shortly the complexion of both highway and terrain makes a drastic change. Approaching Hillsboro through the foothills of the Black Range, the route is tortuous.

In the 1800s **Hillsboro** was a gold and silver mining town and the seat of Sierra County (the seat later moved to T or C). Today you'll discover a sleepy village that depends largely on tourists passing through en route to Silver City.

A popular stop, if you hit the hours right, is the **Black Range Museum and Library,** founded in 1961 by Eve Simmons as a service to the community.

The first collection of relics was accommodated in the auditorium of the local elementary school. The museum moved to an adobe building when the school reclaimed its space, but quickly outgrew its quarters and was conveyed to a building that once housed a bordello and restaurant owned and operated by Miss Sadie Orchard. Sadie was the proverbial madam with a heart of gold. When Percha Creek flooded in 1914 and an influenza epidemic followed, she hiked up her skirts and went out to care for the sick and dying. History relates that she used her fine silk and velvet dresses to line children's coffins, and her fancy buggy was pressed into service as a hearse to carry the deceased to burial in the cemetery above town.

The bordello cook, Tom Ying, assumed proprietorship of the restaurant when Miss Sadie retired, and his café was known as the Chinaman's Place. In addition to the usual flotsam and jetsam of a small-town museum, you will encounter areas retained as Ying left them. The huge meat block and sharp knives wielded by the Chinese cook remain where he abandoned them, and his skullcap is exhibited in a showcase.

It's pleasant walking down the cottonwood-shaded main street lined with shops and cafés. The **Barbershop Café,** which once housed the town mercantile, is now home to a restaurant, a modest gift shop, and a wine shop stocking New Mexico vintages. Angela and Steve Detloff make all their dishes from scratch, including their delicious soups and their bodacious barbecue brisket. Across the street, the **Percha Creek Traders** cooperative shows the work of 23 artists in a variety of media from photography to jewelry to furniture.

The road from Hillsboro to Kingston is another exercise in grand prix driving, and if you're not careful, you'll pass the side road that leads to the tiny community. There's not much left of the 1880s silver mining town, which once had a population of 7,000 people serviced by 22 saloons, three hotels, and three newspapers. A few historic buildings remain: the assay office, the Percha Bank (now a private museum), and **The Black Range Lodge.**

The Black Range Lodge is a rambling bed and breakfast built on the ruins of Pretty Sam's Casino and Monarch Saloon. While most of the construction was completed in 1940, the multilevel brick section dates back to the 1880s, when it housed miners and cavalry.

Catherine Wanek and Peter Fust operate the inn as a combination lodge and retreat center. Both Pete and Catherine are experts in natural building techniques such as straw bale construction, a discipline that engages many of their student groups. The lodge is a rustic, make-yourself-at-home sort of place where the resident cat is likely to join you for an afternoon nap, and self-serve breakfasts feature a plethora of whole-grain breads and fresh fruit. Evening activities may focus on tours of different natural building projects or the occasional hike to view the roosting of a large flock of turkey buzzards on the banks of Percha Creek.

The Black Range Lodge is a bed and breakfast built on the ruins of Pretty Sam's Casino and Monarch Saloon.

From Kingston, you soldier on, climbing higher and higher until you crest Emory Pass, crossed in 1846 by the Army of the West, scouted by Lieutenant William H. Emory of the Topographical Engineers and guided by Kit Carson. Entering Grant County, you gradually descend the mountains toward San Lorenzo and enter the Mimbres.

If it's late afternoon, you should continue on NM 152 past Santa Rita and its huge open pit copper mine. Turn onto US 180/NM 90 and proceed through Arenas Valley to **Silver City,** a total of 24 miles. You need to be fresh for the trip to the Gila Cliff Dwellings, which is long and difficult due to the narrow, winding road offering the real possibility of an encounter with a highballing logging truck. The actual distance to the cliff dwellings does not accurately reflect the time needed for the journey. Allow two hours to navigate NM 35 to the monument visitor's center, at least two hours to hike to the ruins, and another two hours to drive NM 15 back to Silver City—more if you plan to stop at Pinos Altos. You don't want to drive this route after dark if you can possibly avoid it.

If it's the shank of the day and you're still alert, head north on NM 35 out of San Lorenzo into the scenic **Mimbres Valley,** named for the area's prehistoric inhabitants, a branch of the Mogollon people. As you leave the pastoral setting of the valley, you enter the juniper, piñon, and ponderosa pine country of the Gila National Forest. You pass **Lake Roberts,** a 72-acre

Six of the seven naturally formed caves at the Gila Cliff Dwellings contain prehistoric ruins.

man-made lake that offers fishing, boating, and camping. At mile marker 10.1 you may notice an abandoned Meerschaum mine, the only one in the U.S. Meerschaum is a form of hydrous magnesium silicate, a fine, light, white, clayey mineral used in the crafting of fine smoking pipes.

Turn right where the highway reaches its junction with NM 15 and take the scenic mountain road toward the **Gila Cliff Dwellings,** stopping at Copperas Vista (mile marker 33.6) to view the headwaters of the three forks of the Gila River. You will pass the small community of Gila Hot Springs, where you can stop at **Doc Campbell's Post** for gas, a cold drink, or a taste of their special homemade ice cream.

Pass the road leading to the cliff dwellings and continue on a short distance to the **Visitor Center,** where you can watch a 15-minute film and check out the displays on Mogollon country and its people. When you've been well briefed, you can head for the monument. The trail to the cliff dwellings is about a mile in length and begins a short distance from the center. It climbs 175 feet above the canyon floor and is moderately steep as it ascends to the seven naturally formed caves, six of which contain prehistoric ruins. By all means, take the hike if you are able. Cliff Dweller Canyon is a beautiful place any time of the year thanks to its cloaking of Douglas firs standing tall against the warm dun walls of volcanic tuff.

Scientists believe that 40 to 50 people lived in the caves' 40 rooms from 1280 to 1300. They were dry land farmers, and their fields were along the valley of the West Fork and on the mesa across the canyon. They raised squash, corn, and beans, and they supplemented their harvest with wild foods they gathered and animals they hunted. They were weavers and skilled potters, producing brown bowls with black interiors and black-on-white vessels.

What made them leave such a snug harbor? Perhaps there was an extended drought, overuse of natural resources, a shortened growing season, a social schism, or a combination of factors. By the time the Mogollon left the area, their culture largely had been assimilated by other Southwestern groups. Their descendants can be found in today's pueblo people.

After leaving the monument, you'll retrace your steps toward Gila Hot Springs and hook up with NM 15 south. The section between this junction and **Pinos Altos** makes your earlier route appear straight. It is a beautiful but serpentine drive, and you'll breathe a sigh of relief when you arrive in the old mining town, founded in 1860 by Thomas "Three-Fingered" Birch, a prospector who discovered gold in Bear Creek. Miners and settlers followed him, but Apache raids in 1861 and 1864 all but closed down the fledgling town.

Buckhorn Saloon in Pinos Altos overflows with local color and character.

Today Pinos Altos is a pleasant, quiet village snuggled in the tall ponderosa pines. The liveliest spot in town is Karen Campbell's **Buckhorn Saloon.** Housed in an old adobe structure with 18-inch walls, the watering hole has two massive bars, both freighted in on wagons during some distant past. The establishment's resident characters, Indian Joe and Debbie DeCamp, ensure that special Buckhorn ambiance. Debbie, perched on the balcony overlooking the entrance, gives handsome gents the eye. Dressed in a bar girl's net stockings and low-cut gown, the soft-sculpture mannequin commemorates the original Debbie, who is said to have died in a public brawl. Members of her sisterhood penned a rhyme for her:

"Shed a tear for Debbie De Camp,
Born a virgin, and died a tramp.
For 17 years she retained her virginity,
A real good record for this vicinity."

And poor old Indian Joe, another full-size sculpture, warms the end bar stool, reportedly waiting day upon day, month upon month, for someone to buy him a drink. His sad visage, beat-up felt fedora, and hand-me-down clothes reflect his dejection and despair. Myopic or inebriated customers have been known to offer him a beer, but the offer is never acknowledged.

With all its high jinks, the Buckhorn is a good-time bar, and its dining room, decorated with gaslights and scenes of early days, is held in high repute. Offering a basic menu of steaks, seafood, baby back ribs, and homemade desserts, the restaurant draws customers from distant points. The **Pinos Altos Melodrama Theatre** performs in the restored Opera House on most Friday and Saturday nights.

The **Pinos Altos Museum** and adjoining **Log Cabin Curio Shop** are a stop for hard-core small-town museum buffs. Housed in the old schoolhouse, the museum has room after room of household items, arrowheads, pottery shards, an old switchboard, a mineral collection, row upon row of old photographs, and a cider press. You get the idea. The curio shop, which was originally the George Schafer store, carries a selection of souvenirs, T-shirts, books, jewelry, Navajo kachinas, and Casa Grande pottery.

If you're hungry and thirsty, visit the **Pinos Altos Ice Cream Parlor, Café, Gift Shop, and Post Office.** The 1870s multiuse building itself is worth the stop. The food ranges from homemade soups to Frito pie, although the shop is best noted for its ice-cream confections.

Off the main drag down a dusty side street, **Pinos Altos Orchards and Gift Shop** has an excellent selection of local crafts and Mexican imports, but the store really shines with owner Jan Weisling's homemade jellies and jams. More than 50 types are available, but the author's favorite is the chipotle raspberry. Yum! During growing season you will find cider, fruit, and produce for sale.

Leaving Pinos Altos, you have a less arduous route to Silver City. With its spring and marsh, the city was once a popular Apache camping site, and when the Spanish miners discovered copper in the region, they called it San Vincente Cienega and judiciously left the valley to the Indians.

When the English-speaking settlers unearthed the area's silver deposits just above the marsh in 1869, they were not so wise, and incurred the predictable hostile repercussions from the Apache. In spite of this, the municipality, renamed Silver City, grew from one cabin to a boomtown of more than 80 buildings. Prosperity lasted until 1893, when silver prices crashed. Instead of dying a quick death, Silver City survived, first as an industrial center and later, at the turn of the 20th century, as a haven for invalids and tubercular patients.

With new mineral discoveries growth stabilized, and Silver City was named the seat of Grant County. Today the town is a trade center and is becoming an increasingly popular travel destination and retirement haven. Blessed with a beneficent climate and a 6,000-foot elevation, the city is home to an active arts community and Western New Mexico University in addition to serving as gateway to the spectacular Gila Wilderness.

Upon arriving, your first stop should be the **Murray Ryan Visitor's Center** on Hudson Street, where you'll find a plethora of information, including material detailing four historic and scenic tours. Loop Tour One is an excellent guide to the city's attractions, including several sites reminiscent of Billy the Kid's youth. His mother, Catherine McCarthy Antrim, is buried in a town cemetery. Another stop on the tour is **Big Ditch Park,** where from 1895 to 1906 floodwaters destroyed buildings and dropped the level of Main Street 55 feet. In 1980 the city turned the eyesore into what is now a graceful, shaded park.

Don't miss the **Silver City Museum,** located in the H. B. Ailman House. Located on West Broadway in a handsome mansard/Italianate brick Victorian mansion, the building was constructed in 1881 as home to the owner of one of the richest silver mines in the area. Through the years it morphed into a boardinghouse, city hall, and the town fire department. In 1967 it had its final incarnation as the Silver City Museum.

The first-floor galleries include a period parlor with a Jewett grand piano, velvet double-camelback sofa, and marble-top table. Additional rooms display local architectural styles and the history of Silver City from the time of the Apache to the present. A new wing, the Cleveland E. Dodge Memorial Gallery, depicts regional involvement in the Mexican War and the Civil War in the West. A well-stocked gift shop carries a bonanza of Mexican Casa Grande pots, books, Mimbres reproductions, T-shirts, and children's toys.

The second floor houses a room of mining memorabilia, another area devoted to local commerce, and a re-creation of a working mine office complete with an old Underwood Standard typewriter, an Addressograph, two oak desks with matching file cabinets, and a wide-eyed stuffed bobcat. The third-floor cupola offers a vista of the city's historic area.

Broadway's lures do not end with the museum. Galleries line the sidewalks up and down the street. **Silver City Trading Company Antique Mall** houses more than 350 dealers specializing in a whole spectrum of antiques and collectibles. The attractive **Fire Cloud Traders** gallery stocks an eclectic mixture of Native American jewelry, Oaxacan wood carvings, furniture from Chile, fine art, boutique clothing, and handmade items. **What's a Pot Shop** is the studio/home of Harry Benjamin, an artist working his eccentric designs in clay and oils. No shrinking violet, Harry is as much fun as his idiosyncratic constructions. **O'Keefe's Bookshop** on Broadway is bound to attract the inveterate reader with its shelves brimming with used and rare books, tomes of local and Southwestern lore, and photographic prints and cards by owner Dennis O'Keefe.

If all this shopping leaves you hungry, hop over to **Vicki's Eatery,** a little hole-in-the-wall on Yankie. Extremely popular with both locals and visitors, Vicki's lives up to its motto, "We are dedicated to preparing your meal using the freshest, most minimally processed ingredients from the most local sources we are able to locate."

After lunch, be sure to visit the **Western New Mexico University Museum** in Fleming Hall. Anyone fascinated with the Southwest's prehistoric Indian heritage will enjoy the collection of artifacts relating to the Mogollon Mimbres and Casa Grande cultures. Many visitors to this small college museum are drawn by the world's largest permanent display of Mimbres painted pottery. Extracted mainly from the collection of Richard Eisele, these pots are stylized renditions of men and animals in a great variety of whimsical displays. The museum gift shop plays on this theme with Mimbres pottery replicas, jewelry, books, T-shirts, and cards.

For accommodations, you might select either **The Inn on Broadway** if you wish to stay in the downtown area, or **Bear Mountain Lodge,** 3 miles north of the city on 178 acres adjacent to the Gila National Forest.

Bear Mountain Lodge is the ideal choice for hikers, mountain bikers, birders, and nature lovers of all kinds. The 1928 Spanish Territorial has been exquisitely renovated by The Nature Conservancy, which was deeded the property by the legendary Myra McCormick. Myra and her husband, Frederick, purchased the property in 1959, and when Frederick died in 1978, Myra soldiered on, operating the lodge as a bed and breakfast in spite of many financial setbacks. Her indomitable spirit and love of all creatures great and small still hovers over the land. The Nature Conservancy has completely revamped the lodge and outbuildings, turning what were once crumbling structures into luxurious accommodations. You can visit nearby Gila and Mimbres River Preserves with the staff naturalist or participate in daily nature-based activities. An ample breakfast is included in the daily rate, and dinner is available for an additional fee.

The Inn on Broadway is a two-story Queen Ann owned by Sandra Hicks and Ron Belanger. Sandra and Ron have transformed the 1883 Victorian into a cheery bed and breakfast that thankfully does not resort to fussy period furniture and room accessories. The four nicely decorated rooms all have private baths, televisions, and wireless Internet access.

Silver City has multiple evening dining options. Two of the best are **Diane's** and **Shevek and Mi,** both on Bullard. Diane Barrett opened her restaurant in 1997, and it has become a hands-down favorite with locals and visitors. A pastry chef with an impressive background, Diane rises at dawn to turn out her famous confections like her scrumptious coconut cake with lemon curd filling. Son Bodhi Werber rules the kitchen as chef in addition to helping out with management duties. Their food is a blend of European, Pacific Rim, and New Mexican.

Chef Shevek Barnhart and front-of-the-house manager Mike Barnhart brought their tasty bistro cuisine from New York to Silver City. With its pan-Mediterranean emphasis, you'll find dishes like Portuguese curried scallop salad, fava bean and mushroom vegetable ragu, spiced duck breast with pears, and chicken tagine with Turkish apricots and pine nuts. As a veteran of prestigious Eastern restaurants like the Moosewood in Ithaca, New York, the Quilted Giraffe in New York City's SoHo, and the Ivy Inn in Charlottesville, Virginia, Shevek's creations are above and beyond what you might expect from a tiny bistro in a small New Mexico town.

When you leave Silver City, you pass Tyrone's strip mines and head south through the Burro Mountains. Descending through Thompson's Canyon, you pass the place where Apaches ambushed and killed Judge H. C. McComas and his wife, and kidnapped their young son, Charlie. The abduction touched off one of the West's widest searches, but the child was never found.

En route you also pass the remains of Gold Hill, a silver mining town spared by Geronimo and his band of 90 Apaches in 1885. By pure luck the citizens had erected two American flags for Independence Day, and when spotted from afar, Geronimo assumed cavalry troopers were there and he withdrew without attack.

Traversing a section of Gila National Forest and crossing the Continental Divide, you pass into New Mexico's Bootheel with its seemingly endless creosote flats and small volcanic mountain ranges shimmering like mirages in the desert heat.

Lordsburg is an old Southern Pacific town, the kind where every head of household worked for the railroad and people set their watches by the daily comings and goings of the freights. As the fortunes of the railroad diminished, so waned the town. Evidence of the depressed economy stares out of empty store windows up and down the old business district. You can still find a little action at the redoubtable **El Charro Café** across the tracks. Most folks become acquainted with Lordsburg as a stop along I-10, which runs through the state from its borders with Arizona and Texas, or as a jumping-off site for visiting the ghost towns of Steins and Shakespeare.

Shakespeare, a National Historic Site, is the remains of a small settlement on the stage and emigrant trail to California. When silver was discovered in 1870 and news of a diamond mine circulated, Ralston City, or Burro Mines as it was then called, prospered until the counterfeit source of the diamond story was determined. For a while only a few die-hard miners remained, but during the silver mining boom of 1879 to 1893 and the copper boom of 1908 to 1932, the city was again fully occupied with an assortment of wild and lawless characters. Owned since 1935 by the Hill family, Shakespeare is blissfully noncommercial. Tours guided by family member Manny Hough run around two hours and, except for months when a holiday intervenes, occur the second Saturday and preceding Sunday of the month at 10 AM and 2 PM. The town is open to the public only at those times or by special appointment.

Manny takes you back in time, reciting colorful anecdotes from Shakespeare's history as you stroll along the old main street. You'll visit

The unique formations found at City of Rocks State Park in Faywood were created from volcanic ash 35 million years ago.

Grant House, the back portion of which was once the old Butterfield Stage station while the front rooms doubled as a restaurant and hanging parlor. You'll examine the Stratford Hotel, where Billy the Kid is said to have washed dishes, the powder magazine, mail station, saloon, gun museum, blacksmith shop, and assay office. Special reenactments from town history are staged four times yearly.

Steins is west of Lordsburg, just off I-10. Like Lordsburg, it was a railroad town. Named for Enoch Steins, a captain of the U.S. Dragoons who camped there in 1856, Steins was a stop on the Butterfield stage line. After the Southern Pacific pushed track through Steins Pass and established a workstation, the tiny community grew. When the railroad switched from steam to diesel after World War II, however, the workstation was closed and the town began its slow death.

Currently owned by Larry and Linda Link, Steins still sits by the track, looking like some forlorn, jilted Casanova. Crumbling stagecoach station walls, a section house that's rumored to be haunted, and 10 buildings filled with artifacts and furniture await visitors, who can take one of Larry's guided tours or wander at will.

If ghost towns aren't on your list of must-sees, you could bypass Lordsburg by driving east and south from Silver City on US 180 to Deming. This route takes you through the towns of Central, Bayard, and Hurley. If you leave US 180 south of Hurley and take NM 61 about 4 miles northeast, you'll arrive at **City of Rocks State Park.** These wild, eroded formations of Kneeling Nun rhyolite tuff were created 35 million years ago from an ash flow originating in a large volcanic caldera in the Black Range. With a desert garden and picnic and camping areas scattered in the shade of the boulders, the park is a superb place for a bag lunch or an overnight stay.

Returning to US 180, you pass **Faywood Hot Springs** on your left, just 1.5 miles from the park. A multipurpose building houses a visitor's center, museum, gift shop, and restaurant. The springs historically are a popular spot for "taking the waters," and facilities include both public and private flow-through soaking pools and hot tubs, some of which are clothing optional.

Although hardly a "country road," I-10 provides the only reasonable route between Lordsburg and Deming, approximately an hour's drive at interstate speeds.

Your first stop in town should be the old railroad depot, now the **Deming Visitor's Center,** where you'll find a collection of information on Deming and nearby Columbus.

Deming is best known for its **Great American Duck Races,** held the fourth weekend of August. The brainchild of a local businessman who decided to enliven life in their small town, the speedy fowls have been racing since 1980 to continued coverage by national and international media like *Sports Illustrated* and commentator Paul Harvey. Over the years, the festival has grown to include a balloon rally, parade, Main Street outhouse race, chile cook-off, classic car show, tortilla toss, and other special events.

Whether you arrive for the festival or another time of year, you need to reserve a couple of hours to visit the **Deming Luna Mimbres Museum,** one of the finest small town museums in the West. There is a great deal to see, and most people regret not giving more time to their visit. Housed in a building that was originally the National Guard Armory, the museum is a community project operating with all-volunteer personnel and public contributions. The 25,000 square feet of exhibit space house an art gallery, the Gilmore Quilt Room with textiles dating back to 1847, the Southerland Doll room with specimens ranging from china-headed dolls of the late 1800s to today's Barbies, an extensive geode and thunder egg array, and the Indian Gallery with its collection of crafts from the Mimbres, Pueblo, and Alaskan peoples. A new wing is devoted to a transportation exhibit.

Across the street from the museum, the restored **Historic Custom House** was the port of entry from Old Mexico from 1848 to 1900. The all-adobe building is furnished and decorated with period pieces. The main room is especially charming with its marble-top tables and Victorian chairs, carved oak server, and display of fine china and glass.

St. Clair Vineyards is a short distance east of town on NM 549. Master winemaker Florent Lescombes, a seventh-generation vintner, blends a wide selection of wines from grapes grown in nearby fields. The creation of personalized wine bottles is a distinctive service of the winery. A resident artist paints a bottle with one-of-a-kind designs for birthdays, anniversaries, or other special occasions. The tasting room is open daily, and visitors may sample a selection of still and sparkling wines.

Deming is a mineralogist's heaven with its multiple rock shops featuring agate, chert, diopside, garnet, and jasper garnered from nearby sites. If you're a rock hound, you'll want to visit **Rockhound State Park** in the nearby Florida Mountains. The park encourages visitors to take home the agate, jasper, and opal they find.

To fuel all these forays around town, stop at **Si Señor Restaurant** on East Pine. Raul and Margarita Granillo run a justly popular local spot

Besides its extensive cactus gardens, Pancho Villa State Park has a large visitor's center and museum.

where you'll find excellent New Mexican food and fast service in pleasant surroundings. Their carne adovada is especially toothsome.

While in the Deming area, devote a half-day to an excursion south to **Columbus,** a small town on the Mexican border noted primarily as the site of Pancho Villa's raid on March 9, 1916. Villa attacked both Columbus and the nearby 13th Cavalry at Camp Furlong in an attempt to embarrass President Wilson for recognizing Venustiano Carranza as president of the Republic of Mexico instead of Victoriano Huerta, who was backed by Villa. Although the town and its population suffered considerable damage, Villa lost many men to cavalry fire, and the day following the attack, Wilson ordered a punitive expedition, commanded by General John J. "Black Jack" Pershing, to capture the outlaw. After many skirmishes, Villa's forces were decimated, but he was not apprehended. Pershing returned to Columbus with his troops on February 5, 1917.

The military post at Camp Furlong was closed in 1926 and the extensive cactus gardens of **Pancho Villa State Park** now cover the site. A 7,000-square-foot visitor's center and museum display artifacts and exhibits about Villa's raid, the Mexican Revolution, and Pershing's pursuit of Villa.

In addition to the park, the **Columbus Historical Society Museum** is worth a stop. Housed in the restored Southern Pacific Railroad depot, the museum's rooms contain Indian artifacts, military and town memorabilia, and Villa mementos, including his death mask. Also displayed is the telephone switchboard of Susan Parks Kendrick, the town operator who, even though injured, stayed at her post during the raid and summoned help from Fort Bliss and El Paso.

The border crossing between Columbus and Palomas, Chihuahua, Mexico, is New Mexico's only international port of entry open 24 hours a day. You can park your car in the U.S. and walk across into Palomas, a hardscrabble border town. Other than the novelty of strolling into a foreign country, there's little compelling reason for visiting Palomas. However, if you do go, a respectable place for lunch is the **Pink Store,** also known as Casa de Pancho Villa Restaurant and Bar. The restaurant is to the rear of the shop, which sells a variety of Mexican arts and crafts. The dining room is attractive, but the menu predictable.

Las Cruces is your last stop on this tour. With a population of 67,000 and the campus of **New Mexico State University,** Las Cruces is a bustling town. Situated in the Mesilla Valley with the rugged Organ Mountains to the east, the city's long history begins with Paleo-Indian habitation circa 200 B.C., extends through the rise and fall of Puebloan people around A.D. 300, and includes the Spanish Entrada by Alvar Nunez Cabeza de Vaca in 1535 as he made his way from a shipwreck in the Gulf of Mexico. Five years later, Francisco Vásques de Coronado captained the first organized expedition through the Mesilla Valley, and in 1598 Don Juan de Oñate led colonists along El Camino Real, which passed through Las Cruces and Mesilla.

With the ratification of the Gadsden Purchase in 1854, Las Cruces became a major supply center for Organ Mountain miners and soldiers stationed at Fort Selden. Nearby Mesilla was a major stopover on the Butterfield Overland Stage route.

Today Las Cruces is both a cultural and agricultural center. Fields of cotton, groves of pecans, and acres of vineyards dot the outskirts. One of the largest single growers of pecans, with several million pounds harvested annually, **Stahmann Farms'** groves are positioned on the site of an ancient lake bed south of the city. The company store is a good place to buy pecans and pecan candy, and a drive through the groves is a cool treat on a sunny day.

Local products are featured every Wednesday and Saturday morning at the **Farmer's and Crafts Market** on the downtown mall, where more than 200 local growers sell fruit, vegetables, herbs, honey, and baked goods. Artists and craftspeople add their wares to the mélange.

Among the city's galleries and museums, the **New Mexico State University Museum** in Kent Hall stands out. Fronted by a beautifully landscaped courtyard, the museum's eclectic collection includes pottery by San Ildefonso's famous Blue Corn; a Zuni woman's manta; the leather helmet, football, and shoes belonging to Homer Powers, Class of 1916, who captained the Aggies to the Southwest championship; and a lariat said to have belonged to Pancho Villa. A whole gallery and the front room are reserved for changing exhibits, and every object is well displayed and labeled.

Visitors to New Mexico State University Museum in Las Cruces can see everything from pottery to Pancho Villa's lariat.

Anyone visiting Las Cruces should take time to drive out Dripping Springs Road to visit **New Mexico's Farm and Ranch Heritage Museum.** The museum, located on 47 acres at the base of the Organ Mountains, chronicles the 3,000-year history of New Mexico's agricultural and rural life. Children in particular will enjoy visiting the corrals populated by longhorn cattle, dairy cows, churro sheep, Jerusalem donkeys, and all their furry progeny. Milking demonstrations are conducted twice daily in the dairy barn, and other scheduled demonstrations include blacksmithing, weaving, quilting, cooking, and dowsing.

The museum building itself is a commodious structure of 24,000 square feet with space for permanent and changing exhibits, a state-of-the-art theater, a kitchen, and classrooms. The expansive lobby with clerestory and pitched roof is designed to resemble a hacienda or ranch house. The massive stone floor-to-ceiling fireplace wall is reminiscent of early buildings at Chaco Canyon, while the polished concrete floor is reflective of the hardened blood floors found in early Spanish colonial structures.

Adjacent to the lobby, Eagle Ranch Gift Shop imitates an old-time general store. It offers books, gardening supplies, New Mexican food products, jewelry, cowboy gear, and more. There's an outdoor amphitheater for special events, and special living history demonstrations are conducted throughout the year.

The museum's wings stretch out to the right and left. The main gallery in the north wing features a diverse range of artifacts focusing on key aspects of agriculture and rural life. Set against giant backdrops illustrating turn-of-the-20th-century photographs, the exhibit explores a variety of themes: hand tools, horse-drawn implements, harness and tack, making hay, windmills and water, making do, and mercantiles and mail order. Each area includes a segment titled "Voices of New Mexico," a firsthand account of people whose lives were spent in the fields and ranch lands of the state. In addition, the north wing houses a smaller gallery for changing exhibits.

The south wing contains the theater and a restaurant, the Museum Grill, which specializes in New Mexican cuisine such as grilled chicken with chile cream sauce or lighter fare such as black bean nachos or fajita salad.

After catching glimpses of the nearby Organ Mountains from almost every vantage point of the museum, you may be inclined to inspect them up close and personal. Continue east on Dripping Springs Road, up beyond the pavement's ending to the **A. B. Cox Visitor Center of Dripping Springs Natural Area.** From this location you may access the popular La Cueva and Dripping Springs trails.

La Cueva leads to a rock shelter, an archaeological site associated with the Jornada branch of the prehistoric Mogollon culture. In the late 1860s the cave was home to Giovanni Maria Agostini, an Italian nobleman, faith healer, and bona fide hermit, who was murdered in the spring of 1869. His assailant was never found.

Dripping Springs trail leads from the visitor's center to the site of a resort complex built by Colonel Eugene Van Patten in the 1870s. Hikers pass the ruins of the sanatorium, the resort, and the old coach stop. The rocky but beautiful 1.5-mile trail climbs 560 vertical feet and dead-ends above the spring. Be sure to take water and wear sturdy walking shoes.

Las Cruces is blessed with a variety of accommodations, none more appealing than the **Inn of the Arts** in the historic district across from the First National Towers Building. A combined gallery and bed and breakfast, the inn is owned by Linda and Gerald Lundeen, who restored two homes constructed by William Henry Harrison Llewellyn, a member of the New Mexico House of Representatives. Gerald, a noted architect whose passion is the preservation of old structures, designed the addition, which joined the two buildings and provided room for both his office and an art gallery for Linda.

All 20 guest rooms are named for well-known Southwestern artists and are furnished with original art and antiques. The common area, the Merienda Room, soars two stories with massive arched French doors leading to two of many patios and outdoor seating areas. Guests gather here for the ample breakfast or to gossip about the day's adventures. The inn is popular with visitors in the arts community and frequently hosts special Elderhostel programs.

In recent years the Las Cruces gastronomical scene has expanded greatly from a string of chain restaurants to some excellent eating places. For lunch or a casual meal, check out **International Delights Café,** a felicitous combination of a restaurant serving Mediterranean food and a grocery where ingredients for home cooks may be found. The café's menu includes specialties such as Greek salad, falafel, gyros, baba ghanouj, and a variety of baklavas.

If your tastes run to Asian dishes, try **Mix Pacific Rim Cuisine,** owned by Maruya and Chiaki Miyazaki. The beautifully appointed restaurant specializes in food from Thailand, Japan, China, Korea, Vietnam, and the Hawaiian Islands. A complete selection of sashimi and negri are on tap at the sushi bar.

Most visitors to the area spend a day in neighboring **Mesilla,** a historic village dating to the 1500s. The Gadsden Purchase was signed on the plaza in 1854, annexing Mesilla to the U.S. and fixing the international boundaries of New Mexico and Arizona. In 1861 the village was the western headquarters of the Confederacy. The shady plaza is highlighted by San Albino Church, one of the oldest in the valley, and ringed by upscale shops selling everything from fancy Southwestern duds to fine art. The **Galleria on the Plaza** specializes in folk art; **Del Sol** stocks Navajo and Zuni jewelry, imported cottons, South American and Mexican handicrafts, and Zapotec rugs and souvenirs; and sister store **La Zia** features Indian jewelry, pottery, storytellers, fetishes, sandpaintings, and Navajo rugs. You can buy an ice-cream cone or a pound of homemade fudge at **J. Eric Chocolatier,** browse tomes on the Southwest and Americana at the **Mesilla Book Center,** or taste vintages at **Blue Teal Vinyards.**

The plaza also houses two excellent restaurants: **La Posta** and **Double Eagle/Peppers.** Earliest records indicate that La Posta was constructed in the 1840s, and in the 1850s served as a freight and passenger stop for service to Pinos Altos. After the Civil War, it became a stage station on the Butterfield Overland Mail Route, and during the 1870s and 1880s the Corn Exchange Hotel operated from the structure.

In 1939 Katy Camuñez Meeks originated the Posta de Mesilla restaurant in the northwest corner of the old adobe, and she operated it, expanded it, and left her indelible imprint upon it until her death, when the property was acquired by her great-niece, Jerean Camuñez Hutchinson, and her husband, Hutch. The list of habitués runs the gamut from famous to infamous: Billy the Kid, Kit Carson, Pancho Villa, and General Douglas MacArthur, to name a few.

La Posta's unassuming exterior belies a surprisingly exotic interior. You enter through what once was a zaguan, a wide, sheltered entry, and pass several small shops—a jeweler, a clothing boutique, and a store selling New Mexico products. Entering the enclosed patio with its tangle of plants and commodious aviary, you're greeted by the squawks and whistles of parrots, cockatiels, a cockatoo, and Simon, an ancient African gray. Red piranha swim lazily in their tanks.

The dining room fronting Calle de Guadalupe was the original eating house, but as the years passed, additional structures were added and parts of the building devoted to other uses were converted to dining. The Lava Room is the most requested seating thanks in part to its wall covered with basalt boulders, its abundance of plants, and its romantic atmosphere. Food is traditional New Mexican and steaks are an additional specialty.

Double Eagle and Peppers are two restaurants housed in one building. Double Eagle boasts sumptuous, turn-of-the-20th-century rooms and classic continental cuisine, while Peppers is informal and features Southwestern cuisine. Be sure to take a gander at Double Eagle's Maximilian Room with its ceiling covered in 18-carat gold, huge Baccarat crystal chandeliers, and Tiffany-style stained-glass panels. Fine cuts of beef are their forte, and they offer a choice of 14 individual sauces to grace their chateaubriands, filets, sirloins, and New York strips. Save room for dessert. The banana enchiladas are a confection of crepes filled with fresh bananas, bathed in maple syrup and pecans, and graced with a scoop of vanilla bean ice cream.

Military history buffs should make the short journey north to **Radium Springs,** where **Fort Selden State Monument** is located. This post, built in 1865, quartered the famous Buffalo Soldiers, the unit of black cavalry charged with protecting valley settlers from Apache raids. In later years Fort Selden was the boyhood home of General Douglas MacArthur, whose father was post commander. The visitor's center has a 10-minute video on the fort's history and exhibits on day-to-day military life.

Fort Selden's adobe walls are now ruins gradually melting back into the earth, but while walking the sunlit path among sheltering cottonwoods you can almost hear the echoes of bugle calls and the commands of the cavalry officers mustering their troops.

Contacts:

Artesian Bath House, 312 Marr, Truth or Consequences, 87901. Call 505-894-2684. Sun. through Tues. 8–noon and 1–5:30; Fri. and Sat. 8–9.

Barbershop Café, Winery, and Gift Shop, 200 Main Street, Hillsboro, 88042. Call 505-895-5283. Wed. through Fri. 11–3, Sat. and Sun. 8–3. Web site: www.barbershopcafe.com.

Bear Mountain Lodge (The Nature Conservancy), 2251 Bear Mountain Road, mail: P.O. Box 1163, Silver City, 88062. Call 1-877-620-2327 or 505-538-2538. Web site: www.bearmountainlodge.com.

Black Range Business Association, P.O. Box 152, Hillsboro, 88042.

The Black Range Lodge, 119 Main Street, Kingston, 88042. Call 505-895-5652. Web site: www.blackrangelodge.com.

Black Range Museum and Library, Main Street, mail: P.O. Box 454, Hillsboro, 88042. Call 505-895-5233. March 1 through December 31, Tues. through Sat. 11–4.

Blue Teal Vineyards Wine Tasting Room, 1720 Avenida de Mesilla, Old Mesilla, 88005. Call 1-866-336-7360 or 505-524-0390. Mon. through Thurs. 11–6, Fri. and Sat. 11–8, Sun. noon–6. Web site: www.blueteal.com.

Buckhorn Saloon and Opera House, 32 Main Street, Pinos Altos, 88053. Call 505-538-9911. Saloon, Mon. through Sat. 3–11; dinner, Mon. through Sat. 6–10; Opera House shows Fri. and Sat. at 8. Call 505-388-3848. Reservations requested. Web site: www.silvercity.org/restaurant_detail.mvc?CID=93N5FBQE9N.

Buffalo Bill's Exotic Cactus Ranch, 1600 S. Broadway, Truth or Consequences, 87901. Call 505-894-0790. July 4 through Labor Day, Wed. through Sun. 9–5.

The Charles Motel and Spa, 601 Broadway, Truth or Consequences, 87901. Call 1-800-317-4518 or 505-894-7154. Fee. Web site: www.charles spa.com.

City of Rocks State Park, 28 miles northeast of Deming via US 180 and NM 61, Faywood, mail: P.O. Box 1064, Deming, 88030. Call 505-546-6182. Gates open at 7:30 AM, close at sunset. Fee. Web site: www.emnrd.state.nm.us/emnrd/parks/Rockhound.htm.

Coffee, Tea or C, 411 Main Street, Truth or Consequences, 87901. Call 505-894-8800. Summer, daily 7 AM–1 PM; winter, daily 7 AM–5 PM. Web site: www.coffeeteaorc.com.

Columbus Historical Society Museum, P.O. Box 562, Columbus, 88029. Call 505-531-2620. May through August, Mon. through Fri. 10–1, Sat. and Sun. 10–4; September through April, daily 10–4.

Cuchillo Café, 426 Broadway, Truth or Consequences, 87901. Call 505-894-7878. Mon. and Wed. through Sat. 7–7, Sun. 7–3.

Del Sol, 2322 Calle Principal, Mesilla Plaza, mail: P.O. Box 1098, Mesilla, 88046. Call 505-524-1418. Daily 10–6; Memorial Day through Labor Day, open until 9 Fri. and Sat. Web site: www.delsolstores.com.

Deming-Luna County Chamber of Commerce and Visitor's Center, Deming Depot, 800 E. Pine, mail: P.O. Box 8, Deming, 88030. Mon. through Fri. 9–5, Sat. 9–11 AM. Call 1-800-848-4955 or 505-546-2674. Web site: www.demingchamber.com.

Deming Luna Mimbres Museum, 301 S. Silver, Deming, 88030. Call 505-546-2382. Mon. through Sat. 9–4, Sun. 1:30–4. Web site: www.deming lunamimbresmuseum.com.

Diane's Restaurant, 510 N. Bullard, Silver City, 88061. Call 505-538-8722. Brunch, Sat. and Sun. 9–2; lunch, Tues. through Sun. 11–2; dinner, Tues. through Sat. 5:30–9. Web site: www.dianesrestaurant.com.

Doc Campbell's Post, NM 15, Gila Hot Springs, mail: HC 68, Box 80, Silver City, 88061. Call 505-536-9551. Summer, daily 8–6; winter, daily 9–4:30.

Double Eagle de la Mesilla and **Peppers,** 3255 Calle de Guadalupe, Old Mesilla Plaza, mail: P.O. Box 905, Las Cruces, 88004. Call 505-523-6700. Lunch, daily 11–3; dinner, Mon. through Sat. 5–10, Sun. 5–9. Web site: www.double-eagle-mesilla.com.

Dripping Springs Natural Area, A. B. Cox Visitor Center, 15000 Dripping Springs Road, Las Cruces, 88001. Call 505-522-1219. Daily 8–5; gate open until sunset; Dripping Springs Trail closes at 3 in winter. Fee. Web site: www.nm.blm.gov/recreation/las_cruces/dripping_springs.htm.

Dust and Glitter, 404 Main Street, Truth or Consequences, 87901. Call 505-894-3613. Thurs. through Mon. 11–6. Web site: www.dustandglitter.com.

El Camino Real International Heritage Center, County Road 1598, mail: P.O. Box 175, Socorro, 87801. Call 505-835-1829. Summer, daily 8:30–5; winter, closed Tues. Gift shop, year-round Wed. through Mon. 10:30–4. Web site: www.caminorealheritage.org or www.nmstatemonuments.org/about.php?_instid=ECR.

El Charro Café, 209 Southern Pacific Boulevard, mail: P.O. Box 309, Lordsburg, 88045. Call 505-542-9121. Daily 8 AM–11 PM.

Faywood Hot Springs, 165 NM 61, HC71, Box 1240, Faywood, 88034. Call 505-536-9663. RV park, tepee travel trailer lodging. Daily 10–10. Fee. Web site: www.faywood.com.

Fire Cloud Traders, 209 W. Broadway, Silver City, 88061. Call 505-538-5376. Mon. through Sat. 10–5:30.

Firewater Lodge Bed & Breakfast, 311 Broadway, Truth or Consequences, 87901. Call 505-740-0315. Web site: www.firewaterlodge.com.

Fort Selden State Monument, 1280 Fort Selden Road, Radium Springs, 88054. Call 505-526-8911. May through October, daily 8:30–5; closed Tuesday remainder of year. Fee. Web site: www.nmstatemonuments.org/about.php?_instid=SELD.

Galleria on the Plaza, 2310 Calle Principal, Old Mesilla Plaza, mail: P.O. Box 1098, Mesilla, 88046. Call 505-526-9771. Daily 10–6.

Geronimo Springs Museum, 211 Main, Truth or Consequences, 87901. Call 505-894-6600. Mon. through Sat. 9–5. Fee. Web site: www.truthorconsequencesnm.net/members_museums.htm.

Gila Cliff Dwellings National Monument, NM 15, Gila Hot Springs, mail: HC 68, Box 100, Silver City, 88061. Call 505-536-9461. Memorial Day through Labor Day, cliff dwellings and visitor's center, daily 8–5; Labor Day through Memorial Day, daily 8–4:30. Fee. Web site: nps.gov/gicl.

Grapes Gallery, 407–409 Main, Truth or Consequences, 87901. Thurs. through Sat. 11–6, Sun. 11–5. Web site: www.grapes-torc.com.

Happy Belly Deli, 313 Broadway, Truth or Consequences, 87901. Tues. through Fri. 7:05–4, Sat. 8:05–4. Call 505-894-3354.

Hay-Yo-Kay Hot Springs, 300 Austin, Truth or Consequences, 87901. Call 505-894-2228. Mon. through Fri. 10–7, Sat. and Sun. noon–7.

Historic Custom House, 304 S. Silver, Deming, 88030. Call 505-546-2382. Mon. through Sat. 12:30–4, Sun. 1:30–4.

Indian Springs Pools, 200 Pershing, Truth or Consequences, 87901. Call 505-894-2018. Daily 8 AM–10 PM. Fee.

International Delights Café, 1245 El Paseo Road, Las Cruces, 88001. Call 505-647-5956. Daily 7 AM–midnight. Web site: www.internationaldelightscafe.com.

J. Eric Chocolatier, 2379 Calle de Guadalupe, Old Mesilla Plaza, mail: P.O. Box 1073, Mesilla, 88046. Call 505-526-2744. Tues. through Sat. 10:30–5, Sun. and Mon. noon–5. Web site: www.j-eric.com.

La Posta de Mesilla, 2410 Calle de San Albino, Old Mesilla Plaza, mail: P.O. Box 116, Mesilla, 88046. Call 505-524-3524. Tues. through Thurs. and Sun. 11–9, Fri. and Sat. 11–9:30. Web site: www.laposta-de-mesilla.com.

Las Cruces Convention & Visitors Bureau, 211 N. Water Street, Las Cruces, 88001. Call 1-800-343-7827 or 505-541-2444. Web site: www.lascrucescvb.org.

Las Cruces Farmers & Crafts Market, downtown mall, Las Cruces. Wed. and Sat. 8–12:30. Call 505-541-2288.

La Zia, 2340 Calle Principal, Old Mesilla Plaza, mail: P.O. Box 1098, Mesilla, 88046. Call 505-523-2213. Daily 10–6.

Log Cabin Curio Shop and Museum, 33 Main Street, mail: P.O. Box 53083, Pinos Altos, 88053. Call 505-388-1882. Summer, Mon. through Sat. 9–6, Sun. 9–5; winter, daily 9–5.

Lordsburg/Hidalgo County Chamber of Commerce, 117 E. Second Street, Lordsburg, 88045. Call 505-542-9864. Web site: www.lordsburg hidalgocounty.net.

Lordsburg Visitor Information Center, I-10, Exit 20, Lordsburg, 88045. Call 505-542-8149. End of May through end of September, daily 8–6; October through mid-May, daily 8–5.

Los Arcos, 1400 N. Date, Truth or Consequences, 87901. Call 505-894-6200. Sun. through Thurs. 5–9:30, Fri. and Sat. 5–10:30.

Lundeen Inn of the Arts, 618 S. Alameda, Las Cruces, 88005. Call 1-888-526-3326 or 505-526-3327/3326. Web site: www.innofthearts.com.

Main Street Gallery, 108 Main, Truth or Consequences, 87901. Thurs. through Sat. 11–6, Sun. 11–5.

Mesilla Book Center, 2360 Calle Principal, Old Mesilla Plaza, mail: P.O. Box 96, Mesilla, 88046. Call 505-526-6220. Tues. through Sat. 11–6, Sun. 1–5.

MIAO, 409 Broadway, Truth or Consequences, 87901. Call 505-496-3266. Thurs. through Mon. noon–5 or by appointment.

Mix Pacific Rim Cuisine, Las Cruces, 88001. Call 505-532-2042. Mon. through Fri. 11–2 and 5–9, Sat. noon–2 and 5–9. Web site: www.mixpacificrim.com.

New Mexico Farm & Ranch Heritage Museum, 4100 Dripping Springs Road, mail: P.O. Drawer 1898, Las Cruces, 88004. Call 505-522-4100. Mon. through Sat. 9–5, Sun. noon–5. Call for demonstration hours. Museum Grill, Mon. through Sun. 11–4; Eagle Ranch Gift Shop open museum hours. Web site: spectre.nmsu.edu/frhm/welcome.lasso.

New Mexico State University Museum, Kent Hall, University Avenue at Solano, Box 30001, Las Cruces, 88003. Call 505-646-3739. Tues.

through Sat. noon–4; closed Sun., Mon., and university holidays. Web site: www.nmsu.edu/~museum.

O'Keefe's Bookshop, 102 W. Broadway, Silver City, 88061. Call 505-388-3313. Summer, Mon. through Sat. 10–5; winter, Tues. through Sat. 10–4.

Pancho Villa State Park, P.O. Box 450, Columbus, 88029. Call 505-531-2711. Gate open 24 hours; Visitor's center, daily 8–5. Web site: www.emnrd.state.nm.us/emnrd/parks/PanchoVilla.htm.

Percha Creek Traders, Main Street, Hillsboro, 88042. Call 505-895-5091. Wed. through Sun. 10–4 (closes at 3 January through March) or by appointment at 505-895-3363.

The Pink Store (Casa de Pancho Villa Restaurant and Bar), Puerto Palomas, Chihuahua, Mexico. Call 505-531-7243. Store, daily 9–7; restaurant, daily 10:30–6.

Pinos Altos Ice Cream Parlor, Café, Gift Shop, and Post Office, Main Street, Pinos Altos, 88053. Call 505-534-1997. Mon. through Sat. 10–6. Web site: www.pinosaltos.org/icecreamparlor.

Pinos Altos Orchards and Gift Shop, 13 Placer Street, mail: P.O. Box 53004, Pinos Altos, 88053. Call 505-538-1270. Tues. through Sat. 10–5; summer, Tues. through Sun. 10–5.

Rio Bravo Fine Art, 110 Broadway, Truth or Consequences, 87901. Call 505-894-0572. Wed. through Sat. 10–5, Sun. noon–5, or by appointment. Web site: www.riobravofineart.com.

Riverbend Hot Springs Hostel, 100 Austin, Truth or Consequences, 87901. Call 505-894-6183. Daily 8–10. Web site: www.nmhotsprings.com.

Rockhound State Park, 14 miles southeast of Deming via NM 11 and NM 141, mail: P.O. Box 1064, Deming, 88031. Call 505-546-6182. Gate hours 7:30–sunset. Fee. Web site: www.emnrd.state.nm.us/emnrd/parks/Rockhound.htm.

St. Clair Vineyards, 1325 De Baca Road, Deming, 88030. Call 1-866-386-7357 or 505-546-9324. Mon. through Sat. 9–6, Sun. noon–5. Tours Sat. at 11 AM and 3 PM. Web site: www.stclairvineyards.com.

San Albino Catholic Church, 2280 Calle Principal, Old Mesilla Plaza, mail: P.O. Box 26, Mesilla, 88046. Call 505-526-9349. Visiting hours Tues. through Sun. 1–3. Call to confirm.

Second Hand Rose, 414 Broadway, Truth or Consequences, 87901. Call 505-894-4029. Summer, Mon. through Sat. 9–7, Sun. 11:30–7; November through April, daily 11:30–5:30.

Shakespeare Ghost Town, 2½ miles south of Lordsburg, mail: P.O. Box 253, Lordsburg, 88045. Call 505-542-9034. Check Web site for re-enactments and tour dates. Fee. Web site: www.shakespeareghostown.com.

Shevek and Mi, 602 N. Bullard, Silver City, 88061. Call 505-534-9168. Summer, Mon. through Thurs. 10:30–8:30, Fri. 10:30–10, Sat. 8:30–10, Sun. 8:30–8:30; winter, Mon. through Thurs. 10:30–9, Fri. 10:30–11, Sat. 8:30–10, Sun. 8:30–8:30. Brunch, weekends and holidays until 2 PM. Web site: www.silver-eats.com.

Sierra Grande Lodge & Spa, 501 McAdoo Street, Truth or Consequences, 87901. Call 505-894-6976. Web site: www.sierragrandelodge.com.

Silver City/Grant County, Murray Ryan Visitor's Center, 201 N. Hudson, Silver City, 88061. Call 1-800-548-9378 or 505-538-3785. Mon. through Sat. 9–5, Sun. 10–2. Web site: www.silvercity.org.

Silver City Museum and Museum Store, 312 W. Broadway, Silver City, 88061. Call 505-538-5921. Tues. through Fri. 9–4:30, Sat. and Sun. 10–4. Web site: www.silvercitymuseum.org.

Silver City Trading Company Antique Mall, 205 W. Broadway, Silver City, 88062. Call 505-388-8989. Mon. through Sat. 10–5, Sun. noon–4.

Si Señor Restaurant, 200 E. Pine, Deming, 88030. Call 505-546-3938. Mon. through Sat. 9:30–8:30, Sun. 9:30–3.

Stahmann Farms and Country Store, 22505 NM 28 S., La Mesa, 88044. Call 1-800-654-6887 or 505-526-8974. Mon. through Sat. 9–6, Sun. 11–5. Web site: www.stahmanns.com.

Steins Ghost Town, Exit 3 off I-10, mail: P.O. Box 2185, Roadforks, 88045. Call 505-542-9791. Fri. through Wed. 9:30–5. Fee. Web site: www.ghosttowns.com/states/nm/steins.

Truth or Consequences/Sierra County Chamber of Commerce, 400 W. Fourth Street, mail: P.O. Drawer 31, Truth or Consequences, 87901. Call 505-894-3536. Web site: www.truthorconsequencesnm.net.

Tularosa City Hall, 705 St. Francis, Tularosa, 88352. Call 505-585-2771. Mon. through Thurs. 8–5, Fri. 8–1.

Vicki's Eatery, 107 Yankie Street, Silver City, 88061. Call 505-388-5430. Mon. through Sat. 11–3. Web site: www.silvercity.org/restaurant_detail.mvc?CID=1D13333Y5V.

Western New Mexico University Museum, Fleming Hall, 1000 W. College Avenue, Silver City, 88061. Call 505-538-6386. Call for hours. Web site: www.wnmu.edu/univ/museum.htm.

What's a Pot Shop, 300 N. Arizona, Silver City, 88061. Call 505-388-2007. Mon. through Sat. 9–5.

When Gallery, 422 Broadway, Truth or Consequences, 87901. Thurs. through Sat. 11–6, Sun. 11–5. Web site: www.whengallery.com.

White Coyote Café, 113 Main Street, Truth or Consequences, 87901. Call 505-894-5160. Thurs. through Sat. 11–8, Sun. 9–5 (brunch until 2), Mon. 8–3 (brunch until 2).

CHAPTER

10

Gas, Oil, and Chaparral

Getting there: From Albuquerque, take I-40 east 61 miles to Clines Corners, Exit 230. From Clines Corners, take US 285 south, which runs 140 miles through the villages of Encino, Vaughn, Ramon, and Mesa to Roswell. The drive on US 285 south from Roswell to Artesia is 40 miles. Carlsbad lies 69 miles south of Artesia on US 285.

Carlsbad day trips: To access Carlsbad Caverns National Park, from the city take US 180 south to the intersection of NM 7, about 27 miles.

To visit Sitting Bull Falls from Carlsbad, go north on US 285 for 40 miles to its intersection with NM 137.

Rattlesnake Springs is 26 miles south of the city. Take US 62/180 for 26 miles and turn west at the New Cave and Rattlesnake Springs sign. The access road is 2 miles long.

The drive to Slaughter Canyon is 28 miles south off US 62/180.

Carlsbad to Hobbs is 69 miles over US 180/62 east (the Hobbs Highway). Leaving Hobbs, it's a short 22 miles to Lovington on NM 18 north.

To continue on to Portales, take NM 206 north (the Tatum Highway) 87 miles.

Portales to Clovis is 19 miles on US 70 north, and Clovis to Fort Sumner is 60 miles over US 60 west. You will be completing the tour loop when you arrive in Santa Rosa 45 miles north of Fort Sumner via US 84 north.

Detour to Puerto de Luna: From I-40 take NM 91 south 10 miles to the village and the site of Coronado's Bridge.

Access I-40 west in Santa Rosa and return to Albuquerque from Santa Rosa, 117 miles.

Highlights: This is an ambitious trip through parts of New Mexico not visited by the casual traveler. True, your passage will take you to **Roswell** with its UFO lore and **Carlsbad Caverns National Park,** but much of the journey will acquaint you with the state's Staked Plains. Here you'll travel over stretches of lonesome, wind-whipped terrain dotted with oil and gas wells and the small towns of Artesia, Hobbs, Lovington, Clovis, and Fort Sumner.

Let's Go: Up, up, and away you climb, leaving Albuquerque behind. Keeping company with the vast army of behemoths trucking merchandise from west to east, you gain altitude as you climb Sedillo Hill in Tijeras Canyon. Beyond the Sandia and Manzanos mountains you're barreling toward Clines Corners, bypassing the small towns of Edgewood and Moriarty.

Departing the interstate, you head south, through the small village of Encino, now nothing much more than a few deserted buildings and boarded-up homes. At Vaughn you are entering the **Llano Estacado,** or Staked Plains, a region encompassing parts of eastern New Mexico and northwestern Texas. A large mesa or tableland, it is mostly flat, but is dotted here and there by small playas, or seasonal lakes. There are several explanations for the term "staked plains." One is that the dry flower stalks of the omnipresent yucca plant look like stakes. A second is that in 1541 Coronado's men planted stakes along the almost featureless plain to mark their way. A third is that Coronado named the site "Palisaded Plain," for the 300-foot-high edge of the Caprock Escarpment, which marks the western boundary. "Palisaded" was later mistranslated into "staked."

Whatever the truth, the Staked Plains are the high lonesome. Vaughn, on the northeastern boundary, is the biggest settlement you'll encounter until you reach Roswell. In spite of its somnolent appearance, Vaughn is considered one of the nation's top sheep- and wool-raising areas. The town was established as a railroad community in 1919 and is the only town in New Mexico where the main lines of two railroads intersect: the Burlington Northern Santa Fe Railway and the Union Pacific Railroad. If you need to gas up, do it here before the long trek to Roswell through Ramon and Mesa, mere blips on the map. Be sure to stop north of Roswell to have your picture taken at the sign designating the dirt road entrance to Site 131, the location of the reported 1947 UFO crash.

You may be surprised to discover **Roswell** is a bustling, regional trade center. As you enter the city, you pass the usual assortment of big box stores, chain restaurants, and gas stations.

The city has a long history starting in prehistoric times. Originally home to the Mescalero Apache Indians, it was also a part of the Comanche Indians' hunting grounds. With the establishment in 1866 of the Goodnight–Loving Trail, Anglo cattlemen from Texas brought ranching to New Mexico, and in 1870 a settler named Van Smith founded Roswell and named it in honor of his father.

When artesian water was discovered in 1890, the basis of the economy changed from ranching to agriculture. This was the era of grand homes. Roswell's Historic District of 40 city blocks showcases many of these structures constructed in a mind-bending variety of 22 architectural styles.

Oil was discovered in New Mexico in 1924, and by the early 1930s southeastern New Mexico was booming, a trend that continued until the fields peaked in 1967. However, the oil and gas industry still plays a major role as evidenced by the many oil and gas wells dotting the countryside. You'll recognize the oil wells by their rotating pumps and the gas wells by their arrangements of pipes, dubbed "Christmas trees."

The military also played a part in Roswell's growth, starting in 1942 with the construction of the Roswell Army Air Field by German and Italian POWs from World War II. In early 1948, the base was renamed Walker Air Force Base, and it became the largest Strategic Air Command base in the country, employing 5,000 military personnel and an additional 50,000 support personnel. Walker closed in 1967, and the resulting economic hole was difficult to fill. The base location has been turned into an industrial center, and currently companies ranging from a mozzarella cheese manufacturing facility to a German Christmas ornament maker are located there.

All this history is overshadowed by the event that occurred on July 8, 1947, when a mysterious object fell from the sky and landed on Mac Bezel's ranch north of town. There were tales of a flying disk and visitors from another world, and the commotion this generated has lasted to the present day. You'll get many versions of the story in Roswell, but the army's official explanation is that the reported UFO was a downed high-altitude weather balloon. The notoriety of the **"Roswell Incident"** has spawned a museum and a proliferation of UFO-based shops that draw more than a

Pioneer Plaza in Roswell is home to a statue of famed rancher and businessman John S. Chisum.

million visitors a year, but the shrewd traveler will find much more to the city than little green men.

Your first stop on arrival should be **Pioneer Plaza,** home to a statue of John S. Chisum, the rancher and businessman who created a great cattle empire in the Pecos Valley. His ranch headquarters were located near where Roswell was platted. There's plentiful parking in an adjoining lot, which gives you painless access to the little 1920s Conoco service station that serves as the city's visitor's center. While you're in the vicinity, cross North Main and stroll through the **Chavez County Courthouse.** It was built in 1911 in the Beaux-Arts Revival style and was completed just in time for New Mexico's celebration in 1912 as the Union's 47th state. Want to grab a bite to eat? Stop in at **Martin's Capitol Café** for good, inexpensive New Mexican food with an emphasis on green chile.

Roswell is blessed with two excellent small museums. **The Roswell Museum, Art Center and Robert H. Goddard Planetarium** on West 11th Street is a jewel. The collection represents regional, New Mexico modernist, and American contemporary art. You'll find a definitive showing of the work of artists Peter Hurd and Henriette Wyeth, Hurd's wife and daughter of famous illustrator N. C. Wyeth. The Santa Fe and Taos schools of artists are embodied by paintings by Georgia O'Keeffe, Marsden Hartley, Stuart Davis, John Marin, Victor Higgins, Andrew Dasburg, and others. Area history, science, and technology also are represented, and there are periodically changing shows, too.

The Anderson Museum of Contemporary Art on East College Boulevard has more than 200 very diverse works of art highlighting the work of former fellows of the Roswell Artist-in-Residence Program. Established by artist and oilman Donald B. Anderson in 1967, the program provides gifted studio-based visual artists the unique opportunity to concentrate on their work in a supportive environment for a whole year.

Don't be put off by the industrial appearance of the building. Enter and behold serene and spacious galleries amiably interspersed with comfortable seating for informal klatches. You'll find something you like whether you favor the abstract modernism of David Reed or the folk art of Alison Saar. Laugh at the mobile golf bag sharks by Robbie Barber, or study the larger-than-life fiberglass sculpture of Luis Jimenez. You are guaranteed an enlightening and entertaining experience even if you don't know Pollack from Pollyanna.

After a measure of culture, prepare for a dose of kitsch at the **UFO Museum and Research Center.** Housed in a renovated movie theater, the museum exhibits detail the Roswell Incident timeline with testimonies, photographs, maps, copies of newspapers, and a mock-up of a Roswell radio station in 1947. The final exhibit is the famous alien autopsy complete with mannequin doctors and unearthly patient, props from the Showtime movie *Roswell.* The city's biggest celebration is the UFO Festival over the Fourth of July weekend, when outrageous outfits are the order of the day. Street dances, fireworks, a galactic costume contest, and concerts entertain the crowds, and authorities on arcane topics expound on alien abductions and crop circles.

An evening meal is no problem since either **Peppers** in the Sunwest Centre complex or **A Taste of Europe** will fill the bill. Peppers, owned by the Roe family, serves up a varied menu with an emphasis on New Mexican dishes. At Taste of Europe, discreetly tucked into a wing of the Days Inn, Eve Strzyzewski prepares both European and American favorites, but her Polish dishes from her great-grandmother's recipes are the star attraction.

Statues and murals along Artesia's Heritage Walkway and Plaza detail the town's history.

Artesia is the next stop on your southeast tour. Mirroring much the same history as Roswell, the town of 12,000 somehow avoids being dominated by the imposing presence of the huge Navajo Refining Company. The main street welcomes travelers with its attractive shops and small cafés. Browse for antiques among the 25 dealers at **Georgianna's** or check out **Handmade Treasures,** a craft mall. Join the ladies for lunch crowd at **The Garden Café** or order a burger and suds at **The Wellhead Restaurant and Brewpub.**

Downtown also has a couple pocket parks where you can sit back and relax. **Heritage Walkway and Plaza** on Main has murals illustrating Artesia's history and statues of citizens past and present. Fans of old hotels will enjoy the **Heritage Inn,** built in 1905. The 11 rooms are modestly but individually decorated and have either full baths or showers. There's no elevator, so it's not for the movement challenged. All but one room are on the second floor.

If you'd prefer a single-floor adobe hacienda, **Adobe Rose Bed and Breakfast** is for you. The Adobe Rose was originally a building project by the College of Artesia's arts program. Professional artists such as Peter Hurd donated their works for auction to help fund the project. Now owned by Clent and Adriana Schoonover, the Adobe Rose is elegance in the Southwestern style. Rooms have private courtyards opening onto well-tended gardens, and there's satellite TV and wireless DSL throughout. You should make reservations early because they are often fully booked by visitors to the nearby Federal Law Enforcement Academy.

It's just a short hop from Artesia to the city of Carlsbad, but there's a delightful stop along the way. The **Living Desert Zoo and Gardens State Park** is a sanctuary in the Chihuahuan desert. The 1.3-mile self-guided path, arranged in life zones, takes visitors from the windblown sand hills to the life-giving arroyo, and finally to the populated piñon juniper zone. Animals move freely in natural habitats with trees, streams, pools, and other features. You'll see more than 40 species of animals, including kit fox, badger, mule deer, pronghorn, elk, bison, javelinas, a cougar, and others. Lobos, or the endangered Mexican gray wolf, are one of the highlights, as is the walk-through aviary with a population that ranges from songbirds to hawks to eagles. A nocturnal exhibit details how some animals adapt to the scorching heat of the desert by foraging at night. Amateur botanists will enjoy the greenhouse, home to 100 varieties of succulents and cacti from around the world and the many desert plant species along exterior walkways.

You may be surprised to discover the town of **Carlsbad** is 27 miles north of the Caverns. Plan your visit to include some time to explore this city on the Pecos River. Originally a farming community, it was established in 1888 and named Eddy after the founder of the Eddy-Bissell Cattle Company. The area's mineral springs were believed to be salubrious, and in 1899 residents changed the city's name to Carlsbad after Karlsbad health spa in Czechoslovakia.

The rural nature of the city changed with the discovery of large potash deposits, and for years the mines were the base of the economy. Depleted potash reserves and foreign competition have hit hard, and currently Carlsbad depends largely on tourism, light industry, and the booming retirement housing market.

Your headquarters for your stay in the area could be the **Casa Milagro Bed and Breakfast.** The historic 1906 home on 1.7 acres is set in a grove of trees in La Huerta ("the orchard") on the outskirts of Carlsbad. Proprietors Mary and Rob Kamerman originally purchased the property as a residence, but with their children grown they have converted a portion to a warm, welcoming bed and breakfast with five rooms named for the family's sons and daughters. It's a kind of "come as you are" place with an informal atmosphere and family pets in evidence.

Take time to visit the **Carlsbad Museum & Fine Art Center** in Halagueno Park. It has an excellent collection of New Mexican artists' work, particularly The McAdoo Collection by the Taos Society of Artists. Visitors will also find representative work by Gustave Baumann, Emil Bisttram, Glenna Goodacre, Allan Houser, Peter Hurd, Raymond Jonson, Roderick Mead, George Rouault, and others. One wing has a collection of ceramics from early Mogollon, Mesa Verde and period pueblo pottery, to the Heinemann Collection of Peruvian Antiquities. Other areas house the

Hollebeke Collection of historical artifacts from west Texas's early ranching days and the Burns Collection of Tarahumara pieces from northern Mexico. A well-stocked gift shop carries books, cards, original art, handcrafted pottery, and jewelry by both local designers and those from the Spratling Workshops of Taxco, Mexico.

If you're working up an appetite, try the **Court Café** on South Canyon. Mary and George Limbert specialize in Greek and American home cooking, using 21 years of Mary's family recipes. You can order dolmades (stuffed grape leaves with lemon sauce), spanakopita (spinach pie), a Greek salad with feta cheese, or the combination plate. Gyros and a variety of sandwiches, Mexican food, and vegetarian plates are also on the menu. Save room for their baklava sundae.

Looking for a gift to take home? **The Artists' Gallery** on South Canyon carries the work of 36 craftspeople in a variety of disciplines. You'll find paintings and metalwork by Brian Norwood, beadwork by Frieda Bates, Allan Henrikson's exotic wood pens, and Mary Brunt's handwoven baskets.

Or try **Old Pecos Gallery** on West Fox. Karen Johnson carries a good line of Southwestern art and sculpture. You'll find hand-carved santos, pottery storytellers, and a huge selection of handcrafted crosses of clay, tin, glass, copper, pewter, and wood.

Antiques buffs can shop 'til they drop at **Gard'n Gate Antique Mall,** a 3,000-square-foot cooperative with 21 dealers. The converted movie theater has a friendly staff and clean, varied stock.

Tired of shopping? Take a stroll along the **Riverwalk's** more than 4.5 miles of paths along the banks of the Pecos River. You'll find benches for relaxing and many views of the tranquil river.

Dinnertime approaches, and if you're a barbecue fan, you won't do better than the **Red Chimney Bar-B-Que** at the log cabin on Canal Street. Using recipes the Fowler family brought from Sturgis, Kentucky, Red Chimney makes a true Southern-style barbecue, slow cooked in a pit with lots of wood smoke and dressed

A variety of Southwestern art and sculpture can be found at Old Pecos Gallery in Carlsbad.

with a mustard-vinegar-based sauce. You can order turkey, beef, pork, chicken, spareribs, ham, hot link sausages, and chop mixed dinners as well as the Red Chimney Special, a combo of beef, links, and ham. The regular portions are immense, but they provide "small dinners" for less-than-gargantuan appetites. Their sourdough peach and cherry cobblers are a specialty.

You should plan a whole day for a visit to the **Carlsbad Caverns.** Formed within a Permian Age fossil reef nearly 250 million years old, the caves are famed for their massive chambers, great depth, and vast dripstone formations. Interestingly, Carlsbad and the surrounding wild caves were carved not by surface water but by underground waters charged with sulfuric acid.

Texas-born cowhand Jim White is reputed to be the first American to enter and explore the caves in 1898. His descendents still reside in the area, and White's City, the park's closest commercial development, bears their name.

In 1923 the General Land Office, guided by White, surveyed and mapped the caverns, and on October 25 of that year Carlsbad Cave National Monument was established. In 1930 Congress declared it a national park.

Visitors have a choice of three main cave tours. The self-guided Blue Tour begins at the natural entrance and descends nearly 830 feet along the Main Corridor into the Big Room. At 360,000 square feet, the Big Room is the largest cave room in the U.S. The self-guided Red Tour covers easier terrain and much of it is wheelchair accessible. It begins and ends at the visitor's center elevator and follows the same route as the Blue Tour throughout the Big Room. Rangers accompany all self-guided tours to answer questions or, for a small fee, you can rent radio receivers and listen to taped narration. The third tour is led by a ranger and accesses the Scenic Rooms, the Green Lake Room, the King's Palace, the Queen's Palace, and the Papoose Room.

If you visit the caverns from early spring through October, stay for the evening flight of thousands of Mexican free-tailed bats as they emerge from their underground homes in a blackened whirlwind to forage for insects. Prior to the flight, rangers give a short talk at the outdoor amphitheater at the natural entrance.

The park visitor's center has a restaurant, gift shop, and bookstore as well as exhibits and a 3-D model of the caverns. There's a short nature trail and a 9.5-mile Walnut Canyon Desert Drive, a scenic trip over gravel roads.

The park's trail system includes more than 50 miles of backcountry trails. One of the most scenic is **Slaughter Canyon,** which has three main branches: west, middle, and north. A large, open valley, this canyon is best hiked early in the day, when the temperature is lower and wildlife is out. You'll need good hiking shoes, long pants, and plenty of water since you'll be traveling through loose sand and the barbs of catclaw, sotal, cholla, and lechugilla. A detailed map is available from *Trails Illustrated* at the visitor's center bookstore.

Several wild caves are located in the canyon. **Slaughter Cave** has a two-hour, 1.25-mile, ranger-led tour that you must reserve at the visitor's center. Without electricity, paved walkways, or modern conveniences, it is not a casual excursion and requires a strenuous half-mile hike to the cave entrance.

Other backcountry wild caves in the park system include **Goat, Ogle, Corkscrew, Christmas Tree, Wen,** and **Lake.** All require permits available from the park's Cave Resources Department, require technical skills, and may be open at irregular times.

Adjacent to the park, **Rattlesnake Springs** is a birder's paradise, home to a high concentration of rare birds such as Bell's vireo, green herons, and varied buntings. The half mile of wetlands and a small stream also provide habitat for the endangered eastern barking frog, Blanchard's cricket frog, the plain-bellied water snake, and the Pecos western ribbon snake. Under the shade of old cottonwoods, sedges, rushes, and cattails flourish. It's a beautiful spot, a true oasis.

If you have another day in the Carlsbad area, plan to pack a picnic and take a trip to **Sitting Bull Falls,** 40 miles from the city. The box canyon has a 130-foot waterfall, a picnic area, and natural swimming pools. The water from the highly mineralized stream has deposited a massive travertine bluff that towers over the picnic ground, and sprays from the cataract create multiple rainbows. There is a cave system behind the falls that is off-limits to all but tours led by Lincoln National Forest rangers.

If you were to continue on NM 137 from Sitting Bull Falls, you'd eventually end up in Texas in the adjoining Guadalupe Mountain National Park. Instead you're going to veer northeast to **Hobbs,** where you can check in at Beckie Cousins and Bobby Shaw's **En Sueño Bed and Breakfast.** Becky and Bobby are Hobbs natives who purchased the former home of a doctor and restored it. What they bill as a rustic ranch house is more plush than bucolic. The four rooms (two with Jack and Jill baths) are beautifully

Exhibits at the Western Heritage Museum in Hobbs focus on the oil industry and its effect on local culture and communities.

decorated with brass beds, quilts, and antiques. The expansive common room welcomes guests with a fireplace, bookcases, a pool table, and Becky's collection of rocking horses in all sizes. Outdoor amenities include a pool, a hot tub, and, if you've brought along Silver, quarters for your horse.

After one of Becky's hot breakfasts, take time to tour the town, which was settled in 1907 and functioned as an agricultural community before the discovery of oil in the area. Today the oil and gas industry, farming, ranching, and modern dairy farms are the backbone of the city's economy. A regional trade center, Hobbs serves more than 100,000 people in a 55-mile radius.

Spend some time at the **Western Heritage Museum and Lea County Cowboy Hall of Fame** in its spanking new quarters on the campus of New Mexico Junior College, once the location of Hobbs Army Air Field. The entry is a glass structure designed to resemble an oil derrick, and the large exhibit off the lobby, History of Lea County and the Llano Estacado, has sections on petroleum, the first wells, big oil companies, and ranching since the oil boom. Another area has exhibits on the inhabitants of Lea County from the prehistoric Clovis and Folsom people to the Spanish explorers and Comancheros. Visitors can also view a short video, *Petroleum and Prosperity: the Lea County Story.*

The Cowboy Hall of Fame is located along a wide gallery and includes photos of past inductees and items from personal collections such as lariats, Stetsons, and spurs. Both men and women are represented.

For a bite of lunch and a look at the local scene, hop over to **Casey's,** a Hobbs institution since 1976. Owners Kenny and Peggy Smith dish out great burgers, onion rings, and daily specials to the noontime crush. A special incentive to lovers of Coke memorabilia is the decor, Peggy's 20-year collection.

After lunch, antiques shoppers will find fertile ground at **Impressions Antique Mall** on Broadway, home to 30 vendors selling antiques, collectibles, and reproductions. There is strong representation of glassware: Fostoria, Candlewick, Heisey, and Fenton, as well as sets of Lenox and Franciscan china.

Your best bet for dinner is Joe and Sarah Yue's **Pacific Rim.** Billed as "sophisticated Asian," the menu lists signature dishes like the Hawaiian luau chicken salad, medallions of beef tenderloin with two-peppers sauce, and the popular build-your-own stir-fry with a choice of four sauces. In deference to ranch land tastes, Joe tempers the choices with alternatives like Cajun shrimp Alfredo and the Newport rib-eye steak. Portions are not dainty, and the decor is modern and clean with Chinese overtones.

Lovington is a sleepy little prairie town of 9,000 with a ranching and

A former hotel now houses Lovington's Lea County Museum, which details everything from early education to pueblo life.

farming history. Oil was discovered in 1928 but didn't have an impact on the economy until the 1950 discovery of the Denton Pool 9 miles northeast of town. Visit the **Lea County Museum,** housed in an old two-story hotel. First-floor displays include a music room, the Lea Women's Legacy Room with dolls and doll clothing, and the Native American room with mounted projectile points, a pueblo model, and some ceramics. Upstairs guest rooms have been transformed into exhibit areas for everything from early medicine to the military.

Take lunch or dinner at Marilyn and James Dean's **Main Street Café,** which has an old-fashioned soda fountain and country decor. It's a trip back to an earlier age. The menu is pages long, usually a warning sign that food isn't made fresh on premise, and it provided a quandary for the author when she ate there. However, a quick look at a neighboring table revealed some beautiful stuffed spuds, and these certainly were winners—huge Idahos topped with bell peppers, grilled onions, green chiles, shredded cheese, and real bacon bits. You can gild the lily with the addition of diced chicken-fried steak and cream gravy, grilled chicken, or hamburger. Considering your cholesterol count, you might want to add an additional trip to the salad bar.

You will have a 90-minute drive north to Portales, home of Eastern New Mexico University. Sister city Clovis is best known for **Cannon Air Force Base** and **Norman Petty's Seventh Street Studio,** the 1950s recording facility where Buddy Holly cut some of his greatest hits. The studio is not open on a regular basis, but real aficionados can get in touch with the Clovis Chamber to arrange a viewing.

One of the best-known and most significant archaeological sites in North America can be found on the short journey between the towns. **Blackwater Draw,** a National Historic Landmark and a site listed on the National Register of Historic Places, was discovered in 1932 by A. W. Anderson of Clovis. At this location, scientists discovered fluted points and other stone and bone weapons and tools, which provided evidence of human occupation around 11,000 years ago. The site was near a large pond that served as a watering hole and gathering place for game of the Late Pleistocene Era, including the woolly mammoth, camel, horse, bison, saber-toothed tiger, and dire wolf.

The site itself has limited hours and is quite rough walking. However, the **Blackwater Draw Museum** provides a clear picture of the excavations. Opened in 1969 and owned and managed by Eastern New Mexico

University, it focuses on interpreting the life at the site from Clovis times (more than 13,000 years ago) to the present. You can view a model of a mammoth head, a display on Folsom man and his culture, and more. Three films are available for viewing in the auditorium: *Cave Dwellers of Old Stone Age, 64 Million Years Ago,* and *Early Stone Tools.*

Clovis is an antiques hunter's dream, with large stores, great prices, and a wide variety of merchandise. Your first stop should be **Martin Enterprises** in the old Baptist Hospital, listed on the National Register of Historic Places. The two floors are chockablock with everything from Indian artifacts and Western relics to collectible firearms. You might find an Inuit sculpture or a lady's fan. It's a family operation, and with Wayne, Seth, or Henry Wayne II behind the counter, you'll be in good hands.

Sam and Ettie Hardcastle own **Prairie Peddler** in the old, 7,200-square-foot Raton Creamery building. You'll need a guide dog to navigate all the hidden nooks and crannies. Ettie tries to help by arranging the merchandise by category. Their strengths are Depression glass and kerosene lamps.

Some shops handle more than just antiques. **Cydney's Main Street Antiques** in the old Dunlap's Department Store, a blend of old and new, has a roster of 30 merchants. Browse for antiques, home decor, candles, clothing, and jewelry.

The **Main Street Crafters Mall** in the former Woolworth Building is a co-op with 60 booths filled with an assortment of craft supplies, antiques, gifts, apparel, and resale items.

If all this shopping has you fatigued and looking for a good meal, get directions to the **Guadalajara Café.** Clovis's oldest restaurant, it was founded by Librado Casillas, who fled the Mexican Revolution, where he was known to be in cahoots with Pancho Villa. Penniless, he brought his wife and seven children to Clovis and opened a grocery store in the late 1930s. They started serving food in the 1950s, and in 1980 Papa Casillas's daughter Mary took over the business. Mary retired in 1999, and Mike Mendoza, her son, is now carrying on with the traditional family recipes. It's worth seeking out this restaurant down by the railroad tracks. The minute you're seated, your server brings a basket of freshly cut and hand-fried tostada chips and fresh salsa. The menu selections are pure New Mexico, and all sauces, tacos, hand-rolled enchiladas, and chile rellenos are made fresh daily. Take your pick from "Platos Grandes," sufficient for a stevedore, or "Platos Pequeños" for normal mortals. Or you can order a bowl of chile verde or a side of Amelia's frijoles con queso, a blend of beans and spices topped with cheese and served with tostada chips.

After a good meal it's time to hit the road again as you work your way north. Students of history will want to visit **Fort Sumner** and the **Bosque Redondo Memorial** at **Fort Sumner State Monument,** the site of one of the most tragic periods in American history. As Americans settled the New Mexico territory, they met resistance from the native tribes fighting to maintain their land and way of life. To squash and subjugate the Navajo and Mescalero Apache, the U.S. Army conducted a military campaign that verged on genocide. Those who survived were removed from their ancestral lands and forced to march 450 miles to a reservation. Known by the Navajo as the "Long Walk," the harsh journey took almost two months during the winter. Arriving at Bosque Redondo Indian Reservation at Fort Sumner, they were faced with lack of food and supplies. More than 3,000 Navajos died before the U.S. government recognized Navajo sovereignty in the Treaty of 1868, and they were allowed to return to their traditional homelands.

Today the Pecos River gently flows by green fields and trim homes, and the land holds few reminders of the terrible conditions of 1863 to 1868. More than 140 years after the infamous incident, the state of New Mexico built a memorial to the tragedy that occurred there. Designed by Navajo architect David N. Sloan, the visitor's center is filled with exhibits telling the story. The elevated, hexagonal entrance faces the rising sun of the winter solstice, signaling rebirth. A circular pathway funnels visitors clockwise through a grove of cottonwoods cloned from a tree planted by the captives. There's a path leading to the river and an observation deck for contemplation.

Billy the Kid's grave can be found behind the Old Fort Sumner Museum.

Fort Sumner's other claim to fame is the **grave of Billy the Kid** in back of the **Old Fort Sumner Museum,** located 7 miles southeast of town.

After escaping the Lincoln jail following the murder of the sheriff and his deputy, the outlaw hid in the abandoned Fort Sumner. Sheriff Pat

A church in Puerto De Luna is proof that time stands still in this sleepy little town.

Garret heard of his whereabouts, rounded up two of his deputies, John Poe and Thomas McKinney, and set off in pursuit. On the night of July 14, 1880, Garret confronted the outlaw and shot him dead. He was buried where he died. The tombstone has been stolen three times since its placement in the 1940s, so the grave is now enclosed by a metal cage.

Santa Rosa is your exit point from backroads to the interstate. The "City of Bottomless Lakes" is surrounded by artesian spring lakes. You may be surprised to learn there is a well-known scuba diving site here. The **Blue Hole** is an artesian spring connecting to limestone caverns. It is 81 feet deep and 80 feet wide at the surface. The temperature stays a constant 61 degrees, and there's a water flow of 3,000 gallons per minute. You can fish at natural Perch or Park lakes, and enjoy boating, skiing, and camping at the large man-made lake in Lake State Park.

If you have time, take an hour or so for the beautiful 9-mile drive from Santa Rosa to **Puerto de Luna,** where Coronado bridged the Pecos. Twisting and turning through some of New Mexico's finest scenery, old Highway 91 follows the bends of the river. The ancient adobe village, whose intriguing name means "gate of the moon," hasn't changed much since 1880, when it lost its county seat status to Santa Rosa with the coming of the railroad. The sleepy village on a dead-end road is a memory jewel to treasure on your return to mainstream Albuquerque.

Contacts:

Adobe Rose Bed and Breakfast, 1614 N. 13th Street, Artesia, 88210. Call 1-888-748-ROSE or 505-748-3082. Web site: www.adoberosenm.com.

The Anderson Museum of Contemporary Art, 409 E. College Boulevard, Roswell, 88201. Call 505-623-5600. Mon. through Fri. 9–4, Sat. and Sun. 1–5. Donations accepted. Web site: www.roswellAMoCA.org.

Artesia Chamber of Commerce, 107 N. First Street, mail: P.O. Box 99, Artesia, 88211. Call 1-800-658-6251 or 505-746-2744. Web site: www.artesiachamber.com.

The Artists' Gallery, 120 S. Canyon, Carlsbad, 88220. Call 505-887-1210. Mon. through Sat. 10–5.

Billy the Kid's Grave, in back of the Old Fort Sumner Museum, Billy the Kid Road, Fort Sumner. No charge to visit grave site.

Blackwater Draw Museum and Archaeological Site, NM 467, Portales, 88130. Call 505-562-2202. Site: Memorial Day through Labor Day, Mon. through Sat. 10–5, Sun. noon–5; Labor Day through October and March through Memorial Day, Sat. 10–5, Sun. noon–5. Closed November through February. Museum: Memorial Day through Labor Day, Mon. through Sat. 10–5, Sun. noon–5; all other months, Tues. through Sat. 10–5, Sun. noon–5. Fee for site and museum. Web site: www.nmculture.org/cgi-bin/instview.cgi?_recordnum=BWDM.

Carlsbad Caverns National Park, 3225 National Parks Highway, Carlsbad, 88220. Call 505-785-2232. Memorial Day through third weekend in August, daily 8–7; last entry into cave via natural entrance at 3:30, last entry via elevator at 5. Last week in August through Memorial Day weekend, daily 8–5; last entry via natural entrance at 2, last entry via elevator at 3:30. For Slaughter Canyon Cave tours, call 1-800-967-2283. Fee. Web site: www.nps.gov/cave.

Carlsbad Chamber of Commerce and Convention & Visitors Bureau, 302 S. Canal, Carlsbad, 88220. Call 1-866-822-9226 or 505-887-6516. Web site: www.carlsbadchamber.com.

Carlsbad Museum & Fine Art Center, 418 W. Fox, Carlsbad, 88220. Call 505-887-0276. Mon. through Sat. 10–6. Free. Web site: www.nmculture.org/cgi-bin/instview.cgi?_recordnum=CMA.

Casa Milagro Bed and Breakfast, 1612 N. Guadalupe, Carlsbad, 88220. Call 1-866-332-0743 or 505-887-2188. Web site: www.casa-milagro-nm.com.

Casey's Restaurant, 209 Broadway, Hobbs, 88240. Call 505-393-0308. Mon. through Sat. 7 AM–3 PM.

Clovis/Curry County Chamber of Commerce, 105 E. Grand, Clovis, 88101. Call 1-800-261-7656 or 505-763-3435. Web site: www.clovisnm.org.

Court Café, 219 S. Canyon, Carlsbad, 88220. Call 505-887-0238. Mon. through Fri. 7 AM–3:30 PM, Sat. 8 AM–2 PM.

Cydney's Main Street Antiques, 318 N. Main, Clovis, 88101. Call 505-762-0391. Mon. through Sat. 10–5.

En Sueño Bed and Breakfast, 3505 W. Alabama, Hobbs, 88242. Call 505-392-9347. Web site: www.ensuenobandb.com.

Fort Sumner/DeBaca County Chamber of Commerce, 707 N. Fourth Street, mail: P.O. Box 28, Fort Sumner, 88119. Call 505-355-7705. Web site: www.ftsumnerchamber.com.

Fort Sumner State Monument and **Bosque Redondo Memorial,** 3 miles east of Fort Sumner on US 60/84, then south 3.5 miles on Billy the Kid Road, mail: P.O. Box 356, Fort Sumner, 88119. Wed. through Mon. 8:30–5. Fee. Web site: www.nmstatemonuments.org/about.php?_instid=SUMN.

The Garden Café, 318 W. Main, Artesia, 88210. Call 505-746-9030. Mon. through Sat. 10–2.

Gard'n Gate Antique Mall, 105 S. Canyon, Carlsbad, 88220. Call 505-234-9977. Flexible hours. Generally Mon. through Sat. 10–5. Web site: www.gardngate.com.

Georgianna's, 119 W. Main, Artesia, 888210. Call 505-746-3137. Mon. through Sat. 10–5.

Guadalajara Café, 916 L. Casillas Boulevard, Clovis, 88101. Call 505-769-9965. Mon. 11–2, Tues. through Sat. 10:30–8.

Handmade Treasures, 314 W. Main, Artesia, 88210. Call 505-308-3079. Mon. through Fri. 10–5:30, Sat. 10–3.

Heritage Inn, 209 W. Main, Artesia, 88210. Call 505-748-2552. Web site: www.artesiaheritageinn.com.

Hobbs Chamber of Commerce, 200 N. Marland, Hobbs, 88240. Call 1-800-658-6291 or 505-397-3202. Web site: www.hobbschamber.org.

Impressions Antique Mall, 200 W. Broadway, Hobbs, 88240. Call 505-391-3863. Tues. through Sat. 10–5.

Lea County Museum, 103 S. Love, Lovington, 88260. Call 505-396-4805. Tues. through Fri. 1–5, Sat. 10–5. Donations accepted.

Living Desert Zoo and Gardens, New Mexico State Parks, 1504 Miehls Drive, Carlsbad, 88220. Call 505-887-5516. Summer, daily 8–8, last park entry at 6:30; winter, daily 9–5, last park entry at 3:30. Fee. Web site: www.nmparks.com.

Lovington Chamber of Commerce, 201 S. Main, Lovington, 88260. Call 505-396-5311.

Main Street Café, 201 N. Main, Lovington, 88260. Call 505-396-1800. Mon. through Sat. 5 AM–8:30 PM.

Main Street Crafters Mall, 321 N. Main, Clovis, 88101. Call 505-742-2411. Mon. through Sat. 10–6, Sun. 1–5.

Martin's Capitol Café, 110 W. Fourth Street, Roswell, 88203. Call 505-624-2111. Mon. through Sat. 6 AM–8:30 PM.

Martin Enterprises, 515 N. Prince, Clovis, 88101. Call 505-763-0151. Mon. through Fri. 10–5. Call for Sat. hours.

Old Pecos Gallery, 102 W. Fox, Carlsbad, 88220. Call 505-885-5617. Tues. through Sat. 10–5 or by appointment.

Pacific Rim, 1309 Joe Harvey Boulevard, Hobbs, 88240. Call 505-392-0030. Mon. through Thurs. 11–2:30 and 5–9:30, Fri. 11:30–2:30 and 5–10:30, Sat. 11–10:30, Sun. 11–9:30.

Peppers Grill and Bar, 500 N. Main, Roswell, 88201. Call 505-623-1700. Mon. through Sat. 11 AM–1 AM.

Portales/Roosevelt County Chamber of Commerce, 100 S. Avenue A, Portales, 88130. Call 1-800-635-8036 or 505-356-8541.

Prairie Peddler, 100 S. Main, Clovis, 88101. Call 505-763-7392. Mon. through Sat. 10–5.

Rattlesnake Springs, call Carlsbad Caverns National Park for information.

Red Chimney Bar-B-Que, 817 N. Canal, Carlsbad, 88220. Call 505-885-8744. Mon. through Fri. 11–2 and 4:30–8:30.

Roswell Chamber of Commerce, 131 W. Second Street, mail: P.O. Box 70, Roswell, 88201. Call 1-877-849-7679 or 505-623-5695. Web site: www.roswellnm.org.

The Roswell Museum, Art Center and Robert H. Goddard Planetarium, 100 W. 11th Street, Roswell, 88201. Call 505-624-6744. Mon. through Sat. 9–5, Sun. 1–5. Free. Web site: www.nmculture.org/cgi-bin/instview.cgi?_recordnum=ROSW.

Roswell Visitor Center, 426 N. Main, Roswell, 88201. Call 1-888-767-9355 or 505-624-7704. Mon. through Fri. 8:30–5:30, Sat. and Sun. 10–3.

Santa Rosa Chamber of Commerce, 4886 Parker Avenue, Santa Rosa, 88435. Call 1-800-450-7084 or 505-472-3763. Mon. through Fri. 8–5, Sat. 9–noon. Web site: www.santarosanm.org.

Sitting Bull Falls, NM 276, Lincoln National Forest, Guadalupe Ranger District, 114 S. Halegueno, Carlsbad, 88220. Call 505-885-4181. Web sites: www.fs.fed.us/r3/lincoln or www.fs.fed.us/r3/lincoln/recreation/caves.

A Taste of Europe, 1300 N. Main Street, Roswell, 88201. Call 505-624-0313. Tues. through Sat. 5–9, Sun. 11–2.

UFO Museum and Research Center, 114 N. Main Street, Roswell, 88203. Call 505-625-9495. Daily 9–5. Expanded hours during UFO festival first week July. Fee. Web site: www.iufomrc.com.

The Wellhead Restaurant and Brewpub, 334 W. Main, Artesia, 88210. Call 505-746-0640. Mon. through Sat. 11–9.

Western Heritage Museum and Lea County Cowboy Hall of Fame, 5317 Lovington Highway, Hobbs, 88240. Call 505-392-6730. Tues. through Sat. 10–5. Fee. Web site: www.nmculture.org/cgi-bin/instview.cgi?_record num=LCC.

White's City, 17 Carlsbad Caverns Highway, mail: P.O. Box 128, White's City, 88268. Call 1-800-228-3767 or 505-785-2291. Web site: www.whites city.com.

Appendix: Other Sources of Information

Albuquerque Bed and Breakfast Association. Web site: www.abqbandb.com/inns.

"Albuquerque Visitors Guide," Albuquerque Convention & Visitors Bureau, 20 First Plaza, Suite 601, P.O. Box 26866, Albuquerque, 87125. Call 1-800-284-2282 or 505-842-9918. Web site: www.abqcvb.org.

Bureau of Land Management, 1474 Rodeo Road, P.O. Box 27115, Santa Fe, 87502. Call 505-438-7400. Web site: www.nm.blm.gov/field_offices.html.

Highway Hotline. Call 1-800-432-4269. Web site: www.nmshtd.state.nm.us.

Indian Pueblo Cultural Center, 2401 12th Street N.W., Albuquerque, 87102. Call 505-843-7270. Web site: www.indianpueblo.org.

National Forest Service, Southwest Regional Office, 333 Broadway S.E., Albuquerque, 87102. Call 505-842-3292. Web site: www.fs.fed.us/r3.

National Park Service, Southwest Regional Office, 1100 Old Santa Fe Trail, Santa Fe, 87501. Call 505-988-6100. Web site: www.nps.gov.

New Mexico Bed & Breakfast Association, P.O. Box 70454, Albuquerque, 87157. Call 1-800-661-6649. Web site: www.nmbba.org.

New Mexico Department of Fish and Game, One Wildlife Way, P.O. Box 25112, Santa Fe, 87507. Call 1-800-862-9310. Web site: www.wildlife.state.nm.us.

New Mexico Office of Cultural Affairs, 407 Galisteo Street, Santa Fe, 87501. Call 505-827-4378. Web site: www.newmexicoculture.org.

New Mexico Park and Recreation Division, 408 Galisteo Street, P.O. Box 1147, Santa Fe, 87504. Call 1-888-667-2757 or 505-476-3355. Web site: www.nmparks.com.

***New Mexico Road & Recreation Atlas,* Benchmark Maps,** 34 N. Central Avenue, Medford, OR 97501. Call 541-772-6965. Web site: www.benchmarkmaps.com.

"New Mexico Vacation Guide" and/or "New Mexico Outdoor and Recreation Guide," Department of Tourism, 491 Old Santa Fe Trail, Santa Fe, 87501. Call 1-800-545-2040, Ext.751. Web site: www.newmexico.org.

Public Lands Information Center, Santa Fe office, 1474 Rodeo Road, Santa Fe, 87505. Call 1-877-276-9404 or 505-438-7542. Roswell office, 2909 W. Second Street, Roswell, 88201. Call 505-627-0210. Web site: www.publiclands.org.

"Santa Fe Visitors Guide," City of Santa Fe Convention & Visitors Bureau, 201 W. Marcy Street, P.O. Box 909, Santa Fe, 87504. Call 1-800-777-2489. Web site: www.santafe.org.

Ski New Mexico, P.O. Box 1104, Santa Fe, 87504. Call 1-800-755-7669 or 505-982-5300. Web site: www.skinewmexico.com.

Taos Association of Bed and Breakfast Inns, Taos. Go to Web site for listing and availability: www.taos-bandb-inns.com.

"Taos Visitors Guide" and Taos Visitor Center, Taos County Chamber of Commerce, 1139 Paseo del Pueblo Sur, P.O. Drawer I, Taos, 87571. Call 1-800-732-8267 or 505-758-3873. Web site: taoswebb.com.

U.S. Army Corps of Engineers, Albuquerque District, 4101 Jefferson Plaza N.E., Albuquerque, 87109. Call 505-342-3100. Web site: www.spa.usace.army.mil.

New Mexico Native Americans:

Jicarilla Apache, Jicarilla Game and Fish, P.O. Box 507, Dulce, 87528. Call 505-759-3242.

Mescalero Apache, P.O. Box 227, Mescalero, 88340. Call 505-671-4495.

Navajo Nation Tourism, P.O Box 663, Window Rock, AZ, 86515. Call 928-810-8501/8502 or 928-871-7371. Free "Discover Navajo Visitor Guide." Web site: www.discovernavajo.com.

Pueblos:

Acoma Pueblo, P.O. Box 309, Acoma Pueblo, 87034. Call 505-552-6604. Web site: www.skycity.com.

Cochití Pueblo, P.O. Box 70, Cochiti, 87072. Call 505-465-2244.

Isleta Pueblo, P.O. Box 1270, Isleta, 87022. Call 505-869-3111.

Jémez Pueblo, P.O. Box 100, Jémez, 87024. Call 505-834-7235. Web site: www.jemezpueblo.org.

Laguna Pueblo, P.O. Box 194, Laguna, 87026. Call 505-552-6654.

Nambé Pueblo, Route 1, Box 117-BB, Santa Fe, 87501. Call 505-455-2036.

O'ke Owingeh Pueblo (formerly San Juan), P.O. Box 1099, O'ke Owingeh Pueblo, 87566. Call 505-852-4400.

Picurís Pueblo, P.O. Box 127, Peñasco, 87553. Call 505-587-1099.

Pojoaque Pueblo, Camino del Rincón, Suite 6, Santa Fe, 87506. Call 505-455-2278. Visitor's Center, 96 Cities of Gold Road, Santa Fe, 87506. Call 505-455-9023. Web site: www.citiesofgold.com/PuebloMain.

Sandia Pueblo, 418 Sandia Loop, Bernalillo, 87004. Call 505-867-3317. Web site: www.sandiapueblo.nsn.us.

San Filipe Pueblo, P.O. Box 4339, San Felipe Pueblo, 87001. Call 505-867-3381.

San Ildefonso Pueblo, Route 5, Box 315A, Santa Fe, 87501. Call 505-455-2273.

Santa Ana Pueblo, 2 Dove Road, Santa Ana, 87004. Call 505-867-3301. Web site: www.santaana.org.

Santa Clara Pueblo, P.O. Box 580, Española, 87532. Call 505-753-7326.

Santo Domingo Pueblo, P.O. Box 99, Santo Domingo, 87052. Call 505-465-2214.

Taos Pueblo, P.O. Box 1846, Taos Pueblo, 87571. Call 505-758-1028. Web site: www.taospueblo.com.

Tesuque Pueblo, Route 42, P.O. Box 360-T, Santa Fe, 87506. Call 505-983-2667.

Zia Pueblo, 135 Capital Square Drive, Zia Pueblo, 87053. Call 505-867-3304.

Pueblo of Zuni Visitor and Arts Center, 1239 NM 53, Zuni, 87327. Call 505-782-7239. Web site: www.experiencezuni.com.

Visitor Information Centers:

Anthony Visitor Information Center, P.O. Box 1270, I-10, Anthony, 88021. Call 505-882-2419.

Chama Visitor Information Center, P.O. Box 697, 2372 NM 17, Chama, 87520. Call 505-756-2235.

Gallup Visitor Information Center, I-40, Exit 3, P.O. Box 816, Gallup, 87301. Call 505-863-4909.

Glenrio Visitor Information Center, 37315-C I-40, Exit 373, Glenrio, 88434. Call 505-576-2424.

La Bajada Visitor Information Center, 17 miles south of Santa Fe on I-25. Call 505-424-0823.

Lordsburg Visitor Information Center, P.O. Box 132, I-10, Exit 20 rest area, Lordsburg, 88045. Call 505-542-8149.

Raton Visitor Information Center, I-25, Exit 451, 100 Clayton Road, Raton, 87740. Call 505-445-2716.

Santa Fe Visitor Information Center, The Lamy Building, 491 Old Santa Fe Trail, Santa Fe, 87503. Call 505-827-7336.

Texico Visitor Information Center, 336 US Highway 60/70/84, Texico, 88135. Call 505-482-3321.

Index

D

E

F

G

H

I

T

U

V